Waters of Creation

A Biblical-Theological Study of Baptism

Cover Design by Stephen Van Dorn

Fonts:
Cover – Front: Trajan Pro Regular; Back: Adobe Caslon Pro Semi Bold.
Inside – Titles: Garamond; Text: California FB.

ISBN: 978-0-578-02804-0

Waters of Creation
A Biblical-Theological Study of Baptism

Douglas Van Dorn

Waters of Creation Publishing
1614 Westin Drive, Erie, Colorado 80516

CONTENTS

Contents

EXPANDED CONTENTS

ABBREVIATIONS

General

A.D.	Anno Domini (*Year of our Lord*)
ala	in the manner of
B.C.	Before Christ
ca.	circa
Col.	Column
cf.	consult, compare
ed.	editor, edition
e.g.	for example
et al	and elsewhere
etc.	etcetera
Frag.	Fragment
Gk.	Greek
Heb.	Hebrew
i.e.	in other words
lit.	Literally
n.d.	no date
NT	New Testament
OT	Old Testament

Bible Versions

ASV	American Standard Version
ESV	English Standard Version
KJV	King James (Authorized) Version
LXX	Septuagint
NAS	New American Standard
NIV	New International Version
NKJ	New King James
NRS	New Revised Standard
RSV	Revised Standard Version
VUL	Latin Vulgate Bible
YLT	Young's Literal Translation

Modern Works

ABD	*Anchor Bible Dictionary.* Edited by D. N. Freedman. 6 vols. New York: Doubleday, 1992
ALGNT	*Analytical Lexicon of the Greek New Testament.* Edited T. Friberg, B. Friberg, N. Miller.
BASOR	*Bulletin of the American Schools of Oriental Research*
BBCOT	*Bible Background Commentary: Old Testament*
BC	*Belgic Confession*

BCP	*Book of Common Prayer*
BDB	F. Brown, S. R. Driver and C. A. Briggs. *The Brown-Driver-Briggs Hebrew and English Lexicon.* Oxford: Clarendon, 1906.
BECNT	Baker Exegetical Commentary on the New Testament
BR	*Biblical Research*
BSP	*Bible and Spade*
BST	Bible Speaks Today Commentary Series
BT	*Banner of Truth*
CCC	Crossway Classic Commentaries
CCC2nd	*Catechism of the Catholic Church, second edition*
CONTUOT	*Commentary on the New Testament Use of the Old Testament*
CTSJ	*Chafer Theological Seminary Journal*
DAC	*Dictionary of the Apostolic Church*
EBD	*Easton Bible Dictionary*
FJ	*Founders Journal*
HTR	*Harvard Theological Review*
IaVTPSM	*Interpretations ad Vetus Testamentum Pertinentes Sigmundo Mowinckel*
ICC	International Critical Commentary
IVPBBCOT	*InterVarsityPress Bible Background Commentary on the Old Testament*
IVPNTC	InterVarsity Press New Testament Commentaries
JE	*Jewish Encyclopedia*
JETS	*Journal of the Evangelical Theological Society*
JTS	*Journal of Theological Studies*
LNL	Johannes P. Louw, Eugene A. Nida. *Greek-English Lexicon of the New Testament: Based on Semantic Domains.* UBS 2nd ed., 1988.
LBC	*London Baptist Confession of Faith 1689*
MFWJ	*Magazin für die Wissenschaft des Judentums*
MR	*Modern Reformation*
MSJ	*Master's Seminary Journal*
MTJ	*Michigan Theological Journal*
NAC	*New American Commentary*
NDBT	*New Dictionary of Biblical Theology*
NICNT	The New International Commentary on the New Testament
NICOT	New International Commentary on the Old Testament
NIDNTT	*New International Dictionary of New Testament Theology*
NIDOTTE	*New International Dictionary of Old Testament Theology and Exegesis*
NIGTC	New International Greek Testament Commentary
NIVAC	NIV Application Commentary
NTC	New Testament Commentary
PBCD	Puritan Bookshelf CD Rom
PNTC	Pillar New Testament Commentary
RAR	*Reformation and Revival*
RB	*Revue biblique*
RBCD	Reformation Bookshelf CD Rom

RBTR	*Reformed Baptist Theological Review*
RevExp	*Review and Expositor*
SPJ	*Southern Presbyterian Journal*
TCEC	*Twentieth Century Encyclopedia of Catholicism*
TDNT	*Theological Dictionary of the New Testament*
TNCE	*The New Catholic Encyclopedia*
TWOT	*Theological Wordbook of the Old Testament*
UBS	United Bible Societies
VT	*Vetus Testamentum*
W&W	*Word and World*
WBC	*Word Biblical Commentary*
WBCS	Westminster Bible Companion Series
WCF	*Westminster Confession of Faith*
WDTT	*Westminster Dictionary of Theological Terms*
WTJ	*Westminster Theological Journal*
ZAW	*Zeitschrift für die alttestamentliche Wissenschaft*

Apocrapha/Pseudepigripha

ApZeph	*Apocalypse of Zephaniah*
Did	*Didache*
En	*Enoch*
Esd	*Esdras (or Ezra)*
Jub	*Jubilees*
Jud	*Judith*
LetAris	*Letter of Aristeas*
Mac	*Maccabees*
Odes Sol	*Odes of Solomon*
PsPhilo	*Pseudo Philo*
SibOr	*Sibylline Oracles*
Sir	*Sirach*
TBen	*Testament of Benjamin*
TIsaac	*Testament of Isaac*
TJac	*Testament of Jacob*
TJud	*Testament of Judah*
TSim	*Testament of Simeon*
TLevi	*Testament of Levi*
Vita AE	*Vita Adae et Evae (Life of Adam and Eve)*
Wis	*Wisdom*

Ancient Jewish Sources

ALD	Aramaic Levi Document
AvZar	*Avoda Zarah*
CTLevi	Cairo Geniza *Testament of Levi*

Erub	*Erubin*
m.	*Mishnah*
MasKid	*Ma'aseh Kiddushin*
Mek	*Mekilta*
Midr	*Midrash (+ biblical book)*
Mik	*Mikwaoth*
Pes	*Pesahim*
1QH	Qumran: *1QHodayot*
1QS	Qumran: *1QRule of the Community*
4Q266^a	Qumran: *4QDamascus Document^a*
4Q270^e	Qumran: *4QDamascus Document^e*
4Q418	Qumran: *4QInstruction*
Suk	*Sukkah*
TgJon	*Targum of Jonathan*
Vita	Josephus: *Vita*
Yeb	*Yebamoth*
Zad	*Zadokite Fragments*

Early Christian Writings

AdvHaer	Ephiphanius: *Against Heresies*
CHipp	*Cannons of Hippolytus*
Dial.	Justin Martyr: *Dialogue with Trypho*
Eph	Ignatius: *Ephesians*
GMatt	Chrysostom: *Gospel of Matthew*
Hom.	Cyril of Alexandria: *Homily*
Paed.	Clement of Alexandria: *Paedagogus*
Or.	Gregory Nazianzen: *Oration Holy Lights*
Rev.	*Revelation*
Smyr	*Letter to the Smyrnaeans*
TAHN	*Treatise Against the Heretic Novatian*
Vis	*Vision*

Foreword

Afavorite professor in seminary often postulated that the state of Biblical interpretation could be greatly improved, if we would only learn like men of old, to read our Bibles whole.

Many credobaptists read their Bibles with the presupposition that unless explicitly uncovered by chapter and verse, that the New Testament theology of baptism is something radical and new, with no continuity whatsoever with Old Testament theological covenants and themes.

Paedobaptists, on the other hand, are convinced that there is indeed continuity between the Testaments, with obvious joints hinging the Abrahamic covenant (circumcision) and the New Covenant praxis of baptism.

When Doug Van Dorn first introduced me to his Biblical Theology of baptism, I was immediately struck by the inimitable conclusions of his thesis. Doug has demonstrated, in my view, both cogently and powerfully, that this thesis is the only hypothesis able to bring together the seemingly irreconcilable strands of discontinuity and continuity in the theology of baptism.

Far from being "novel," Doug has carefully and responsibly supported his conclusions with extensive and vigilant research of ancient biblical literature. He has demonstrated this care with copious notations, enabling anyone to easily trace the evidence brought to bear in his arguments.

I highly commend this work to you dear brethren, whatever your theological presuppositions happen to be. I am quite certain that you will be encouraged by the irenic spirit of his labor of love, and challenged by its rigor.

More than anything, it is my prayer (along with Doug) that you will discover that the light of this work shines solely and truly upon the splendor of our blessed and beautiful savior, Jesus Christ. First and foremost, this book is about Him.

Washed Clean,

Tony Jackson, MDiv.
Member of the Reformed Baptist Church of Northern Colorado

Introduction

Baptism is ancient. However, what is ancient to you may not be ancient to me. To a child, its grandparents are ancient. To an American living in Colorado, two hundred years is ancient. That's longer than Colorado has been a state and older than almost every building in it. To someone living in Rome, ancient might mean two thousand years. That's about how long the average Christian thinks that baptism has been around. Most assume that the rite started with John the Baptist or maybe a few years before him. That would put its origin back near the birth of Jesus Christ. Because of this, many Christians only look as far as the NT in their investigation into the meaning and mode of baptism.

When we say "baptism is ancient," we do not mean it as a child or someone from Colorado or even someone from Rome would think of it. The pagan (and we will argue in great detail later – the Jewish) practice of baptism was ancient and universal. It is found in the worship of the Egyptian goddess Isis, in Roman Bacchic consecrations, in Greek Pelusium festivals and Apollinarian games. Mystery cults like the Mithras, Attis, and Eleusinians all incorporated baptism. Babylon, Persia, and India practiced baptism in sacred rivers (see Opeke, 'baptō, baptizō', TDNT 1:531). The idea of baptism even crossed the Atlantic Ocean. An ancient Aztec Prayer reads, "Merciful Lady Chalchiuhtlicue, thy servant here present is come into the world... wash him and deliver him from impurities... cleanse him of the contamination he hath received from his parents: let the water take away the soil and the stain, and let him be freed from all taint. May it please thee, O Goddess, that his heart and his life be purified, that he may dwell in this world in peace and wisdom. May this water take away all ills... wash from him the evils which he beareth from before the beginning of the world" (Alexander 1920: 11.73).

The 19th century theologian A.A. Hodge summarizes that, "No other religious symbol is so natural and obvious, and none has been so universally practiced. Its usage is distinctly traced among the disciples of Zoroaster, the Brahmen, the Egyptians, Greeks, and Romans, and especially the Jews" (Hodge 1999, 603). Paul Myers adds, "History records that lustration rites have been practiced by nearly all primitive people" (Myers 1985: 2).

In light of this one must wonder, how do such religiously and geographically diverse cultures just "happen" to practice the same religious rite and ascribe the same general meaning to it? Scripture and logic dictate that they derive it from one ancient source. In fact, the LORD God prescribed this rite to the sons of Adam. God is the Source of the waters (Jer 17:13). But the pagans took the rite, twisted and distorted it, all while retaining partial elemental truths of baptism, even in their own practice of it.

In actuality, the oldest cultures on earth do not predate the first explicitly recorded baptism, which Scripture says was Noah's flood (1 Pet 3:20-21). But the Christian church has not stopped investigating the origins of baptism here. The fact is, baptism finds its origins in the very creation of the world: on day three when God gathered the waters together and called them seas (Gen 1:10). Some even see it as far back as the preface of the creation days, when the Spirit hovered over the waters (Gen 1:2).

Tertullian (ca. 155-230 A.D.), in what is one of the oldest works on baptism to come down to us (*de Baptismo*), connects the element of baptism (water) to creation saying, "In what respect, pray, has this material substance merited an office of so high dignity?... Water is one of those things which before all the furnishing of the world, were quiescent with God in a yet unshapen state. 'In the first beginning God made the heaven and the earth.'" (Gen 1:2). He adds, for "water is a perfect, gladsome, simple material substance, pure in itself" (Tertullian, *On Baptism*, ch. 1, 3). His point is that the preface to all baptism comes in Genesis 1:2. Jerome (ca. 347–420 A.D.) makes the connection even clearer saying,

> Sing the praises of water and of baptism. In the beginning the earth was without form and void... The Spirit of God above moved, as a charioteer, over the face of the waters, and produced from them the infant world, a type of the Christian child that is drawn from the laver of baptism... The first living beings come out of the waters; and believers soar out of the laver with wings to heaven. Man is formed out of clay and God holds the mystic waters in the hollow of his hand. In Eden a garden is planted, and a fountain in the midst of its parts into four heads. This is the same fountain which Ezekiel later on describes as issuing out of the temple and flowing towards the rising of the sun until it heals the bitter waters and quickens those that are dead.
> (Jerome, Letter LXIX.6)

Following the lead of the Fathers, Western Christianity has been unified on this. The second entry in the section titled "Prefigurations of Baptism in the Old Covenant" of the *Catechism of the Catholic Church* says, "Since the beginning of the world, water, so humble and wonderful a creature, has been the source of life and fruitfulness. Sacred Scripture sees it as 'overshadowed' by the Spirit of God[1]: 'At the very dawn of creation your Spirit breathed on

---

[1] *CCC2nd*, Part 2, Section 2, Chapter 1, Article 1, Paragraph 2 #1218.

the waters, making them the wellspring of all holiness.'"[2] The Anglican *Book of Common Prayer* has this prayer offered up by the bishop *during baptism*, "We thank you, Almighty God, for the gift of water. Over it the Holy Spirit moved in the beginning of creation" (*BCP*, "Consecration of a Church"). Thus, Herman Westerink (Reformed) summarizes, "Is baptism a strange sign? Is it a sign Israel can comprehend only with difficulty? Absolutely not! We must keep in mind that centuries of divine instruction precede the Lord Jesus instituting the sacrament of baptism" (Westerink 1997: 63).

Drawing from these ancient and diverse reservoirs of interpretation, it is our contention that God baptized the earth itself. In doing so, he established a baptismal precedent for our sake, in order to teach us how things work in the heavenly realm. In other words, there is a direct and deliberate correspondence between what God established on earth, and what exists in heaven. In this way, baptism is a physical sign of an invisible and *eternal* reality. It is a rite belonging to the Temple of God, where earthly temples become created microcosms of the Temple in heaven.

When theologians try to identify the meaning of baptism, most stop at its redemptive significance. That is, they think of baptism chiefly in categories *post*-fall: cleansing, washing away filth, and forgiveness of sins. While baptism certainly took on this meaning, it cannot be that this is *all* that it means, if baptism is a part of the heavenly temple (for there is no sin in heaven). Furthermore, if baptism existed prior to the fall, then this could not even be its first and most important function. So, our theology must also incorporate the meaning of baptism prior to the fall. The significance of baptism in this regard is that it is God's way of setting apart or initiating his priest to work out his holy temple-task with the very blessing of heaven itself.

Martin Luther wrote, "All Christians are truly of the spiritual estate, and there is no difference among them except that of office... whoever comes out of the water of baptism can boast that he is already a consecrated priest," because, "We are all consecrated as priests by baptism, as St. Peter says in I Peter 2[:9], 'You are a royal priesthood and a priestly realm.' The Apocalypse says, "Thou hast made us to be priests and kings by thy blood' [Rev. 5:9-10]" (Luther, *Luther's Works*, 44:127, 129).[3]

---

[2] Roman Missal, Easter Vigil 42: Blessing of Water.

[3] Luther goes on to say that there are different roles within the priesthood, even as there were between the various families of Levitical priests (Kohathites, Gershonites, Merarites) and the sons of Aaron the High Priest. "It follows from this argument that there is no true, basic difference between laymen and priests, princes and bishops, between religious and secular, except for the sake of office and work, but not for the sake of status. They are all of the spiritual estate, all are truly priests, bishops, and popes. But they do not all have the same work to do. Just as all priests and monks do not have the same work. This is the teaching of St. Paul in Romans

Luther was not alone in connecting baptism and the priesthood. Peter Leithart tells us, "The typology of priestly ordination and baptism is a truism of our tradition" (Leithart 2003: 44). He cites the following Church Fathers as men who have to one degree or another made this connection: Tertullian, Cyril of Jerusalem, Ambrose, Prudentius, Jerome, Augustine, Leo, Salvian the Presbyter, Fastidius, Cassiodorus, Origen, Basil the Great, Gregory Nazianzus, Didymus of Alexandria, John Chrysostom, pseudo-Dionysius, and Procopius of Gaza. From the medieval period they are joined by the likes of John the Deacon, Isidore of Seville, Leidradus of Lyons, Theodulf of Orleans, Maxentius, Amalarius, Hincmar of Reims, Atto of Vercelli, Peter Damien, Lanfranc of Bec, Ivo of Chartres, Rupert of Deutz, Peter Abelard, Master Simon, Peter Lombard, Peter of Celle, Martin of Leon, Innocent III, Alexander of Hales, and Thomas Aquinas. There are a number of Eastern theologians who likewise make such connections: Anastasius of Sinai, Theodore the Studite, Photius, Arethas of Caesarea, Oecumenius, Serronius, Theophylactus the Bulgar, Germanus, archbishop of Constantinople, and Symeon of Thessalonica (Leithart: 44 n. 59).

It has been our experience that many Christians do not think of their lives (i.e., their service to God) in terms of the priesthood. Certainly they do not think of their baptism in this way. They think through the lenses of contemporary Evangelicalism that the priesthood has been done away with; or they have a more medieval/Roman view that the priesthood belongs to a select few, intelligent, educated clergy. But the NT sees the work of Christians as the fulfilment of OT priestly work.

The NT has much to say about the *"priesthood* of all believers." (The doctrine of the priesthood of all believers was a pillar of Reformation theology). The NT language of our worship and service as Christians is cast in OT sanctuary-priestly language. For instance, Hebrews says, "Do good and to share what you have, for such *sacrifices* are pleasing to God" (Heb 13:16). Paul says that his suffering is a *drink offering* poured out for the Philippians (Php 2:17). Paul calls their gift of money a *fragrant offering,* a *sacrifice* acceptable and pleasing to God (4:18). Paul calls his gospel ministry a *fragrant aroma* to God as he calls us the aroma of Christ (2 Cor 2:14-15). Romans 12:1 says, "Brothers, by the mercies of God, present your bodies as a living *sacrifice,* holy and

---

12[:4–5] and I Corinthians 12[:12] and in I Peter 2[:9], as I have said above, namely, that we are all one body of Christ the Head, and all members one of another" (p. 129). In this way the Reformation did not do away with the distinction between pastors and laity, but actually emphasized it in such a way so as to preserve the integrity of both.

acceptable to God, which is your spiritual worship." We could multiply these kinds of verses many times.

The work described here is unmistakably referencing OT priestly duty. Many Christians do not have the lenses to notice this. But it is obvious once our attention is caught. The fact that we are each priests means that no matter where we serve—be it in the church, the state, the family, or in secular vocation—our whole lives are to be lived out in holy service before a holy God as his temple expands throughout the whole earth. We do not have the luxury of being "Sunday-only Christians."

This is just one practical implication of our baptism. But it is derived from our first realization that baptism is ancient. The ancient origin of baptism provides the key to understanding the NT practice and purpose of baptism. It also holds the key to overcoming long-standing differences between Baptists and paedobaptists. The OT beginnings of baptism are the missing ingredient in baptistic arguments against our paedobaptist brothers.

George Beasley-Murray once wrote, "It seems to me that some difficulties are going to be solved only by walking, and that in unaccustomed paths. I am prepared to believe that problems at present apparently insoluble may receive light from further study of the Word of God" (Beasley-Murray 1962: 387). In this book we will walk in some "unaccustomed paths." Yet, we will belabour the point that these paths are *forgotten* paths, *biblical* paths, and *orthodox* paths. Every mile of this path was at one time well-worn, even if most seem to have wandered off the path at different points along the journey so that no one reached the destination in quite the same way that we will.

This book seeks to work out the implication of the idea that baptism is ancient. First, we will prove—through a variety of methods (exegetical analysis, typology, temple comparisons, and covenant theology)—the assertion itself. Then we will look to the implications of these findings for the debate between Baptists and paedobaptists. This in turn will help us explain why the NT practices the rite in the way that it does.

Baptists have been absolutely correct to practice immersions of non-infants, because this *is* the way the NT practices baptism. Now we are able to understand why the NT holds baptism in such high esteem, and why they practiced it the way they did. Only a thorough-going study of baptism *from all of Scripture* is able to give an answer to this, until now, unanswerable (because it is often the unasked) question. Through this journey, our goal will be to strengthen our theology of baptism so that we might bring greater glory to God through his Son Jesus Christ. During the course, you might find yourself learning to read the Scripture in new and exciting ways. This study of baptism may actually bring a unity to your understanding of the Bible that few possess, but many wish they had; just as it has for many of my friends and colleagues that had the opportunity to read the manuscript prior to publication. My prayer is that God through the Holy Spirit would expand your faith in Scripture and transform the way you live your life day to day. These are the fruits that God promises to those who earnestly seek to know Him in a deeper way. These are the fruits promised to us in our baptism.

Part I – THE BAPTISM OF JESUS

Perhaps the best place to start a study of baptism is with Jesus. We learn from all four Gospels (Matt 3, Mark 1, Luke 3, John 1) that Christ was baptized in the Jordan River by John the Baptist. Christian baptism follows after Christ's baptism. Therefore, whatever Christ's baptism meant, it must be directly related to the meaning of Christian baptism. But what was the purpose of Christ's baptism? If we do not know why Christ was baptized, then we cannot possibly understand the meaning of our own baptism *into* Christ.

John the Baptist asked the same question. "I need to be baptized by you, and do you come to me?" (Matt 3:14). In other words, John asked Jesus why he needed to be baptized. Like us, John wanted to know the purpose of Christ's baptism. Jesus gives John the answer. Before we explore this, let's review the story.

John the Baptist is Jesus' older cousin through Elizabeth his mother who is the relative/cousin of Mary (Luke 1:36). Elizabeth was a Levite (Luke 1:5, 13; cf. 1 Chron 24:10, 19). Zechariah, John's father, was also a Levite and a priest (Luke 1:5). John is therefore a Levitical priest, inheriting the office from his father (Ex 29:9; Num 25:13). John was Isaiah's "voice crying in the wilderness" preparing the way for Messiah in the fashion of Elijah (Matt 3:3; cf. Isa 40:3; Matt 11:14; 17:12). The preparatory ministry of John included a message of repentance (Matt 3:2) and a rite of passage commonly known as "*baptism*" (Matt 3:6).

Why was John baptizing? This was the very question that troubled the religious leaders of the day. It is recorded that, "The Jews sent *priests* and *Levites* from Jerusalem to *Bethany beyond the Jordan*[4] to ask [John], 'Who are you?... Why are you baptizing, if you are neither the Christ, nor Elijah, nor the prophet? [emphasis mine]" (John 1:19, 25).

It must be kept in mind at just this point that John is himself *a priest and a Levite*. In the passage above, the priests and Levites from Jerusalem are sent all the way to the other side of the Jordan to inquire about his practice of

---

[4] Some scholars have suggested that this "Bethany" is the one located a couple miles east of Jerusalem, nowhere near the Jordan River. Long ago Origen put forth the theory that Bethany should be *Bethabarah* (represented in several early manuscripts), since it made no sense that John was baptizing in the Jordan yet was nowhere near the Jordan in this incident. Leon Morris suggests that the manuscript evidence changed because of Origen. He believes that Origen was incorrect, but that this Bethany was not the one close to Jerusalem. It was rather lost to time and impossible (as of yet) to identify with accuracy (Morris 1995: 125). This puts the baptism of Jesus along the *eastern* boundary of the land; a fact we will see time and again in relation to baptism.

baptism. Why send the priests and Levites? Why send priests and Levites from *Jerusalem*? Is this a hint that baptism was something familiar to them? We suggest that there was a problem with John's baptism in the eyes of the Pharisees. It was not a problem with John's *legal status* to baptize, but with the *place* of John's baptism—namely that it was not being done in the temple in Jerusalem. This raised the ire of the religious leaders who sent representatives to inquire into the answer.

John eventually answers their question, "I came baptizing with water, *that [Messiah] might be revealed to Israel*" (John 1:31). He then recalls the baptism that he performed upon Jesus sometime earlier, "I saw the Spirit descend from heaven like a dove, and it remained on him. I myself did not know him, but he who sent me to baptize with water said to me, 'He on whom you see the Spirit descend and remain, this is he who baptizes with the Holy Spirit. And I have seen and have borne him witness that this is the Son of God" (John 1:31-34). (It is striking to note that John's gospel records no more of the exchange between the Baptist and the priests. Perhaps it is because the Baptist's answer settled their minds for the time being).

Now we will look more closely at the baptism of Jesus as recorded in the Synoptics (Matthew, Mark, Luke). We will pay particular attention to Matthew's account. Matthew gives two different *kinds* of answers for the baptism of Jesus. The first is an explicit statement. The second is an implicit argument built from the order that Matthew and Luke tell their stories. *Both* answers find their origin in the priesthood of the OT.

Explicit Purpose of Jesus' Baptism

Let us deal with the explicit statement first. Prior to baptizing Jesus, even John was confused about why Jesus would want to be baptized. Recall again, John is baptizing and people are *repenting* of their sins. John's was a baptism of repentance (Mark 1:4).

Jesus now comes to John to be baptized by him (Matt 3:13). But it says, "John would have prevented him, saying, 'I need to be baptized by you, and do you come to me?" (Matt 3:14). Obviously, John has in mind the purity and sinlessness of Christ. John had the same notion about baptism that many have had since. He thought Christ was being baptized for sin in some way.[5]

---

[5] So for example, Francis Turretin speaks for many when he says that Christ "not needing baptism was himself baptized for our sake by John" (Turretin 1997: 380). The implication is that we are sinners and Jesus was baptized for our sin.

John can't, he *won't* baptize Jesus for repentance. John is the sinner. He needs to be baptized by Jesus.

So Jesus offers to John *another reason* for being baptized. "'Let it be so now, for thus it is fitting for us *to fulfill all righteousness*.' Then [John] consented" (Matt 3:15).[6] "To fulfill all righteousness" is the explanation that causes John to see the light. He immediately stops his objection and baptizes Christ in the water. In this way James Dale correctly observes, "The baptism of Christ was not a 'Johannic baptism'... It is one thing to be baptized by John and quite another to receive the 'baptism' of John" (Dale 1874: 27).[7]

Why? What did Jesus' answer mean to John? Again, John explains it that he was baptizing "That [Messiah] might be revealed to Israel." But this is still fairly cryptic to our modern ears, not accustomed to thinking like Jews with the OT in our minds. The key to understanding John's explanation is to look into the meaning of Jesus' words, "to fulfill all righteousness." This is what we need to turn our attention to understanding.

Speculation abounds in the literature as to what Jesus meant. Davies and Allison tell us this question has "scarcely cancelled further discussion. There has been no dearth of conjectures on the query" (Davies and Allison 1988: 321). They then proceed to give eleven different popular interpretations.[8]

---

[6] This is not the only time that John has a wrong understanding of Messiah's fulfilling the OT. See his doubts in Matt 11:3. Jesus answers John by quoting from the OT Scriptures, especially Isaiah (11:5-6; cf. Isa 8:13-14, 26:19, 29:18-19, 35:5-6, 61:1). In receiving these OT quotes, John could piece together the works of miracles and teaching that Jesus was doing were in fulfillment of the Scripture. John needed this because like most prior to the resurrection, he just didn't get it.

[7] This goes against the grain of one stream of thought dating at least to the time of Theodore of Mopsuestia (circa 400 A.D., and teacher of the Nestorian heresy). Theodore said, "The baptism of John was at one and the same time perfect and imperfect. It was perfect according to the precept of the law, but it was imperfect in that it did not supply remission of sins but merely made people fit for receiving the perfect one. For this reason, even Christ, since he was perfect with regard to the law, was baptized with this baptism, that is, the baptism of John. And he makes this clear, saying, 'For thus it is fitting for us to fulfill all righteousness'" (Theodore of Mopsuestia, *Fragment 13*).

[8] 1. Jesus went to John in order to repent and find forgiveness. 2. Jesus only wished to join the saved remnant, the new Israel, and saw its formation in the ministry of John, to which he then submitted. 3. Jesus, conscious of being the servant of Deutero-Isaiah, had himself baptized in order to identify himself with sinners. He had to be numbered with the transgressors. Baptism was the first step in bearing the sins of the world. 4. God's call to all Israel had gone out through the Baptist: repent and be baptized. Jesus, humbly and obediently, responded to the call: it was religious duty to be accepted without question. 5. According to Jerome, the Gospel according to the Nazoraeans contained this: 'Behold, the mother of the Lord and his brothers said to him: John the Baptist baptized unto the remission of sins. Let us go and be baptized by him. But he said to them: Wherein have I sinned that I should go and be baptized by him? Unless what I have said is ignorance'. When invited to accept John's baptism, Jesus saw no need for any act of repentance, for he was not conscious of having transgressed God's will. But he shrank from following his conscience because he knew the united teaching of the Scripture to the effect that no human being is free from sin. 6. Perhaps as Messiah and Son of Man and therefore as representative person, but in any case as he came to seek and to save those who were lost, Jesus took his stand with the publicans and sinners against the self-righteous. He was thus compelled to join the ranks of those who came to the Jordan confessing their sins and in need of deliverance. 7. According to Justin Martyr, the Jews believed that 'the Messiah is unknown and does not even know himself and has no power until Elijah comes to anoint him and make him manifest to all'. Maybe, then, Jesus went to the Jordan to be anointed as Messiah by one he took to be

Among the more conservative answers (listed in note 8), "identification with sinners" is probably the most popular today.[9] Though it is not wrong to think of Jesus' baptism as an identification with sinners, sanctifying of the waters, being our representative, being an example, and teaching submission (they are not mutually exclusive); one solution not usually considered today is hinted at in the explanation offered by Justin Martyr. This makes it per-haps the oldest explanation in the Church's interpretive history.

Justin (100-165 A.D.) explains in his *Dialogue with Trypho* what Trypho the Jew saw as common Jewish expectation concerning Messiah. Trypho says,

> But Christ – if He has indeed been born, and exists anywhere – is unknown, and does not even know Himself, and has no power until Elias [Elijah] come *to anoint Him*, and make Him manifest to all... For all expect that Christ will be a man [born] of men, and that Elijah when he comes *will anoint him*. [Emphasis added].
>
> (Justin, *Dialogue with Trypho*, 8, 49)

To "make Him manifest to all" is strikingly similar to John the Baptist's own answer, "That he might be revealed to Israel." Justin's reply is as fol-lows,

> We know that this [anointing] shall take place when our Lord Jesus Christ shall come in glory from heaven; whose first manifestation the Spirit of God who was in Elijah preceded as herald in [the person of] John, a prophet among your nation; after whom no other prophet appeared among you. He cried, as he sat by the river Jordan : "I baptize you with water to repentance; but He that is stronger than I shall come, whose shoes I am not worthy to bear : He shall baptize you with the Holy Ghost and with fire : whose fan is in His hand, and He will thoroughly purge His floor, and will gather the wheat into the barn; but the chaff He will burn up with unquenchable fire."
>
> (Justin, *Dialogue with Trypho*, 49)

So Justin understands the baptism of Christ to be his *anointing* as Messiah by Elijah (cf. Matt 11:14; 17:12).[10] After this, Justin points out that John—the

---

Elijah. 8. Jesus interpreted his prospective dark fate in terms of eschatological trial. John saw his baptism as preparing Israel for the tribulation and judgment of the latter days. Therefore, Jesus could have gone to the Baptist not in order to obtain the forgiveness of sins but rather to receive a pledge of ultimate deliverance, a seal of divine protection from the imminent eschatological flood of fire. 9. Jesus wished to sanctify the waters of baptism. 10. Jesus was giving an example to Christians. 11. Jesus wanted to teach submission to priests. These last three all have roots in the Fathers. See Ignatius, *Eph.*, 18:2; Justin, *Dial*. 88; Clement of Alexandria, *Paed.* 1.6; Jerome, *Adv. Pelag.* 3.2; Gregory Nazianzen, *Or. Holy Lights* 14; Cyril of Alexandria, *Hom. On Lk.* 11. (Davies and Alli-son, 321-23).

[9] At least as far back as Chromatius (3rd century) it was said, "The Lord did not want to be baptized for his own sake but for ours, in order to fulfill all righteousness. Indeed, it is only right that whatever someone instructs another to do, he should first do himself. Since the Lord and Master of the human race had come, he wanted to teach by his example what must be done for disciples to follow their Master and for servants their Lord" (Chro-matius, *Tractate on Matthew* 12:2-3).

[10] Leon Morris is a contemporary commentator who seems to agree. Without making the priestly connection he nevertheless concludes of Jesus' baptism that he was "so to speak, commissioned for his work as Messiah" (Mor-ris 1992: 72).

last OT prophet of Israel—pointed only to Christ, and this unambiguous fact should prove to Trypho that Messiah has come in the person of Jesus Christ (Justin, *Dial*, 51).

Justin's explanation to Trypho makes perfect sense given the descent of the Holy Spirit immediately after the baptism. Luke records Jesus' words that begin his ministry – a quote from Isaiah 61:1-3, "The Spirit of the Lord is upon me, because he has *anointed* me to proclaim good news to the poor. He has sent me to proclaim liberty to the captives and recovering of sight to the blind, to set at liberty those who are oppressed, to proclaim the year of the Lord's favor" (Luke 4:18-19). This is said *immediately* after Jesus is baptized and the Spirit descends upon him like a dove (and then comes out of the wilderness). This is because there is a connection between Jesus' ministry and his baptism (as we will see shortly).

The quote from Isaiah 61 needs to be understood not merely as the anointing of Messiah, but as Jesus being anointed *into the priesthood*. As we will see, Jesus' baptism was a baptism ordaining him to serve before God as his High Priest. This is why scholars like Jay Adams say, "Christ was made a priest by John's baptism" (Adams 1975: 18). Everywhere in Isaiah 61 we find allusions to the priesthood and the Levitical Law. In fact, not only are these allusions, they are the very details of ordaining the priest! It says, "You shall be called priests of the Lord; they shall speak of you as the ministers of our God" (61:6).[11]

The reference to "anointing" is a priestly term used when consecrating a priest for his office, "After you put these clothes on your brother Aaron and his sons, anoint and ordain them. Consecrate them so they may serve me as priests" (Ex 28:41). The text says, "Grant to those who mourn in Zion - ... to give them a beautiful headdress instead of ashes" (Isa 61:3). The law of ordaining the priest also demands that a headdress be placed upon him, "Put the turban on his head and attach the sacred diadem to the turban... Bring his sons and dress them in tunics and put headbands on them" (Ex 26:6, 8-9). Isaiah says, "Grant to those who mourn in Zion - ... the garment of praise instead of a faint spirit" (Isa 61:3). Again, garments were to be made for the priests as his consecration, "Weave the tunic of fine linen and make the turban of fine linen. The sash is to be the work of an embroiderer. Make tunics,

---

[11] John Oswalt notes the following in relation to the term "minister" in his discussion of the related passage in Isaiah 56:6-7, "The word used, šārēt, *minister*, refers typically to cultic service (60:7, 10; 61:6)" (Oswalt 1998: 459). By "cultic service," he is talking specifically about the Levite (Ibid., n. 38).

sashes and headbands for Aaron's sons, to give them dignity and honor" (Ex 28:39-40).[12]

These laws concerning the ordaining of the priest are found in Exodus 28-29. The central passage explaining the actual service is Exodus 29:1-9. It reads,

> [1]Now this is what you shall do to them to consecrate them, that they may serve me as priests. Take one bull of the herd and two rams without blemish, [2] and unleavened bread, unleavened cakes mixed with oil, and unleavened wafers smeared with oil. You shall make them of fine wheat flour. [3] You shall put them in one basket and bring them in the basket, and bring the bull and the two rams. [4] You shall bring Aaron and his sons to the entrance of the tent of meeting and wash them with water. [5] Then you shall take the garments, and put on Aaron the coat and the robe of the ephod, and the ephod, and the breastpiece, and gird him with the skillfully woven band of the ephod. [6] And you shall set the turban on his head and put the holy crown on the turban. [7] You shall take the anointing oil and pour it on his head and anoint him. [8] Then you shall bring his sons and put coats on them, [9] and you shall gird Aaron and his sons with sashes and bind caps on them. And the priesthood shall be theirs by a statute forever. Thus you shall ordain Aaron and his sons.

The key here is verse 4 (cf. Ex 40:12). In the middle of the ceremony, Aaron and his sons are to be brought before the entrance of the tabernacle and washed (*rachats*) with water. The Hebrew word *rachats* is the same word used of Bathsheba when she "bathed" on the roof in front of David (2 Sam 11:2), and of the leprous Naaman who was commanded by Elisha to bathe (LXX has "baptize") in the Jordan seven times (2 Kings 5:10). Elmer Martens explains,

> The vb. is frequent in priestly legislation with instructions for the ceremonial washing of priests, and sometimes the washing of parts of the sacrifice (Num 19:7, 8; Lev 1:9, 13; 9:14). At their investiture and also on the Day of Atonement priests were to wash their bodies (Ex 29:4; Lev 8:6; 16:4, 24, 26). Before stepping to the altar or into the tent of meeting, priests were to wash hands and feet on penalty of death (Ex 30:19-21). Lavers for the tabernacle (30:18) and a brass "Sea" in Solomon's temple (2 Chron 4:6) facilitated the ritual.
>
> (Martens, '*rachats*,' *NIDOTTE* 3:1098-99)

Rachats is therefore a full body (or part of the body) bathing or washing. It often times includes full body immersion as one would undergo in a bath.[13]

---

[12] Other priestly references in Isaiah 61 include the priestly duty of bringing good news to the poor (Isa 61:1; cf. Rom 15:16), and proclaiming the year of the Lord's favor (Isa 61:2; cf. Heb 4:9).

[13] See Appendix 1: The Mode of Various Old Testament Baptisms.

Though we have no statement that Jesus was clothed with *physical* garments at his baptism,[14] we do have this curious statement made by Paul that, "As many of you as were baptized into Christ have *clothed yourselves* with Christ" (Gal 3:27). It is entirely probable that Paul is linking baptism with the ordination ceremony of the priest here, for nowhere else do we see washing being described in such close proximity than in the ordination of the Priest.

The NT gives us several other clues that Jesus is in fact being baptized in accordance with Mosaic Law. At least eight compelling tidbits of information converge at the beginning of Jesus' ministry.

1. Jesus was baptized (Matt 3:16; Mark 1:10; Luke 3:21; John 1:31-32).
2. Jesus was thirty years old at his baptism, the moment prior to the beginning of his ministry (Luke 3:23).
3. Jesus was called directly by God at his baptism (Heb 5:4-10; cf. Matt 3:17; Mark 1:11; Luke 3:22).
4. Jesus was baptized by John the Baptist, a Levitical priest in the line of Aaron (Luke 1:5, 13).
5. Jesus was without spot or blemish (Heb 5:9; 1 Pet 1:19; cf. Matt 3:14).
6. Jesus was a male (Matt 1:21).
7. Jesus begins his ministry immediately after his baptism (Luke 4:18ff).
8. Jesus' "genealogy" stems from Melchizedek, the High Priest of [Jeru]Salem (Heb 7:11; cf. Ps 110:4).

Each of these are arresting in light of the requirements for the Levitical priesthood. There are at least eight:

1. A priest had to be washed in water at his ordination (Ex 29:4).
2. A priest could not begin ministry until age 30 (Num 4:3; 47).[15]
3. A priest (especially the High Priest) had to be called of God as was Aaron (Ex 28:1).
4. A priest had to be washed by one already a priest (Ex 29:9; Num 25:13).
5. A priest had to be without defect in several special ways (Lev 21:16-23).[16]
6. A priest had to be a male (Num 3:15).

---

[14] However, Jung Kim does make the observation that early Christian and Jewish proselyte baptisms may have included going into the water naked and coming out to be clothed with new clothes (Kim 2004: 96-99).

[15] Darrell Bock comments on the meaning of age thirty in the OT. "The age of thirty has been taken as symbolic of the appropriate age for the beginning of service, since many OT offices could be filled at that Age. Among the OT references to thirty are the age for the priesthood (Nu. 4:3), the age of Joseph on entry into Pharaoh's service (Gen. 41:46), the age of Ezekiel when called to ministry (perhaps Ezek. 1:1), and most importantly, the age of David when he started reigning (2 Sam. 5:4). However, the number should not be taken as merely symbolic or theological, since Luke gives only an approximate number... The age of thirty connects Jesus with OT notables" (Bock 1994: 351-352). J.C. Ryle rightly notes, "This was the age, it will be recalled, when the Levites were first allowed to work in the tabernacle (Numbers 4:3)" (Ryle 1997: 54). See also Dionysius, Rom. Ant. 4:6.

[16] This includes blindness, lameness, disfigurement, deformity, crippleness, hunchbacks, dwarfism, eye defects, festering or running sores, or damaged testicles.

7. A priest began his ministry immediately after the ordination ceremony was completed (Ex 29:1).
8. A priest had to be descended from Aaron (Ex 28:1).

Only the eighth qualification is changed with Jesus. But this is exactly why Hebrews goes to such pains to explain it. Obviously, the writer of Hebrews was aware of the difficulty raised by Jesus' lineage so far as it concerns his priestly ministry. (This presupposes that Jesus' priestly ministry was in accordance with the Law). The explanation the writer gives is that in this instance, *his* genealogy could override the Law, because *his* lineage stems from Melchizedek, the High Priest of Salem, prior to Aaron. He even explains that Melchizedek was greater than Levi (the ancestor of Aaron), as is demonstrated by the tithe that Abraham (and therefore Levi as he was "in the loins" of Abraham; cf. Heb 7:9-10) paid to Melchizedek.

The interpretation that Jesus is being baptized into the priesthood is truly ancient. In the ancient document the *Testament of Levi* (dated to 100-200 B.C.),[17] there is a section that reads, "The heavens shall be opened, and from the temple of glory shall come upon him sanctification, with the Father's voice as from Abraham to Isaac. And the glory of the Most High shall be uttered over him, and the spirit of understanding and sanctification shall rest upon him in the water" (*TLevi* 5:21-22). This is strikingly similar to the Gospel's account of Jesus' baptism. The kicker here is that the entire chapter focuses upon the coming of "a new priest" (5:13) whose "priesthood the Gentiles shall be multiplied in knowledge upon the earth, and enlightened through the grace of the Lord. In his priesthood shall sin come to an end, and the lawless shall cease to do evil" (5:25). Though not inspired Scripture, it is clear that someone a very long time ago was either anticipating the coming Messiah or commenting upon the meaning of Jesus' baptism into the priesthood.

Jesus himself seems to make the connection between his priestly ministry and his baptism. These things are not a coincidence. Immediately after he cleanses the temple (Matt 21:12-13[18] - cleansing the temple was a *priestly* duty;

---

[17] Portions of the *Testament of Levi* were found among the Dead Sea Scrolls, which *predate* the Common Era. Thus, it is impossible for the entire book to be a NT Christian commentary. However, scholars debate whether or not parts of this book were in fact redacted later by a Christian author. We have said here that the Testament is a commentary on Christ's baptism. This takes the more conservative approach. If this is the case, it shows at the very *least* that the ideas we are expounding in this book have an incredibly ancient source. On the other hand, if it predates the baptism, then this is a prophecy that came true with remarkable accuracy when Jesus was baptized. This would lend more credence to the idea that Jesus was baptized into the priesthood. Whether the portion we quote here is pre or post Jesus' baptism, we will leave for the scholars to debate.

[18] In the very next verse, Jesus begins to heal the blind and the lame *in the temple* (Matt 21:14). Matthew tells us that this is in fulfillment of the *priestly* work of Messiah predicted by Isaiah 56:3-8. G.K. Beale writes, "Jesus'

cf. Lev 16:17-19; 2 Chron 29:15-16; Heb 9:6), the Pharisees ask him what authority he has to do this. He responds by asking them about the authority that John had to *baptize* (Matt 21:23).

Paul Myers (citing Dahl 1955:37-38) explains the answer to the question of John's authority.

> Jewish lustrations were performed by the priests. 'The priestly laws of the Old Testament and the corresponding rabbinic rules may seem to establish merely a casuistic system of purifications. But there can be no doubt that a deeper, spiritual meaning has been attached to them, just because the washings had the character of initiatory rites to temple worship.'... Since John came from a priestly family, it is assumed he would carry on this application.
>
> (Myers 1985: 27)

The biblical answer to Jesus' question is that John received his authority *to baptize* from God via the Torah. In asking this, Jesus is also connecting his own authority to dutifully cleanse the temple, like a good High Priest should, to his baptism performed by John in accordance with the Law. Thus, Jesus is implicitly arguing that his own baptism was his ordination into the priesthood. That is why he has the authority to cleanse the temple.

If Jesus is obeying a law from the OT in his baptism, it should not surprise us that he fulfills many other laws from the OT during his life. He was presented in the temple (Luke 2:22-23; cf. Lev 12:1-4, 6; Ex 13:1-2, 11-15; Num 3:11-13, 41, 414, 45, 47-51; 18:16), went to the Passover (Luke 2:42; cf. Ex 34:23), and observed the Jewish feasts (Mark 14:12; Luke 22:3; John 17:10), all in accordance with the Law.

Why did Jesus do these things? It is because he came as one "born under law" (Gal 4:4). The meaning of this is that Christ was obligated by the covenant of works to obey all of the Law of God. This was for him his righteousness (e.g., Deut 6:25).

Besides these things, Jesus was circumcised on the eighth day (Luke 2:21; cf. Lev 12:3). Jesus was both circumcised *and* baptized. This has not seemed to present a problem to paedobaptists who nevertheless suggest that baptism is the NT equivalent of *circumcision*. Perhaps they would think twice if

---

violent act in the temple would briefly have stopped the offering of sacrifices by shutting down the procedure by which animals were bought and sacrificed. If the temporary ceasing of sacrifices is to be inferred to any degree from the passage, then in performing this action, Jesus would have been indicating that the temple's purpose in offering sacrifices for forgiveness was passing away and that the temple was awaiting judgment. Directly after this episode, those who were forbidden to enter the temple because of the deformity were now accepted by Jesus: the 'blind and the lame came to Him in the temple, and He healed them' (Matt 21:14). This suggests... that he is beginning to clear the way for the eschatological temple, since the OT prophesied that in the future sanctuary eunuchs and other outcasts could worship even together with Gentiles. That which was formerly unclean will be considered clean for worship in the true temple (Is. 56:3-8). (Beale 2004b: 179).

they understood that Jesus' baptism was also done in fulfilment of OT Law, but not the law of circumcision. If we are correct, it would be strange indeed for baptism to replace circumcision when both laws existed side by side, together, in OT law.

Most Christians do not understand that baptism comes from the OT Law. F.C. Burkitt expressed the opinion of most when he said, "The Christian sacraments are certainly not part of the inheritance taken from Judaism. They are not derived from the Temple worship, nor (except in minor details) from the service of the Synagogue" (Burkitt 2003: 71). But this is not the view of everyone. Arland Hultgren writes,

> Can the origins of Christian baptism be traced to analogous customs in the Old Testament? Yes and no. Yes, in the general sense that there are washings of various kinds prescribed for various persons on various occasions, such as the self-immersion of Naaman seven times into the Jordan River (2 Kings 5:14) and a host of ritual washings (Ex 40:12;[19] Lev 11:32; 15:11, 13; 16:4; Sir 34:30). Yet these acts are not understood to be initiatory rites in the sense that Christian baptism is.
>
> (Hultgren 1994: 7)

Arthur McCormack says that Christian baptism was foreshadowed in the OT first ". . . obscurely in the ceremonial washing, which was intended to give ritual purity to persons and objects that had been defiled by contact with what was impure or unclean according to the law" (McCormack 1969: 50:20). H. Mueller says that the OT washing rites *lead* to Jewish proselyte baptism, which then *leads* to Christian baptism (Mueller 1967: 2:55). These authors are getting warmer. Still, it is rare to find a scholar making a direct link between OT washing ceremonies and NT baptism.

Jay Adams is one of the few who recognizes that Jesus' baptism fulfills a water-rite of the OT. Unfortunately, he pegs the wrong rite. "The law of the Old Testament which Jesus was obeying when he was baptized is found in Numbers 8:6-7" (Adams 1975: 17).[20] To his credit, Adams is trying to establish an OT link for baptism. But the law he identifies was for *all Levites*. On the other hand, Exodus 29:4 belonged only to the High Priest; the son(s) of

---

[19] It is odd, *to say that least*, that he would include Exodus 40:12 in this list, since this is the carrying out of the Exodus 29:4 law which is said to "*ordain* Aaron and his sons" (vs. 9). Is not "ordination" just another word for "initiation?"

[20] See also Rose 1949: 10-11. But Peter Leithart understands the correct OT ritual that corresponds to baptism. Repeatedly he insists that "baptism replaces ordination," with "ordination" being the entire ceremony of Exodus 29 (see Leithart 2003: 87, 100, 102, 107, 131). In this way baptism initiates a person into the priesthood and their various priestly privileges (pgs. 52, 96, 105-06, 112, 102). The troubling thing is that Leithart remains a committed *paedo*baptist, because he never bothers to question his presuppositions about circumcision.

Aaron.[21] Jesus was not an ordinary Levite. In fact, he wasn't a Levite at all. He was the High Priest of Israel (Heb 4:14). This is the law we suggest that Jesus was obeying, as one "in the order of Melchizedek" (see page 132).

The former law contained a sprinkling (*nazah*) of water and a washing (*kabas*) of clothes. As already mentioned, the ritual of Exodus 29 was a washing, bathing, or immersing (*rachats*) in water. In this way, Adams' mis-identification causes him to argue that sprinkling is the proper mode of baptism and that Jesus must have been sprinkled in the Jordan. He even goes so far as to say, "If Jesus was immersed, then He did not thereby 'fulfill all right-eousness,' for remember, we have seen that there was no requirement in the entire Old Testament ritual of immersion which He was obligated to fulfill" (Adams: 20). As *we* have seen, this is simply incorrect. As we will see later, sprinkling baptisms are fulfilled at *another baptism* in Jesus' life. It is true that sprinkling was a mode of baptism in the OT. It is not true that Jesus was sprinkled at his water baptism. It is correct to relate the mode of Christian baptism to the OT. When the proper law is understood, it becomes clear that sprinkling is not the appropriate mode for baptism today (see Part V - "Implications for Christian Baptism").

Now we can understand Jesus' explanation to John the Baptist. What did Jesus mean when he said he needed baptism in order to fulfill all right-eousness? First we should consider the meaning of "fulfill" in Matthew. Up to this point in Matthew's book, every time the word has been used it has meant that Jesus fulfills something *from the OT* (Matt 1:22; 2:5; 15, 17, 23 etc.). After this, Christ fulfills the Law, by both teaching its true meaning as the True Prophet, and by enacting it in his daily ministry as the True Priest (e.g., Matt 5:17). Since this is the way the word is normally used, it is reasonable to conclude that it is being used in the same way here.

The term "righteousness" is equally related to the OT as "fulfill" is. According to Deut 6:25, "righteousness" is directly linked to *obeying the Law.* "And it will be righteousness for us, if we are careful to do all this commandment before the LORD our God, as he has commanded us." Matthew usually uses the term in the same way. Michael D. Goulder points out, "Righteousness is normally in Matthew good works: (3:15; 5:20; 6:1; 21:32 and probably 5:10)" (Goulder 1974: 262).

---

[21] Raymond Abba correctly distinguishes the ordinary Levite from the priest when he says, "The evidence [does] warrant the commonly held assumption that in Deuteronomy Levites and priests are virtually synonymous terms, all Levites being priests or potential priests... Far from using the terms 'priest' and 'Levite' indiscriminately, the Deuteronomist reserves the term 'Levite' for a subordinate order of cultic official not altogether dissimilar to that portrayed in the Priestly Code" (Abba 1978: 1).

Fleshing this out in the actual obedience of Christ, Ulrich Luz says, "The Son revealed by the Father 'fulfills all righteousness' (3:15) and obeys the will of the Father as revealed in the Scriptures (4:1-11). As the inclusion of 3:15-4:11 with 27:43-54 shows, the obedience of the Son of God is highly significant for the Gospel" (Luz 2005; 93). Paul Myers concludes, "Perhaps the simplest way to view this saying is as a declaration of duty – to fulfill all that God asks. Viewed this way, baptism is presented as a motif of obedience" (Myers 1985: 94).

We have given several reasons to believe that Jesus is obeying the Law of Moses at his baptism. Though Justin did not relate the baptism directly to the Law, it is reasonable to conclude that Trypho and Jewish expectation of the day understood that Messiah needed to be anointed by Elijah from the prophets and the Law.

Following similar understanding, several commentators (especially in the early church) understand Jesus as fulfilling the Law of Moses at his baptism. While not necessarily tying the baptism to the particular rite of Ex 29:4, Theodore of Heraclea (d. 319) nevertheless wrote, "When he who is perfect according to the law was baptized with the baptism of John, he became the first to achieve the perfection of the law. For this reason even Christ, who was perfect in the law, was baptized with the baptism of John. For this reason he says, 'For thus it is fitting for us to fulfill all righteousness" (Theodore of Heraclea, Frag 21). It is difficult to understand how Jesus would "achieve the perfection of the law" if he was not in fact obeying any law at all. Likewise Chrysostom writing in 386 A.D. taught,

> And then he shows how this baptism is fitting. Why? "For thus it is fitting for us to fulfill all righteousness." The whole law is fulfilled by "all righteousness," by which all the commandments are performed. He is in effect saying, "Since then we have performed all the rest of the commandments, this baptism alone remains. I have come to do away with the curse that is appointed for the transgression of the law. So I must therefore first fulfill it all and, having delivered you from its condemnation, bring it to an end."
>
> (Chrysostom, *GMatt*, Homily 12.1)

Perhaps the earliest reference to this idea is found in Ignatius (d. 98-117 A.D.). He writes, "Our Lord was. . . baptized by John in order that righteousness might be fulfilled by Him" (Ignatius, *Smyr* 1:1). This is important because of how others in the early church were interpreting the event. Edouard Massaus explains,

> Undoubtedly, this passage recalls Mt. 3:15: Christ responds to the Baptist who is astonished to see him come to him in order to be baptized... Of all the evangelists, only Mt.

furnishes this motive for the baptism of Jesus: it is fitting to fulfill all righteousness. The same words of Ignatius are found in Mt. ... Moreover, the apocryphal gospels give a totally different motive for the baptism of Jesus. So it is that, according to Jerome,[22] the Gospel according to the Hebrews notes a certain reticence on the part of Jesus to be baptized, since he is not a sinner. In the Gospel according to the Ebionites, the sequence of words is different, and the word dikaiosu,nhn is missing. The Predicatio Pauli,[23] on the other hand, mentions that, urged by his mother and almost against his will, Christ allowed himself to be baptized.[24]

(Massaus, 1990: 89)

Our investigation into this matter leads us to a very specific conclusion. Christ "fulfilled all righteousness" at his baptism *by obeying the Law of Moses* in Ex 29:4, thereby *initiating him into the priesthood* so that he could begin his priestly ministry. The next three years of his life, going all the way to his sacrifice on the cross, are done in priestly service to the LORD his God. This could not have been done legally (i.e., biblically) without first undergoing the initiation ritual of the priest.

When read through this lens, NT writer's connections between baptism and the priesthood make perfect sense. Luke tells us that the baptismal event was the moment of time where Jesus began his *ministry* (Luke 3:23). Hebrews seems to directly relate the high priestly work of Christ (begun in baptism) to his temptation (the very next life-event of Christ). "For we do not have a high priest who is unable to sympathize with our weaknesses, but we have one who has been tempted in every way, just as we are, yet was without sin" (Heb 4:15; see also Heb 2:17-18 which connects the same priestly service with temptation). Paul directly relates Christian baptism (Rom 6:1-4) to the priestly service of making offerings of our bodies and lives each day before a Holy God (Rom 6:13ff). Thus, the NT repeatedly connects baptism and priestly service.

Implicit Purpose of Jesus' Baptism

There is another line of evidence suggesting that Jesus is fulfilling other things from the OT at his baptism. These also have to do with OT baptisms. We arrive at this conclusion by examining the order in which the early life of Jesus takes place. When we understand the implications of Jesus' life as fulfilling OT types and shadows, the possibilities for developing our theology of

---

[22] Jerome, *Contra Pelag.* 3.2.

[23] Cyprian, *Retract. De Baptism.* 17.

[24] It is misguided when Ignatius explains what he means by fulfilling righteousness in Ephesians 18:2 where he says, "He was born and was baptized in order that by his suffering he might cleanse the water." This does not seem to us to explain sufficiently how *Christ* is actually fulfilling all righteousness as he said elsewhere.

baptism explode with all sorts of interesting lines to pursue. Consider the following relationships between Jesus and Moses taken from Exodus and Matthew.

> 1a. Pharaoh tried to kill Moses and the other Israelite boys under two years of age (Ex 1:22).
> 1b. Herod tried to kill Messiah by calling for the extermination of all boys in Bethlehem under two years of age (Matt 2:13-15).
>
> 2a. Moses fled his home until "those seeking [his] life [were] dead" (Ex 4:19).
> 2b. Jesus fled his home until "those who sought the child's life [were] dead" (Matt 2:20).
>
> 3a. Moses comes out of Egypt (Ex 13:18).
> 3b. Jesus comes out of Egypt (Matt 2:15; cf. Hos 11:1).
>
> 4a. Moses leads the people through the Red Sea (Ex 14:22).
> 4b. John leads Jesus through the Jordan in his baptism (Matt 3:15-17).
>
> 5a. Moses leads the people from their baptism into the wilderness (Ex 15:22).
> 5b. The Holy Spirit leads Jesus from his baptism into the wilderness (Matt 4:1; cf. Luke 4:1).
>
> 6a. Israel goes into the wilderness for 40 years (Num 14:33-34).
> 6b. Jesus goes into the wilderness for 40 days (Matt 4:2).
>
> 7a. Israel is tested by God (Ex 16:4).
> 7b. Jesus is tempted by the Devil (Matt 4:1).[25]
>
> 8a. Moses leads the people to the foot of Mt. Sinai to receive the Law of God (Ex 19:17ff).
> 8b. Jesus leads the people to the foot of a new mountain to receive the Law of God (Matt 5:1ff).

Clearly, Matthew is developing a theme of promise-fulfillment between Moses and the life of Christ. Several people have noticed this.[26] Points 4 and 5 are of particular interest to a study of baptism. In Exodus, the crossing

---

[25] "Tested" and "tempted" are the same Greek word. LXX says God tested (*peirazō*) Israel (Ex 16:4). Matthew says Jesus was led into the wilderness to be tempted (*peirazō;* Matt 4:1).

[26] For example, Michael D. Williams notices many of these same comparisons and writes, "Matthew includes in his presentation the theme of Jesus as the true Israel... Matthew draws the correspondence vividly... Jesus is not just the savior of Israel; he is also the embodiment of what Israel was meant to be" (Williams 2005:225). Cf. Blomberg 2007, Motyer 2005: 22-23.

of the Red Sea takes place *immediately prior* to entering the wilderness to be tested. The same thing occurs in Matthew (and Luke).

This is fascinating, but made even more so by Paul's discussion of the Red Sea in 1 Cor 10:2. He writes, "All were *baptized* into Moses in the cloud and in the sea."[27] This is very important to understand. The very event that corresponds to Jesus' baptism from the OT is itself called a baptism by Scripture. Baptism is foreshadowed by *baptism*.

Many people do not take the time to consider the importance of this for a theology of baptism. It is not right to start our theology of baptism in the NT. But it is also not right to start a theology of baptism with Abraham (especially linking it to something totally organically unrelated to baptism like circumcision). Instead, our theology of baptism should begin in the *baptisms* of the OT. The idea that baptism is found in the OT is made explicitly by the NT several times.

Israel's Baptism

We have just seen the baptism of Israel "into Moses." Paul identifies two separate but related things in this baptism: the crossing of the Red Sea and the pillar of cloud. For Paul, this "baptism into" language is a clear sign that he sees a relationship between Moses and Christ and OT baptism with NT

---

[27] Paul immediately makes explicit Christological connections in the happenings of Moses and Israel in the manner that Matthew draws implicitly. For example he says, "All ate the same spiritual food, and all drank the same spiritual drink. For they drank from the spiritual Rock that followed them, and the Rock was Christ" (1 Cor 10:3-4). He says, "We must not put Christ to the test, as some of them did and were destroyed by serpents" (1 Cor 10:9). And he says, "These things happened to them as an example, but they were written down for our instruction, on whom the end of ages has come" (1 Cor 10:11). Perhaps most importantly of all, we read that "God was not pleased with most of them; their bodies were scattered over the desert" (1 Cor 10:5). This is the opposite declaration that God made towards his Son at his baptism, "This is my Son, whom I love; with him I am well pleased." Apparently this pronouncement shows that Jesus is True Israel, standing where the nation fell flat.

It is important to notice what Matthew and Paul are doing in this regard, because they see the life and events of Moses and Israel as foreshadowing and typifying Jesus Christ. Later in this book, we will make similar comparisons following the example of the Apostles and the hermeneutic taught by Christ himself. As we read in Luke, "And beginning with Moses and all the Prophets, he interpreted to them all the Scripture the things concerning himself" (Luke 24:27). The word for "interpret" is *diermēneuō*, from which we get the English word "hermeneutics." Thayer's Lexicon has for the meaning in this verse, "*To unfold the meaning of what is said, explain, expound.*" In other words, Jesus is not receiving some Dictaphone message from the Father, but is actually *interpreting* the Scripture according to the Christo-centric principle he explains to the disciples. This is the same principle they use throughout the NT (cf. Paul's similar explanation of his own interpretation of the Scriptures for the Corinthians in 1 Corinthians 2:13-15. The word for interpreting in vs. 13 is *sugkrinō*. LNL says that the word means to *judge whether something is like something else, hence a comparison.* Friberg's Lexicon says "it speaks of things brought together for explanation: *interpret, explain, combine* [1C 2.13]." The word in *1 Cor 2:15* is *anakrinō*. LNL says that "generally it is the process of evaluation: *examine, question, study carefully.*" Friberg's Lexicon says it is "generally of the process of evaluation: *examine, question, study carefully.*" Thus, the idea of interpretation plays a key role for Paul and his expectations for his churches).

baptism. For, he says elsewhere, "For as many of you as were *baptized into Christ* have put on Christ" (Gal 3:27).[28]

Fundamental to these baptisms is the element of water. The Red Sea is made of water and clouds are made of water. It is important to notice that when the NT relates *Christian baptism* to something in the OT, water is always involved. (As we will see, there are also baptisms of blood and baptisms of fire in the Scripture, but these are not identical to the sacrament of Christian baptism in water).

The baptism of the Holy Spirit (which is related to fire, cf. Acts 1:5; 10:47 etc.), or baptisms that unbelievers go through (cf. Rev 20:10, 15), or even the baptism-circumcision link made in Col 2:11-12 are *not* referring to the water-immersion rite of baptism, but to *other kinds* of baptism altogether. These other kinds of baptism do not have ordination in mind so much as cleansing or even punishment.

There are several ways of getting at this so that we can understand. We can remember John's baptism was "for repentance." Yet, Jesus gives a *different reason* for being baptized. A different reason assumes a different purpose for baptism.

Then there is the idea that Jesus himself gives that his baptism into water was not the only baptism he underwent. In Mark 10:38-39 Jesus says, "'Are you able to drink the cup that I drink, or to be baptized with the baptism with which I am baptized?' And they said to him, 'We are able.' And Jesus said to them, 'The cup that I drink you will drink, and with the baptism with which I am baptized, you will be baptized.'" Jesus is not talking about water baptism (which the disciples had all undergone already[29]), but a baptism of death. Luke 12:50 makes the same point, "I have a baptism to be baptized with, and how great is my distress until it is accomplished."

Jesus was not distressed about going under the water because he couldn't swim. He was distressed about his upcoming crucifixion *baptism*.[30] For now

---

[28] In this regard, the *Testament of Levi* as found in the Cairo Geniza (Dead Sea Scrolls) says the following as it talks about a priest, "And when you stand up to enter the house of God, bathe yourself in water, and dress yourself with the clothes of the priesthood. And when you are dressed, go back again and wash your hands and your feet before you offer on the altar anything at all" (CTLevi ar *Bodleian* Col. c 2).

[29] This point is not explicit in Scripture, but is easily inferred. It is reasonable to assume that the disciples of John the Baptist were baptized by John. Some of John's disciples later became Jesus disciples. Besides this, the disciples of Jesus baptized many later followers of Christ (John 4:1-2). Finally, the repeated message of the disciples was to "repent and be baptized." Surely each of these facts demonstrates that the disciples were baptized very early on in the ministry of Jesus.

[30] It is *this* baptism that we believe fulfills the *sprinkling* baptisms of the old covenant. Therefore, to sprinkle today is akin to going back to type and shadow which has been fulfilled in the death of Christ. We will say more about this later.

we will leave it at this, though we will return to these subjects again: we must not confuse the different kinds of baptisms, or say that baptism has the same meaning for everyone by conflating different ideas into a single category. As we will see, Jesus was fulfilling a particular law, and this is the fundamental reason why we practice baptism the way that we do.

Noah's Baptism

Peter regards Christian baptism as the "antitype" of Noah's flood.[31] "Because they formerly did not obey, when God's patience waited in the days of Noah, while the ark was being prepared, in which a few, that is, eight persons, were brought safely through water. Baptism, which corresponds to this, now saves you, not as a removal of dirt from the body but as an appeal to God for a good conscience, through the resurrection of Jesus Christ" (1 Peter 3:20-21).

"Corresponds to this" is the Gk. word *antitupos*, from which we get our English word: antitype. Some people may say that the flood was only *symbolic* of baptism; i.e., that it was not a real baptism. This is possibly because they get hung up on the type-antitype relationship. But just because the flood is a type of Christian baptism, it does not follow that it was not a *real* baptism, any more than it follows that animal sacrifices are not real sacrifices because they were types of Christ's sacrifice on the cross. Types are not related to antitypes as forgeries are to originals, but as an acorn is to an oak, as shadows are to the substance. There is an organic relationship to them (for more on types and antitypes; see Part II, Section 1).

Peter's reference to the flood as baptism is critical on three accounts. First, in telling us that the flood anticipates Christian baptism Peter sets up another direct baptismal relationship between the OT and the NT. Second, the relationship is comparable because both baptisms take place with the same element: water (see Appendix Two: Typology and Allegory, Substance and Identity). Following these, the third point establishes that baptism *predates* circumcision. Baptism goes at least back to Genesis 6 while circumcision is not introduced until Genesis 17. Now the problem for the circumcision-baptism connection is even greater. Not only did baptism exist side by side with circumcision in the Law, it actually *predated* circumcision in

---

[31] Marianne Micks shows how Protestants have recognized in Noah's Flood the idea of baptism saying, "Curiously, the flood was the chief archetype featured in Martin Luther's prayer at baptism, and this co-called Flood Prayer found its way into the 1549 Book of Common Prayer, thanks to Thomas Cranmer. Luther's prayer repeats the scriptural analogy of eight persons saved in the ark and goes on to add that by the baptism of Jesus God 'did sanctify the flood Jordan, and all other waters to the mystical washing away of sin'" (Micks, 1996: 15).

history.   We wonder how baptism can replace circumcision when it predates circumcision by hundreds or thousands of years.[32] We will argue later that this has significant implications in trying to identifying NT baptism as the equivalent sign of OT circumcision.

Legal Baptisms

We have assumed, but not yet argued, that the Mosaic Law contained baptisms. Perhaps you are wondering if it is even legitimate to call Exodus 29:4 a baptism.[33] But Scripture is *explicit* about this. Hebrews 9:10 tells us that *in the Mosaic Law* there were "various baptisms." Among English translations, only the NRS and YLT make this clear. The Greek term used in this verse is a form of the noun *baptismos* or "baptism."[34]

There are basically five root words for baptism in the Scripture. *Baptizō* is the verbal form. It is found only one time in the OT LXX—in 2 Kings 5:14 where Naaman dips himself seven times into the Jordan (it is also found in Jud. 12:7 to describe ceremonial *bathing*, in Sir. 34:25 to describe ceremonial washing after touching a dead body, and in Isaiah 21:4 where it metaphorically describes overwhelming terror). *Baptisma* is the most common noun describing Christian baptism. It occurs some 19 times in the NT and never

---

[32] Paedobaptists have made some intriguing arguments trying to connect the flood with circumcision. For instance, Meredith Kline writes, "In Gen. 9:11 the flood is viewed as the cutting-off curse of the covenant: 'I establish my covenant with you, that never again shall all flesh be cut off by the waters of a flood.' The same play on 'cut (off),' is used with reference to the flood waters here as is found with circumcision in Gen. 17:14. (Note, too, the coincidental use of 'flesh,' in both passages.) From a biblical viewpoint, therefore, circumcision and baptism are related to a common symbolic source; for the waters of the flood were a proto-circumcision as well as a proto-baptism" (Kline 1968: 62 n. 24). This is an interesting and perhaps even a valid comparison. Yet this same exegete sees the same parallel between circumcision *and the Sabbath* saying, "Note also the use of the same pun on the idiom of cutting, i.e., making, a covenant to denote the curse of the cutting off of the covenant-breaker in the case of violations of both circumcision (Gen 17:14) and Sabbath (Exod 31:14)" (Kline 2006b: 82). Since the first pun is supposed to be evidence for why baptism should replace circumcision in the NT, we wonder—on the same grounds—why puns showing similarity between the Sabbath and circumcision are not also used to show how the Sabbath replaces circumcision as the covenantal sign in the OT? Our explanation is that similarity does not mean anything more than that. It is exegetically improper to create an artificial edifice connecting circumcision with baptism covenantally, when the Sabbath is every bit as much a sign of the covenant as the flood was. A significant problem that paedobaptists have is that they are not consistent in their reasoning. They will rightly say that the Sabbath does not replace circumcision, since circumcision continues parallel to the Sabbath as a sign. Yet, as we will see, the same holds true for baptism. It continues parallel to circumcision as a sign that God never suggests "replaces" circumcision in the OT. Overlapping signs do not make for identical signs. We must seek the origins of baptism in *baptism*. For more, see Appendix Two.

[33] Two church fathers are worth quoting, as they agree that Hebrews 9:10 refers to baptisms. James Dale explains Ambrose's (d. 397 A.D.) view, "Among these 'many, very many kinds of baptisms,' he enumerates as 'one kind, the healing of the leprosy of Naaman; another kind was the purging of the world by the deluge; a third kind, when our fathers were baptized in the Red Sea." Gregory Nazianzen (328-389 A.D.) writes, "Moses baptized, but with water, and previously with the cloud and sea" (Both quotes in Dale 1869: 380, 382).

[34] The word here (*baptismos*) is a different word from the Greek normally employs for Christian Baptism (*baptisma*). However, as Anthony R. Cross has pointed out, the former word "is the more all-encompassing term and could include [the latter], while the peculiarly Christian term *baptisma* could not include the broader [term]" (Cross 2002: 165). A good defense of this can be found in Duncan.

in the LXX. *Baptismos* is used by the NT to describe ceremonial or OT washings (Mark 7:4, Heb 6:2; 9:10), but it also incorporates Christian baptism in two of its four usages (Col 2:12 and Heb 6:2). It is likewise not used in the OT. *Baptistēs* is the formal name of John the Baptist. Finally, *baptō* is a separate verb describing dipping. It is most common in the LXX where it discusses ceremonial dipping of something into blood (Ex 12:22; Lev 4:6, 17; 9:9; 14:6, 51), water (Lev 11:32; Num 19:18; 2 Kgs 8:15; and probably Josh 3:15), oil (Lev 14:16; Deut 33:24); as well as non-ceremonial dipping of food into wine (Ruth 2:14; John 13:26), of a staff into a honeycomb (1 Sam 14:27); of cloth into water (2 Kgs 8:15); and of garments into blood (Rev 19:13). There are also metaphorical uses of the word in Job 9:31 and Ps 67:24 (also Sir. 31:26).

As pointed out above, besides Hebrews 9:10, *baptismos* is used only in Hebrews 6:2 to incorporate both OT and NT baptisms;[35] in Mark 7:4 (along with the verb *baptizō*) to discuss ceremonial hand washing; and in Colossians 2:12 where it talks about our being "buried with Christ in baptism." This last reference is probably not referring to Christian baptism in water, but to Spirit-baptism upon repentance.[36] The other references demonstrate that it is used of ceremonial baptisms either from the OT or from Jewish tradition. Once more the NT is establishing here a type-antitype relationship between OT baptism and NT baptism.

---

[35] *TDNT* says of this verse, "'*Baptismōn didache*' [teachings of baptisms] denotes instruction on the difference between Jewish (and pagan?) 'washings' (including John's baptism?) and Christian baptism" (Oepke, '*baptō*, *baptizō*', *TDNT*, 1:545). Interpreters since at least the time of Chrysostom have completely missed this point. Chrysostom said of the plural "baptisms" (Heb 6:2) that it refers to baptizing over and over again (Chrysostom, *Homily IX: Hebrews vi. 1-3*). Calvin takes another interpretation saying, "By baptisms are meant the solemn rites, or the stated days of baptizing" (Calvin: 2005: 133). And so on.

[36] For support on this from a paedobaptist, see Reymond 1998: 929-930. For a brilliant baptistic analysis of these verses, see Barcellos 2005: 3-23. We really only differ with him on one point which is the meaning of the genitive "of Christ" in "the circumcision of Christ" (vs. 11). He opts to call it a possessive genitive; that is a circumcision *that belongs to* Christ. He says, "Paul has been talking about what has happened *in* and *to* the Colossians not *for* them. Paul discusses what Christ did *for* the Colossians in vv. 13b and 14. Verses 11 and 12 discuss what happens *in* the Colossians and *to* them." (p. 10). We would suggest that it is neither a possessive genitive, nor a subjective genitive (that is the circumcision *done by* Christ – the view taken by most infant Baptists because it allows them to maintain their infant baptism by suggesting that Paul is alluding to the physical rite of circumcision and later, the physical rite of baptism in vs. 12). Rather, it is an *objective* genitive. Thomas Schreiner is helpful here, "The 'circumcision of Christ' probably refers to his death, for the participial clause in verse 12 indicates that the circumcision Paul describes occurred when 'we were buried together with him in baptism.' Thus, the decisive circumcision for believers is the 'cutting off' of Christ at the cross. Entrance into the church is based on Christ's work at the cross, not the acceptance of circumcision" (Schreiner 1993: 168-169). Finally, a good quote from Spurgeon is appropriate, "It is often said that the ordinance of baptism is analogous to the ordinance of circumcision. I will not controvert that point although the statement may be questioned. Supposing it be, let me urge on every believer here to see to it that in his own soul he realizes the spiritual meaning both of circumcision and baptism and then consider the outward rites. For the thing specified is vastly more important than the sign" (Spurgeon 1868: 695; see also Kingdon 1973; Conner 2007: 113-117).

Why do most English translations obscure the typology by opting to translate *baptismos* as "washing?" It is difficult to know for sure. This is the only form of the word "baptism" that is *ever* translated anything but "baptism," and here only half of the time (two out of four occurrences). In one of those occurrences (Mark 7:4), the verb *"baptizō"* is also used, indicating that it is correct to see ceremonial washings as baptisms.[37] Since the word obviously means baptism in half of its uses, and since the other forms of "baptism" are always translated "baptism" by English translations, perhaps the answer to the question is that there is a preconceived bias against the idea that there could be baptisms in the OT Law.[38] As Peter and Paul have already demonstrated, baptism is present in the OT. This verse adds for us that at Sinai the very idea of baptism was codified into Law.

We mentioned the distinctions in various types of baptism when we discussed Israel's baptism into Moses. Now is the time to discuss this in more detail, since we are dealing with legal baptisms. Leonard Badia writes,

> According to the Jews, baptism means a religious ablution [immersion] signifying purification or consecration...[39] Perhaps it would be well to point out that there are two types of washing purifications or baptisms. One is initiatory. It is a rite required of someone who wishes to enter a group. It does not have to be repeated. The second is a rite that is repeated at intervals as a sign of purification from evil thoughts, words or deeds.
>
> (Badia 1980: 12, 47)

The question has sometimes been raised as to where John the Baptist (and other of his contemporaries like the Qumranians and Essenes) got the idea to baptize in the first place. We believe it clearly comes from the OT Law. This is not our opinion alone.

Dwight Hervey Small expresses the point in unequivocal terms. "The Law prescribed Baptism. It was ceremonious and symbolic" (Small 1959: 119). Matthew Henry agrees, "Water baptism then, when our Lord appeared, was no new thing: it had been applied, in every age of the church, and especially under the Mosaic dispensation, to religious uses" (Henry, *n.d.*:

---

[37] Here, the most popular translation for baptize is "wash." This is the *only* time this verb is ever translated with the more generic "wash." The NAS is better: "cleanse." The idea is clearly ceremonial purity, not physical dirt and the spread of disease. Of course, what word better represents this to a modern mind than baptism? See also YLT and VUL (*baptizentur*).

[38] While water-rites are certainly part of what Hebrews has in mind in Heb 9:10 (that is why translators go with the "washing" word), it is possible that bloody sprinklings are also in view, especially given that the previous verses (vs. 7, 9) have just talked about sacrifices while the later verses (vs. 12, 13, 14) talk about Christ shedding his blood. But "washing" is not a word we normally associate with blood! "Baptism" encompasses this well.

[39] Originally in Singer 1901: 499-500.

489). If we are correct on this point, then the words of William Barclay explaining the uniqueness and novelty of Christ's baptism are surely off base. "It is the fact that *never in all history before this had any Jew submitted to being baptized*. The Jews knew and used baptism, but only for proselytes who came into Judaism from some other faith" (Barclay 1975a: 59-60).

This fact, that baptism was ritually codified into Law, has great significance for our practice of baptism today. While one-time baptismal event-signs like the flood and the Red Sea are useful to study (and we will throughout this book), it is the fact that baptism became a *sacramental* institution (and that as a particular sign of a particular covenant, see Part IV) that grounds our theology of Christian baptism deep in OT history. When this is understood properly, the burden of proof shifts to the paedobaptist. He must now demonstrate why baptism is replaced by something other than baptism, why its mode changes from the OT practice of "bathing" to something like sprinkling, and why its application changes from its OT application to now includes infants, something it was never applied to in the OT administration of the rite.

Naaman's Baptism

We want to mention one more example of baptism in the OT. Like the others in this section, this is an explicit reference that we do not have to infer from anything. Bringing this up here will help ground the claim that in the *Law* there were various water baptisms.

Though it is not derived from the NT, it is found in the LXX. The Greek verb for baptism is used only one time in the LXX – in 2 Kings 5:14.[40] It is the story of Naaman the leper who is told to "wash" in the *Jordan River* seven times. The verse in question says, "So he went down and dipped (*baptizō*) himself seven times in the Jordan." As this rite is called a baptism in the Greek and is so very much like the baptism of Christ (especially the fact that both are in the Jordan River), it is certainly fair to identify it as yet another type of Christian baptism.

As far back as Irenaeus (177 A.D.), the Church has understood Naaman's washing to be a baptism. "[Naaman] dipped himself, (says the Scripture,) seven times in the Jordan. It was not for nothing that Naaman of old, when

---

[40] See above, including the other instances found in *Jud* 12:17, *Sir* 34:25, and *Isa* 21:4 LXX. The two apocryphal references demonstrate that the Greek word *baptizō* was being used prior to the writing of the NT as a synonym for *lutron* (washing), which is the usual Greek word to describe ceremonial washings.

suffering from leprosy, was purified upon his being *baptized*" (Irenaeus, Frag. 34).[41] Marianne Micks rightly points out,

> When [Naaman] reemerges, his flesh is restored; the Bible says his flesh is like that of a child's, suggesting not only healing and cleansing, but rebirth... the story [of baptism] achieve[s] a remarkably powerful illustration of the role of the river in Christian tradition. The river brings freedom, yet the journey to the Promised Land is inextricably linked to death and resurrection. We go under the water in death. We rise to newness of life.
>
> (Micks 1996: 8, 5)

In this way the faithless words of Joram ("Am I God, to kill and to make alive;" 2 Kgs 5:7) are fulfilled in Jesus Christ. "All of us who have been baptized into Christ Jesus have been baptized into His death[.] Therefore we have been buried with Him through baptism into death, in order that as Christ was raised from the dead through the glory of the Father, so we too might walk in newness of life" (Rom 6:3-4).

Comparing the baptism of Naaman the leper with the law of cleansing lepers in Leviticus 14:6-8 (where it says to dip[42] a sacrifice in the blood of a bird killed over running water and then bathe[43] in water) is important in light of the fact that Moses required baptisms for the lepers after they were cleansed (like Naaman) from their disease.[44] In other words, we may ask why Elisha commanded this of Naaman? (Naaman thought Elisha would just wave his hand over him, but instead the prophet tells him he must be baptized, and that only in the Jordan River; cf. 2 Kings 5:10, 11, 12, 14). Because, Elisha was going back to the Law. Thus, if Naaman's washing is called a baptism, then we must infer that the cleansing rite of the leper was also a baptism. This is one of many baptisms found in the Law, and it is an example of why Hebrews says there are diverse baptisms in the OT Law.

These four references to baptism in the OT are explicit and important. They ground our theology of baptism in a place much older than Jesus and

---

[41] Likewise Gregory of Nyssa (ca. 335-394 A.D.) said, "Naaman the Syrian [is cleansed] by washing in the Jordan, clearly indicating what should come, both by the use of water generally, and by the dipping in the river in particular. For the Jordan alone of rivers, receiving in itself the first-fruits of sanctification and benediction, conveyed in its channel to the whole world, as it were from some fount in the type afforded by itself, the grace of Baptism" (Gregory of Nyssa, *On the Baptism of Christ*). And Ambrose of Milan (ca. 340-397 A.D.) said, "The Syrian Naaman bathed seven times under the old law, but you were baptized in the name of the Trinity" (Ambrose, *On the Mysteries* ch. 4).

[42] Heb: *tabal*; Greek: *baptō*!

[43] Heb: *rachats*; meaning: to wash. See rachats in the Naaman story in 2 Kgs 5:10, 12, 13.

[44] It was obviously the washing with water that *instrumentally* made Naaman clean. Later, he says he will offer sacrifices only to Elisha's God [2 Kgs 5:17], and this corresponds to the sacrificial part of the rite of the leper, and it is done for sin [vs. 18] rather than the external leprosy.

John. This in turn means that if we wish to truly understand baptism, we must look deep within the pages of the OT Hebrew Scripture. When we do this, our entire focus of baptism is radically altered. It is allowed to change, to grow, and to incorporate many more things than a neo-Marcion "NT only" theology of baptism can give us.

We are going to turn our attention now to the study of baptism from the OT. There are two tracks we will take in this study. First, we are going to look at baptism from the perspective of the temple motif. As we have seen, baptism was a rite of the priest. It was performed around the tabernacle/temple in the OT. But baptism is an important element of *all* temples in the OT, not just the two commanded by God to be built by the Israelites.

After this, we will turn our attention to the deliberate comparisons that Scripture makes between various baptismal stories in history. Having already seen the baptism of Jesus, we will compare his baptism with several other baptismal stories. This in turn will deepen our theology of baptism and why it is such an important rite for NT Christians to undergo.

Part II - Baptism and the Sanctuary

Introduction

The temple motif is basic to the OT's worldview. A tremendous amount of literature has been published on this in the past couple of decades.[45] But not much of anything has been done on the element of baptism as found in each of those sanctuaries. As we take a look at the sanctuaries of the Bible, we want to pay special attention to baptism. In order to understand these connections clearly, however, we need to take a closer look at the biblical hermeneutic called typology. That is the focus of Part II, Section I.

---

[45] Probably the best overall treatment of the theme of sanctuary is G. K. Beale's *The Temple and the Church's Mission: A Biblical Theology of the Dwelling Place of God* (Beale 2004b). Two other important and recent works are Meredith Kline's *God, Heaven and Har Magedon* (Kline 2006a) and Vern Poythress' *The Shadow of Christ in the Law of Moses* (Poythress 1991). Smaller summaries of individual temples include Gordon Wenham's "Sanctuary Symbolism in the Garden of Eden Story" (Wenham 1994), and Steven Holloway's "What Ship Goes there" (Holloway 1991).

Section I: Baptism and Typology

What is Typology: Definition

What exactly is typology? One theological dictionary says that typology is "the study of Old Testament types as anticipating New Testament persons or occurrences" (*WDTT* 1996: 290). "Type," used in the way we are defining it here, is a biblical word (cf. Rom 5:14; 1 Cor 10:6; Heb 8:5; cf. Ex 25:40 LXX). Types may consist of persons, actions, events, and institutions (Goppelt 2002: 18). They occur as part of *real* history. History does not take a backseat in typological interpretation as it sometimes does in allegorical methods of interpretation (Estelle 2005: 69). Typology presupposes, then, that historical events in redemptive history were predetermined ahead of time by a single Author.

Not everything in creation and history are actual types. Rather, only those acts of grace and judgment that point to the final salvation/judgment in Christ would normally be considered (Goppelt 2002: 219). At least, this seems to be the way the NT understands types to work. Why would this be the case? It is because the key to unlocking the meaning of Scripture is *only* found in Christ (Luke 24:27, 44; 2 Cor 1:20; 3:15ff). Unless Christ is understood *from the* OT, a veil remains over the eyes. This is why Paul says that when the Jews read the OT, a veil remains over their eyes until they understand and see Christ (2 Cor 3:14-16). Christ-o-centric interpretation keeps interpretation from becoming a guessing game open to everyone's personal opinion, speculation, and imagination.

Furthermore, the types that we know exist (because the NT talks about them) always relate the same kinds of things. For example, types contain similar substance (like water) or time frames (like Jonah's three days in the fish and Jesus' three days in the earth) or institutions (the tabernacle is a type of the heavenly tabernacle), or events (baptisms) or laws and morality (the disobedience of Israel as a "type" for us) etc. This forms another barrier against some kinds of allegorical methods that make the Scripture say whatever the interpreter feels like it should say (for more see Appendix: Substance and Identity). *Typology is not allegory.* Edmund Clowney makes an important point about temple typology (which we will look at in detail below as we come to a better understanding of baptism through it), "Above all we must recognize that [typology] is not spiritualization in our usual sense of the word, but the very opposite. In Christ is realization. It is not so much that Christ fulfills what the temple means; rather Christ is the meaning for which the temple existed" (Clowney 1973: 177).

Probably most important of all, typology is Scripture's own language; its own hermeneutic. A good case can be made that "typology was the hermeneutic normative for Judaism and is the hermeneutic of the New Testament - which is to say that both Old and New Testament are bound together in their mutual witness to redemptive history consummated in Christ" (Riesen 1988: 41; also Hummel 1964). Jesus himself used typology many times (Matt 12:6, 39-40, 42; John 1:51; 2:19; 3:14; 6:41 etc.), as did many other NT writers (as we will see shortly, this concerns baptism specifically). When Jesus taught the Disciples how to read the Scripture, he taught them to use typology; that is to see everything in the Law and prophets as concerning himself (Luke 24:27, 44).

How does typology work?

Types (Gk: *tupos*) and antitypes are related to each other like the image of Abraham Lincoln on the front of a penny is related to the actual man of history. The image is the type (like a *type*writer that strikes an image onto a piece of paper). The man is the antitype.

In this example, the antitype comes *prior* to the type. We will call this kind of antitype the "archetype." This is not a biblical word, but it helps maintain clarity. The archetype stands before all other types, as the model or original pattern upon which all others were copied. Archetypes are *preexisting heavenly realities*. For example, God commanded Moses to make a tabernacle. He was to build it exactly like God told him, "In accordance with all that I show you concerning the pattern of the tabernacle and of all its furniture, so you shall make it" (Ex 25:9). Why? It is because that earthly tabernacle was a replica of the heavenly tabernacle (Heb 8:5; 9:23-24). (Note: Because there are typological relationships that exist between biblical sanctuaries, then what is true or meaningful in the type will have the same function and meaning in the next type or antitype. This truth extends from the architecture to the furnishings. In this way not only is the meaning of baptism enriched, but the correct application(s) of it may be deduced).

The first *created* example of the archetype is what we will call the "prototype." Here prototype does not refer to something flawed, but something that is first. The tabernacle is not the prototype of the heavenly reality. It was one of many types (more properly "ectypes") that followed the prototype. The prototype distinction belongs to a *created* sanctuary that *God* built.

This is the heaven/earth/Eden sanctuary. We will have more to say about this in the next section.

When using the Bible's own language, the type usually comes *before* the antitype. Antitype *is* a biblical word (1 Pet 3:21). It refers to the substance, reality, or fullness that the type foreshadows. Generally speaking, types are in the OT. Antitypes are in the NT.

But if the type foreshadows the *antitype*, how can it also be patterned upon an *arche*type? The answer is that the archetype bears a special relationship to the antitype. We may think of the antitype as the archetype *come down out of heaven*. Christ is both Archetype (pre-existing Lord upon whom image bearers are patterned) and Antitype (the greater Adam, David, Jonah come down etc.); there is a sanctuary that is both archetype (in heaven) and antitype (on earth in the form of Christ and his church); etc.

Obviously, this complicates the matter of typology to some degree, but it is important to try and get a firm grasp of this concept. So take the time to try and understand this. It is important to our study of baptism. There is a triangular relationship to what we just said. Geerhardus Vos (Vos 1994: 38) created a diagram explaining this.

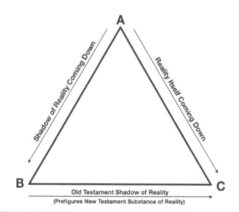

Key:
A Represents the Heavenly Reality
B Represents the OT which is a "shadow" of the Heavenly Reality
C Represents the NT which is the substance of the Heavenly Reality
B Prefigures C because B is the "shadow" of A.
C Equals A manifested physically.

I would prefer to take Vos' equilateral triangle and turn it into an obtuse triangle.

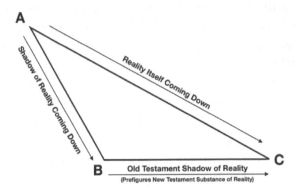

The benefit of this change is that is shows how "Reality" is *temporally* antecedent to anything in created history (imagine "B" as the beginning of history). For example, Christ the Lamb was slain before the foundation of the world (Rev 13:8). Yet, Reality still resides "above" the created order, showing its heavenly origin. History still had to occur, because what is ordained is distinct from what occurs in time. For example, Christ was slain two thousand years ago outside of Jerusalem. Now we want to proceed to the question, how does typology relate to baptism?

Baptism and Typology

We have already seen that typology is the way Peter refers to the flood. As noted in the first chapter, Peter says that baptism "corresponds" to the flood. "Corresponds to" is the Greek word *antitupos*, from which we get our English word: antitype. What is being typified by the flood? In answer to the question, Goppelt is worth quoting at length,

> 1 Peter uses a type from primeval history to illustrate the way in which baptism separates the church from the world. Like the saying of Jesus in Matt 24:37-39, 1 Pet 3:20f. compares this age, which is hastening to the end (1 Pet 4:7) and in which the judgment will begin (4:17), with the time of the first world judgment. At that time only eight people from the whole human race were saved (3:20; cf. Gen 6:18; 7:7), so now only a few from this blind generation, which is sunk in worldliness, will permit themselves to be saved (cf. 1 Pet 1:14f.; 2:9f.; 4:3f.). Our passage, however, relates the flood directly to baptism, not to the final judgment as Jesus and late Judaism do... As was true in 1 Cor 10:1f., it is not simply the eternal event that is being compared. Passing through the water of baptism is symbolic of passing through a water of judgment. According to the NT and for Paul especially, baptism saves in that it judges the old man, and, therefore, the final judgment is fulfilled in it proleptically.
>
> (Goppelt 2002: 156-157)

Judgment is a theme of baptism that many people miss, but because it is so important, we will dedicate some space to it at the end of this section (see Excursus: Baptism as Ordeal).

As the quote above intimates, Paul also refers to baptism with typological language. He explicitly calls the Red Sea baptism and its associated events "types" (*tupos*; 1 Cor 10:6).[46] The verse says specifically that "these things happened as examples[47] for us." "Baptized into Moses" language strengthens the typological connection, which is parallel in essence (as opposed to just form) to being "baptized into Christ" (Gal 3:27). Thus, the Belgic Confession beautifully says, "The Son of God... is our Red Sea, through which we must pass to escape the tyranny of Pharaoh, who is the devil, and to enter the spiritual land of Canaan" (*BC* Art. 34).

Matthew mentions two types of baptism. In the broader typology between Moses/Israel and Christ (ch. 2-5) stands the crossing of the Red Sea and Jesus' baptism in the Jordan. But there is also a typological relationship between Jonah and Christ's death. This is almost certainly another type of baptism (see *Excursus* below). Finally, there is the typological relationship that Hebrews develops in the baptismal Levitical laws. Peter Leithart believes these biblical relationships are so basic to baptism that he says this is not "typological ornamentation but a necessary dimension of the theology of baptism" (Leithart 2003: 43).

These relationships can be seen clearly only by taking the time to examine the common baptismal themes of the sanctuaries. We are now prepared to begin discussing these sanctuaries in the next chapter.

---

[46] Heinrich Müller comments on Paul's use to *typos* ("type") here to show how the same serious judgment that fell upon the people in the wilderness can also fall upon NT Christians, especially in relationship to the sacraments. "[In] 1 Cor 10:6, 11, Paul uses *typos* to interpret the events in the Corinthian church in the light of Israel's experiences in the wilderness. The punishment of God's ancient people which followed their disgraceful practices is seen as a prefiguration of judgment on those who abuse the Lord's Supper. It carries a specific warning to the 'strong' at Corinth not to abuse the sacrament. The typological method developed by Paul thus consists in expounding the analogous relationship of concrete historical OT events, in the sense of the past prefiguring present or future eschatological happenings... It is God himself who creates this 'typical' relationship, in so far as his Word of revelation (the Scriptures) fulfils it (cf. Rom. 4:23 f.; 1 Cor. 10:11). In this prefiguration of eschatological saving events in OT history, witness is born to the participation of the community in the saving work of Christ" (Müller 1978: 905-06). His comments appear to us to bolster our understanding that OT baptisms were not just *figurative* baptisms, but literal baptisms, typologically speaking, that pointed to a greater spiritual reality outside of themselves.

[47] *Tupos* is often translated as "examples." Goppelt writes, "Here *tupos* does not mean example in the ordinary sense of the word, as it does several other times in Paul (1 Thess 1:7; 2 Thess 3:9; Phil 3:17; cf. 1 Tim 4:12; Titus 2:7; 1 Pet 5:3). It refers to the fact that future events are represented in redemptive history" (Goppelt 2002: 146).

Excursus: Baptism as Ordeal

We mentioned in this chapter the idea that baptism is an ordeal, closely related to judgment. While not the only meaning of baptism, it is surely an important element oft forgotten. Unless we can understand this, many OT baptismal motifs will be hidden from our view. For in the OT, water as an ordeal is a common theme.

Theological Dictionaries point out that the secular sense of "*baptizō*," though sometimes used for "bathing" or "washing," was more generally used for perishing or drowning. In other words, the verb is an ordeal. Albrecht Opeke explains,

> The intens. baptizō occurs in the sense of 'to immerse' from the time of Hippocrates, in Plato and esp. in later writers... "to sink the ship"... "to suffer shipwreck," "to drown," "to perish"... "to bring the city to the border of destruction"... "to go under"... "to sink into"... "to be overwhelmed"... "thou lettest thyself be overborn." ... The idea of going under or perishing is nearer the general usage"
>
> (Opeke, 'baptō, baptizō', TDNT 1:530)

Opeke goes onto write, "The NT uses... baptizō only in the cultic sense, infrequently of Jewish washings (Mk 7:4) and otherwise in the technical sense 'to baptize.' *This usage shows that baptism is felt to be something new and strange*." In other words, he argues, the NT usage does *not* include the idea of "ordeal."

What is strange is that, given the common usage of the term in that day, the NT writers would *not* have ordeal in mind. In fact, we believe it clearly does. Isa 21:4 LXX uses *baptizō* metaphorically. It translates the Heb. word "*baath*," which means to be terrified, frightened, or overwhelmed. The metaphor is that the vision Isaiah saw washes over him like a flood. Clearly, baptismal ordeal is in mind in this Greek translation.

If *baptizō* is used in conjunction with a non-water event as a metaphor for being overwhelmed, what about those Scriptures where the Hebrew writer uses water as an image of terror? One thinks of the Psalms. "Save me, O God, for the waters have come up to my neck. I sink in deep mire, where there is no foothold; I have come into deep waters, and the flood sweeps over me... rescue me from sinking in the mire; let me be delivered from my enemies and from the deep waters. Do not let the flood sweep over me, or the deep swallow me up, or the Pit close its mouth over me" (Ps 69:1-2, 14-15; cf. Gen 1:2 with Gen 8:2; Ex 15:5; Ezek 31:15; Jonah 2:3, 5; Hab 3:10; Rom 10:7).[48] Though the LXX does not use any form of *baptizō* here (are there any Hebrew words that it could translate?), it is clear that the ordeal element of the

---

[48] At least seven of the thirty-six verses in this Psalm are directly quoted in the NT as referring to Jesus Christ. For example, Ps 69:4 is quoted in John 15:25, "They hated me without cause." Ps 69:9, "Zeal for thy house consumes me" are Christ's words in John 2:17. Ps 69:21 is quoted in each Gospel in Jesus' death "so that the Scripture would be fulfilled" (cf. John 19:29). Therefore, given that Christ calls his death a baptism (Mark 10:38; Luke 12:50), it is perfectly reasonable to see baptism in Ps 69:1-2 and other places.

word is staring us in the face (see also Job 22:10-16;[49] Ps 18:4, 15-16; 88:17; 124:4; Isa 8:6-8 etc.).

Among these passages, one thinks of Jonah's song, "You cast me into the deep, into the heart of the seas, and the flood surrounded me; all your waves and your billows passed over me. Then I said, 'I am driven away from your sight; how shall I look again upon your holy temple?' The waters closed in over me; the deep surrounded me; weeds were wrapped around my head at the roots of the mountains. I went down to the land whose bars closed upon me forever; yet you brought up my life from the Pit, O LORD my God" (Jonah 2:3-6). (Note the overlap of words [e.g., *metsulah*, "the deep"; *tehom*, "the deep"; and *suf*, "seaweed"] used in this song and also in Moses' song of the Red Sea baptism in Exodus 15. See Estelle 2005: 94).

In Jonah, the theme of death and resurrection is clear, even as it is in many of the Psalms. This is clearly a picture of baptism. Death is an element that is symbolized in baptism (at least when immersion is present). People go down into the water. If they are not brought up again, they drown. This is their ordeal and their judgment.[50] But they *are* brought up, and so they live anew, a perfect picture of resurrection.

This is true be it the story of Jonah, of Noah, or of Israel in the Red Sea. Byran Estelle sums this up nicely for us, "Just as God delivered them through their ordeal at the Red Sea, so he has acted again especially on Golgotha to deliver his people safely through the raging waters, defeating their foes, subduing their sin, and bringing them safe upon dry ground on the other side" (Estelle 2005: 95). As it says in Isaiah, "But now, this is what the LORD says- he who created you, O Jacob, he who formed you, O Israel: 'Fear not, for I have redeemed you; I have summoned you by name; you are mine. When you pass through the waters, I will be with you; and when you pass through the rivers, they will not sweep over you... For I am the LORD, your God, the Holy One of Israel, your Savior" (Isa 43:1-3).

But what about the NT writers? It seems more than obvious that Peter's reference to the flood as a baptism *must* have ordeal in mind. Though Noah is saved, most of the world is *not*. They perish in the flood. This is exactly what *baptizō* means in secular Greek. Obviously, Peter has in mind Christian baptism, and so he is focused on the salvific element that ritual baptism always signifies. But he does mention that only eight in all were saved through the water (1 Pet 3:20). This obviously calls to mind the ordeal element for the rest of humanity (cf. Gen 7:21).

The Red Sea is similar. Again, Paul is focused upon Israel's baptism into Moses. His focus is the salvific aspect of the rite. They came safely through the sea. But what about Pharaoh and his army? They went into the water too. But they never came out. Moses sings about this, "I will sing to the LORD, for he has triumphed gloriously; horse and rider he has thrown into the sea" (Ex 15:1). Moses obviously has the death of Pharaoh in mind... a death that came from a flood of water.

---

[49] This is a particularly striking passage, because in it the flood (which Peter calls a baptism) is metaphorically related to Job's ordeal.

[50] One scholar notes, "In the Mesopotamian materials, a primary function of *id*, the (divine) River, was, as is well known, to serve as a judge in certain legal cases. Trial by river ordeal was a widespread phenomenon, in which the accused was plunged into the river, where his success in withstanding the rushing waters was supposed to determine his guilt or innocence" (McCarter 1973: 403). A biblical example of something along these lines is the "bitter waters" ordeal in Numbers 5:11-31.

In an interesting metaphor, Ezekiel 29:3 and Psalm 74:13-14 each refer to Pharaoh as the sea monster (lit: *tannin*, often translated as sea monster, dragon [LXX], serpent, or leviathan) whom God hurled into the sea. In Genesis 1:21 we read how God created the great *tannins*. These come to represent danger and evil in the world of the Bible (cf. Job 40; Isa 27:1).

In the Exodus story, Moses is told to throw his rod onto the ground where it first becomes a snake (*nachash*; Ex 4:3) and then a serpent (*tannin*; Ex 7:9-12). The words are used interchangeably, and yet *nachash* is the term used for Satan in the Garden of Eden (Gen 3:1). We will remember that the magicians of Egypt duplicated the feat, until Aaron's *tannin* swallowed the two serpent-rods of Jannes and Jombres.

This was a foreshadowing of God's swallowing up Pharaoh and his serpentine army in the sea. This in turn is a foreshadowing of the hurling of the beast into the lake of fire (Rev 19:20), while those nearby sing the Song of Moses and of the Lamb (Rev 15:2-3). The point is, redemptive history is a progressive movement wherein God will finally destroy the evils that lay hidden just below the murky waters. Jesus has defeated, through his baptism into death, the serpentine-seraphim (seraphim used in Isa 6:2 means "fiery ones," but it is only used elsewhere of the fiery serpents sent by God as his instruments to inflict on the people the righteous penalty of sin) named Satan. And how will Satan be destroyed? By a baptism in a lake of fire that was foreshadowed death of the ancient human snake-king named Pharaoh.

Secular writers would have had no problem understanding this as a baptism for Pharaoh. Indeed, this is exactly what they *would* have understood—which is why coming out of baptism *alive* (like Noah, Israel, and Jonah did) is such an important element of *Christian* baptism. In the ancient world, Herodotus tells us,

> When an Egyptian or a foreigner is dragged into the water by a crocodile and killed, or destroyed by the water itself, and it is known, then the inhabitants of the city where he comes to shore have the solemn obligation of embalming him, of arraying him in the most gorgeous robes and of placing him in a sacred sarcophagus. No one may touch him, whether relatives or friends, apart from the priests of the Nile, who must tend him with their own hands and treat him as one who is more than an ordinary being.
>
> (Herodotus Book II. 90)

When this happens, the drowned man is said to have been "immersed." In this way the Egyptian god Osiris is thought as a god in conjunction with the river as he is given up to the Nile. Antinous was drowned in the Nile and so proclaimed as a god.[51] These men died and were not risen, yet proclaimed as gods. Christian baptism takes the death theme but adds the true resurrection element (either symbolically or literally) and in this way shows the incomplete (and therefore devastating) conclusion of the pagan beliefs. In order for baptism to be a good thing, one must truly be raised from the dead.

But resurrection *assumes* death. Death, and therefore the idea of ordeal, is present in many NT references to baptism. Rom 6:2 says, "Do you not know that all of us who have been baptized into Christ Jesus were baptized into his *death*? We were

---

[51] Antinous was the male lover of Emperor Hadrian. After his death in the Nile, Hadrian had an entire cult devoted to Antinous as a god after the order of Osiris. For more, see Opeke, '*baptō, baptizō*', *TDNT* I:531-532.

therefore *buried* with him by baptism into *death...*" Col 2:12 says, "You were *buried* with him in baptism." 1 Cor 1:13 teaches, "Has Christ been *divided*? Was Paul *crucified* for you? Or were you *baptized* in the name of Paul?" Here "division," "crucifixion," and "baptism" are parallel ideas. Obviously ordeal is in mind in this verse.

The idea of crucifixion as baptism is in the mind of Christ where in Mark 10:38-39 it says, "But Jesus said to them, 'You do not know what you are asking. Are you able to drink the cup that I drink, or be baptized with the baptism that I am baptized with?" They replied, 'We are able.' Then Jesus said to them, 'The cup that I drink you will drink; and with the baptism with which I am baptized, you will be baptized.'"[52] He was speaking about his death and their own (vs. 34; cf. John 21:19). Luke 12:50 is a parallel passage. It says, "I have a baptism with which to be baptized, and what stress I am under until it is completed!" Jesus would not have been distressed if ordeal was not present in his theology of baptism.

Christ calling his death a *baptism* is related to another thing that he says refers to his death and resurrection: *The Sign of Jonah* (Matt 12:39-40; 16:14; Lk 11:29-30). Jesus says that as Jonah was in the belly of the sea monster three days and three nights, so he will be in the belly of the earth. Think about this in light of the song that Jonah sang (above). When we put Jonah 2:3-6, Mark 10:38-39, Luke 12:50 and Matthew 12:39-40 *et al* together, the only biblical conclusion one can come up with is that the NT is calling Jonah's experience a baptism ordeal, a prototype of Christian baptism, which symbolizes death and resurrection.

Finally, John the Baptist says just prior to Jesus' baptism, "He will baptize you with the Holy Spirit and with fire. His winnowing fork is in his hand, and he will clear his threshing floor and gather his wheat into the barn, but the chaff he will burn with unquenchable fire" (Matt 3:11-12). The close relationship of baptism, the Holy Spirit, and fire can be seen in places like Gen 15:17 (cf. Kline 2006b: 296); Gen 19:24, Ex 14:24 (cf. Isa 63:9-11; 1 Cor 10:2), Deut 4:24; Dan 3:22; Acts 2:3; 1 Thess 1:8; Heb 10:27 etc. Obviously, baptism has a close link to judgment from its very first mention in the New Testament, though the work of the Spirit and the fire in this verse are not meant to convey final judgment for believers (cf. Ex 3:2, Ex 14:19-21; Num 9:17, Dan 3:23-27; 1 Cor 2:13-15 etc.). This fits with the idea that baptism for believers is *resurrection* after judgment (which occurs in Christ).[53]

---

[52] The water and blood from his side, hands, and sweat make this more than a metaphor for baptism.

[53] For more on baptism as ordeal, see Kline 1968: 65-73.

Section II: Baptism and the Archetypal Sanctuary

E dmund Clowney explains, "To seek the meaning of the temple, as the Old Testament presents it, is to ask: What has God revealed through this symbolism he has instituted?" (Clowney 1973: 157-58). In this and the next section we will survey how types work in the biblical motif of "sanctuary." The idea of sanctuary is critical to help us develop our theology of baptism, because baptism is found in each and every biblical sanctuary. This chapter and the next will be an explanation of Chart 1, which is a summary of the various sanctuaries in Scripture.

Archetypal Sanctuary

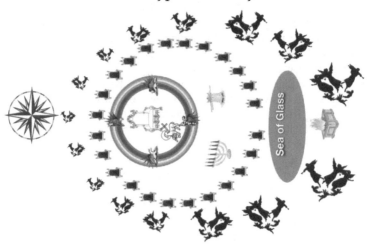

Diagram of the Temple Described In Revelation 4-5

The Temple consists of three "layers." Since Moses' tabernacle is a pattern of the Archetypal Temple, we will use some of the terminology of the tabernacle to describe this sanctuary.

1. *The "Outer Court."* Here "myriads of Angels" (5:11) and "every creature in heaven and on earth and under the earth and in the sea" (5:13) sing praises around the Throne. In this space there is a "Sea of Glass" (4:6) and a "Sacrificial Altar" (6:9).

2. *The "Holy Place."* This is separated from the outer court by "24 elders who surround the throne" (4:4). In this space there are "seven blazing lamps" (4:5) and a golden altar of incense (8:3).

3. *The "Most Holy Place."* This is separated from the holy place by "four living creatures" (4:6) and an "emerald rainbow that encircles the throne (4:3). In this space is lightning and thunder (4:5) around a throne where God, whose brilliance resembles "jasper and carnelian" (4:3), sits (4:2).

Hebrews 9:24 says some important things about the archetypal sanctuary. "For Christ did not enter a man-made sanctuary that was only a copy of the true one; he entered heaven itself, now to appear for us in God's presence." First, this sanctuary is not "man-made." Second, this sanctuary is the "true" sanctuary. Third, it is the place where Christ now resides. This place is "heaven." Finally, heaven is the place of "God's presence." Since this sanctuary is the model upon which all later types are patterned, it is imperative to become familiar with it. As we will see, baptism is greatly informed by it.

There are various places in Scripture where men have been allowed a glimpse of this heavenly sanctorum.[54] Isaiah says, "I saw the Lord on a throne, high and exalted, and the train of his robe filled the temple" (Isa 6:1). This is no ordinary temple. For Isaiah also saw angels. "Above God were seraphs, each with six wings" (vs. 2). They sang a song, "Holy, holy, holy is the LORD Almighty; the whole earth is full of his glory" (vs. 3). When they sang, their voices shook the doorposts and thresholds and the temple was filled with smoke (vs. 4). This caused Isaiah to fear, and he was struck with an acute sense of his sin (vs. 5). In response, the one of the angels went before the altar and touched Isaiah's lips (vs. 6).

The scene takes place in heaven. God's presence is in heaven. His throne is in heaven. Isaiah 66:1 says, "Heaven is my throne." It is probable that "heaven" in this verse is the invisible spiritual realm (see next paragraph). The place where God resides is parallel to the "Most Holy Place" in typological temples. It is filled with smoke and completely taken up with the train of God's robe. Here, there are angels that fly around praising God and doing his bidding.

God's presence is not limited to heaven. It extends to fill the earth. "Earth" should be understood as the visible cosmos: heavens and earth. God is everywhere. Isaiah 66:1 continues, "Earth is my footstool." King Solomon (at the dedication of the temple) echoes this sentiment, "But will God really dwell on earth? The heavens, even the highest heaven, cannot contain you. How much less this temple I have built!" (1 Kgs 8:27; cf. Acts 7:49). If the heavens cannot contain God, then they must be referring to the physical creation, not the spiritual heavens. In other words, all created sanctuaries are but copies of the spiritual sanctuary where God resides.

The heavenly sanctuary that Isaiah saw is given more detail by the Apostle John in Revelation 4-5. Just like Isaiah, he saw this same place.

---

[54] 1 Kgs 22:19; Isa 6, Ezek 1; Dan 7; Zech 3-4; Rev 4-5 etc.

Common Space (The Outer Court)

This diagram (above) clearly shows three gradations of holiness or three spaces separated one from another. Space 1 is filled with an uncountable number of invisible angelic creatures that encircle the throne (Rev 5:11). These provide the outer limits (or "wall") of the sanctuary. It is also filled with all of the creatures that God has made in the visible realm (5:13). Obviously, this must be a gigantic space to fit all of these creatures. The fact that visible and invisible creatures are interacting together, shows that from heaven's perspective, the lines between them are meaningless. The fact that every creature is invited into this space shows that this is a *common space*.

In this area there is an altar (Rev 5:9). This altar is where the blood of the martyrs [God's people] has been spilt and has become a sacrifice pleasing to the Lord (Ps 116:15; 2 Tim 4:6; Heb 11:37, 12:24). God sees the death of his people far differently than the world does.

The Glassy Sea and Baptism

In this area there is also something described as a "glassy sea" (4:6). What is this? It is said to be as "clear as crystal." Elsewhere in Revelation (21 times), "sea" (*thalassa*) always refers to water.[55] *2 Enoch* 27 probably has the closest parallel to this in ancient literature, "It became water, and I spread it out over the darkness, below the light, and then I made firm the waters, that is to say the bottomless, and I made foundation of light around the water, and created seven circles from inside, and *imaged [the water] like crystal wet and dry, that is to say like glass*, [and] the circumcession of the waters and the other elements, and I showed each one of them its road, and the seven stars each one of them in its heaven, that they go thus."

It may be asked where there are other precedents for such a sea *in Scripture*? Samuel Hooke cites possible sources that include the "upper sea, the waters in the heavens, separated by the firmament from the waters below" (in Gen 1:6-7),[56] the pavement of sapphire in Ex 24:10, and the firmament, like the color of the crystal, over the four living creatures, upon which is the throne like sapphire in Ezek 1:22, 26 (these two citations do not directly

---

[55] Some have been of the opinion that this "sea" actually refers to the pavement of heaven (cf. Ex 24:10; Ezek 1:2, 26; Rev 21:21). But Greg Beale notes that this is not incompatible with a water interpretation (see Beale 1999: 327-28).

[56] To this, Hooke gives a parallel in the ancient near east, "This is directly connected with the Babylonian chaos-myth of the conquest of the chaos-dragon Tiâmat by Marduk. Moreover, in the Babylonian cosmogony the heavenly universe is divided into three parts corresponding to those of the earthly universe, the third and lowest division being the heavenly ocean" (Hooke 1918: 464).

refer to water[57]), and finally the fiery stream issuing from the throne in Dan 7:9-10[58] (Hooke, 'Sea of Glass', *DAC* 2:464).

Beale concurs, adding that Ezek 1:22 is a reflection of Gen 1:8 (Beale 1999: 328). Here he is comparing "the likeness of the firmament upon the heads of the living creature," with "God called the firmament heaven." He also cites Ps 29 as a source. This refers to God in his glory living "on many waters" (vs. 3) in direct relationship with "his holy court" (vs. 9) where God sits "a king forever," "enthroned above the flood" (vs. 10).[59]

There is much biblical and extra-biblical precedent for understanding this sea of glass to be a *watery* sea. Francis Bodfield Hooper reluctantly admits that this is "a very ancient opinion" that "appears to have been entertained as early as the time, when high views of the *sacrament of baptism* began to prevail. The sea of glass came then to be interpreted as representing the laver of regeneration, and denoting the necessity of baptism to all who would approach the throne of God; and since that time the same view has commonly been taken by high Sacramentarians [emphasis added]" (Hooper 1861: 174). Let us seek to understand why the ancients would connect this sea to baptism.

This is a *watery* sea, which is clear as crystal. This may be a way of describing a liquid sea that is calm, especially since the Lamb is pictured as being resurrected (i.e., "standing"; 5:6), having conquered evil thereby calming the chaotic sea waters. Or, it may mean that the sea has been congealed, frozen solid.

Delving deeper here will help us expand our theology of baptism. Jewish interpreters have a parallel to John's "sea of glass."[60] It is the Red Sea ordeal (of course we have already seen that the NT describes this event as a baptism). Some of the Jews called the Red Sea a "sea of glass" because the deeps were congealed (Ex 15:8).

---

[57] The heretical Koran has a curious take on Solomon's temple that is akin to these passages. The Queen of Sheba enters the temple and it says, "When she saw it, she thought it was a lake of water, and she tucked up her skirts, uncovering her legs. He said: 'This is but a palace paved smooth with slabs of glass" (*Sura* 27:44).

[58] Daniel's vision has a close parallel in *1 En* 14:10-17 where there is similar house and throne of God, a floor in the first house is of crystal and in the second house is of fire. But also underneath the throne there are (four?) streams of flaming fire (cf. *1 En* 71:6). See also *SibOr* 2:196-200.

[59] Two other extra-biblical passages are worth citing here. *2 Enoch* 3 says, "And there I looked, and again I looked higher, and saw the ether, and they placed me on the first heaven and showed me a very great Sea, greater than the earthly sea." The *Testament of Levi* is almost identical, "And behold, the heavens were opened... and I entered from the first heaven, and I saw there a great sea hanging" (*TLevi* 1:9-10).

[60] See Mekilta de Rabbi Ishmael, *Beshallah* 5.15 (on Ex 14:16-21) and 'Abot de Rabbi Nathan 30a. This second source even says that fire was present in the midst of the glass. *Midr Pss* 136:7 adds that the sea was "a crystallized... kind of glass." Cited in Beale 1999: 791-792.

This sea returns in Rev 15:2 where it is now mixed with fire. Though the sea was clear like crystal in 4:6, there was also fire *nearby*. Thunder and lightning surrounded the throne; but also seven lamps (or torches) of fire burned "before the throne" (which happens to be the identical phrase describing the location of the sea).

The "sea mixed with fire," which is before the throne, has a clear OT parallel already mentioned in our discussion of Rev 4:6. It is Dan 7:9-10. "As I looked, thrones were set in place, and the Ancient of Days took his seat. His clothing was as white as snow; the hair of his head was white like wool. His throne was flaming with fire, and its wheels were all ablaze. *A river of fire* was flowing, coming out from before him. Thousands upon thousands attend him; ten thousand times ten thousand stood before him. The court was seated, and the books were opened."[61]

Revelation puts the language of Daniel's vision into three different (but overlapping) chapters.[62] Besides Chapter 15, Chapters 4-5 talk about the myriads and myriads of heavenly hosts that attend God (5:11) and all the creatures in the physical order (5:13). Chapter 20 incorporates the judgment themes of Daniel. There is a Great White Throne with One seated on it (20:11). There is a host standing before the throne (20:12). There are books that are opened (20:12), and it is a judgment scene (20:13).

For the purposes of baptism, the most striking thing here is the *lake of fire* in Revelation 19:20; 20:10, 14, 15; and 21:8. This is very similar to Daniel's "river of fire," and the previous glassy sea mixed with fire (15:2).[63] In Revelation 21-22, John sees a heavenly city. We will discuss this in detail in Section

---

[61] Fanciful imaginations of the river of fire are attested time and again in pagan, apocryphal, and even Christian sources. Clement of Alexandria wrote, "Did not Plato know of the rivers of fire and the depth of the earth, and Tartarus, called by the Barbarians Gehenna, naming, as he does prophetically, Cocytus, and Acheron, and Pyriphlegethon?" (Clement of Alexandria, *Elucidations* 5.14). The Greeks understood there to be five rivers that separate Hades from the world of the living. Cocytus (the "river of lamentation"), Acheron (the "river of woe"), Phlegethon (the "river of fire"), Lethe (the "river of forgetfulness"), and Styx (the "river of hate"). On Phlegethon see Pseudo-Clementine, *Recognitions*, Book 1.4. I. Howard Marshall notes that "Sometimes the wicked are plunged into a river of fire" (Marshall 1978: 147). For people crossing or washing or being plunged into the river of fire, see 4 Esd 13:10; 1 QH XI, 28-32; TIsaac 5:21-26; TJac 7:13; the *Apocalypse of the Holy Mother*, V; *The Vision of Paul*, 31-32; *The Revelation of Paul*; SibOr 2:252-54; Origen, *Against Celsus*, Book 4.13 and the Gnostic *Gospel of Bartholomew, Book of the Resurrection*. (We will look at several of these passages later).

[62] Unfortunately, we do not have the time to explain the common reading of Revelation, which sees events taking place in a series of progressive parallelisms or cycles (as opposed to chronologically). In this reading, Chapter 4, 15, and 20 all take place simultaneously. They are rather like different camera angles capturing the same event. For a good introduction to this see Herman Hoyt's *Amillennialism* (in Clouse 1977: 156-159).

[63] For another kind of image of a "river of fire," see 2 Sam 22:5 and Ps 18:4 where you have torrents of "Belial." Belial is sometimes used as a demonic name, perhaps for Satan (2 Cor 6:15). 1 QH III, 28ff has a kind of eschatological "river of Belial" in much the same vein. Here the torrents of Belial, "is a symbol of the forces of evil, depicted as a river of fire which sweeps through the entire world and destroys everything in its path" (Knibb 1987: 181).

IV. But for now, it is fascinating to read the description of this heavenly city in the *Apocalypse of Zephaniah*. "I turned back and walked, and I saw a great sea. But I thought that it was a sea of water. I discovered that it was entirely a sea of flame like a slime which casts forth much flame and whose waves burn sulfur and bitumen" (*ApZeph* 6:1-2).

Do these all represent the same thing? Since the chapters all appear to describe the same place (heaven), it is probable that they do. The fire is not physical, since Satan (who is thrown into it) is a spiritual being.[64] It probably represents spiritual punishment or judgment that comes from God himself. Isaiah 30:27-28 is helpful, "See, the Name of the LORD comes from afar, with burning anger and dense clouds of smoke; his lips are full of wrath, and his tongue is a consuming fire. His breath is like a rushing torrent, rising up to the neck. He shakes the nations in the sieve of destruction; he places in the jaws of the peoples a bit that leads them astray" (cf. *4 Esd* 13:10-11).[65] The idea surrounding the lake of fire is that Satan, the beast, the false prophet, and anyone whose name was not written in the book of life are thrown into the lake (cf. *SibOr* 2:252-54).

The kind of judgment that comes to the mind with the "lake of fire" is a mixed metaphor. The image of fire obviously calls to the mind *burning*. But the image of a lake calls to the mind *drowning* (the two are often put together, as in Isa 43:1-3). This second image often escapes the contemporary mind. Now, recall the discussion of the usage of baptism in secular Greek (Excursus: Baptism as Ordeal in the previous chapter). It chiefly meant *drowning*. Two facts make this all the more interesting. First, the lake of fire seems to be before the throne, just like the glassy-fiery sea and the river of fire. Therefore, they all represent the same thing.

Second, we need to ask about the context of the fiery-glassy sea in Rev 15. This is quite fascinating in light of baptism. Rev 15:3 *clearly* has the *Red Sea* in mind. In the next verse (15:3) the saints begin singing a new "Song of Moses." They are singing this song because they have triumphed over the beast, who is the antitypical "sea monster" (Rev 13:1) of which Pharaoh (who was called the sea monster; cf. Isa 51:9-11; Ps 74:12-15; Ezek 32:2) was a type.

---

[64] The strange book of 3 *Enoch* has the rather bizarre image of "ministering angels" going down "into the River of Fire" to "bathe themselves in the fire of the River of Fire" (3 *En* 36:1-2). The note in the James Charlesworth edition of the *Old Testament Pseudepigrapha* says, "'Bathe themselves': a literal 'baptism of fire'" (Alexander 1983: 289). It then cites another ancient source which tells us that "all the angels and all the camps bathe in fiery rivers seven times and restore themselves 365 times."

[65] Origen (*Against Celsus*, 4:13) writes, "The divine word says that our God is 'a consuming fire,' and that 'He draws rivers of fire before Him;' nay, that He even enters in as 'a refiner's fire, and as a fuller's herb,' to purify His own people."

(Their triumph is pictured as "standing" beside[66] the sea, which also happens to be the way the victorious conquering resurrected Christ was pictured previously).

What happened to Pharaoh? He was "thrown into the sea," and *this* was the song of Moses: "The horse and rider he has thrown into the sea" (Ex 15:1). In the same way, Revelation says that God throws the antitypical sea monster (the beast) into the lake of fire (Rev 19:20).[67] Similarly, what happens to the people of the earth in Noah's day? They are thrown into the flood. The same thing happens to the people whose names are not written into the book of life (Rev 20:15). It is probable that people are about to be thrown into the river of fire in Daniel 7 as well, along with the beast who is "burned with fire." This confirms not only that baptism contains imagery of ordeal, but that the sea in front of the throne in the archetypal sanctuary contains *baptismal* waters.

(Moving east to west in the common space of this archetypal sanctuary), the movement from slain saints at the altar (Rev 6:9) to standing saints at the sea (Rev 15:2) is probably a picture of death and resurrection. Since this resurrection of the saints is pictured by *the sea*, we are not out of line to ask, is this a picture of baptism? Greg Beale doubts it because, "This is nowhere explicitly affirmed. In Revelation fire and sea are always images respectively of judgment and evil and never connote the saint's trials or baptism" (Beale 1999: 789).

Yet, the baptismal interpretation has a recent[68] as well as ancient pedigree. Victorinus (circa 270 A.D.) in his *Commentary on the Apocalypse* says.

> "And before the throne there was, as it were, a sea of glass like to Crystal." That is the gift of baptism which He sheds forth through His Son in time of repentance, before He executes judgment. It is therefore before the throne, that is, the judgment. And when he says a sea of glass like to crystal, he shows that it is pure water, smooth, not agitated by the wind, not flowing down as on a slope, but given to be immoveable as the house of God.
>
> (Victorinus, *Commentary on the Apocalypse* 4:6)

Another interesting take on this is found in the eighth Sibylline Oracle (circa 175 A.D.), in a particularly interesting acrostic poem spelling "Jesus Christ, son of God, savior, cross," (making it obviously Christian). "A river of fire and brimstone will flow from heaven. There will then be a sign for all

---

[66] Or "on" the sea, depending upon whether the sea is liquid or solid.

[67] I am indebted one of our church Elders, Sean Kielian, for this insight.

[68] See Farrer 1964: 171, 173.

men, a most clear seal: the wood among the faithful, the desired horn, the life of pious men, but the scandal of the world, illuminating the elect with waters in twelve streams" (*SibOr* 8:243-247). The note in the Charlesworth edition reminds us, "The language of illumination is commonly used for baptism from the second half of the 2nd cent. A.D., e.g. Justin, *Apologies* 1.61.14)" (Collins 1983: 424). So it seems that baptism is directly linked in the Oracle with the heavenly river of fire and with waters in twelve streams.

We believe the baptismal interpretation is legitimate. Beale does not seem to take into account the idea that baptism *does* picture ordeal. As we have seen, John clearly has the Red Sea in mind, including the destruction of the beast (who is typologically preceded in death by Pharaoh). There is no doubt that the Red Sea was a baptism. Given only what we have said so far, it seems justifiable to conclude that the glassy sea is also a picture of baptism. As we make our way through the various sanctuaries, this will become absolutely certain.

Holy Place (The Sanctuary)

For now, let us briefly describe the rest of this archetypal sanctuary. As you move past the sea you come into a second "wall" of sorts. This is space 2. This wall is made up of "24 elders who surround the throne" (Rev 4:4). It is most likely that these elders represent the OT church (12 Tribes) and NT church (12 Apostles).

This interpretation is further confirmed by the "seven lamps" that reside in this space. Preceding this in Revelation is a discussion of seven churches (Rev 2-3). These churches are each said to have a "lampstand" (Rev 2:5). Earlier it says, "The seven lampstands are the seven churches" (1:20). Given what we will learn about typical sanctuaries, the seven lampstands would be the same thing as the seven lamps that reside in this holy place.[69] (By way of

---

[69] We may talk here about the identification of the seven lamps as the "seven spirits of God" (4:6). It is tempting to see this as a reference to the Holy Spirit. And while it is true that the Holy Spirit is in the background, it is not proper to identify the seven spirits as the Holy Spirit. Rather it is the Church as empowered by the Spirit. This language all harkens back to Zechariah 4:2-6. Beale writes about this passage, "The seven lampstands" represent the church (cf. Rev 1:20). In Zech 4:2-6 the lampstand with its seven lamps is a figurative synecdoche: part of the temple furniture stands for the whole temple, which by extension also represents faithful Israel (Zech 4:6-9), which is required to live "'not by [earthly] might nor by power, but by my Spirit,' says the Lord" (Zech 4:6). Jewish writings also understand the lampstand of Zechariah as symbolizing Israel, especially the righteous gathered from all generations at the end time. The lampstand in the tabernacle and the temple was in the presence of God, and the light that emanated from it apparently represented God's presence (see Num 8:1-4); in Ex 25:30-31 the lampstand is mentioned directly after the "bread of Presence"; likewise 40:4; 1 Kgs 7:48-49). Similarly, the lamps on the lampstand in Zech 4:2-5 are interpreted in 4:6 as representing God's presence or Spirit, which is to empower Israel (= lampstand) to finish rebuilding the temple despite resistance (cf. Zech 4:6-9). So new Israel, the church, is to draw its power from the Spirit, the divine presence, before God's throne in its drive to stand against the world's resistance" (Beale 1999: 206-7).

passing, I also want to note that in this same place there are "seven spirits of God" (4:6). Also there is a direct visible/invisible relationship between the churches and the angels (1:20). Here, the angels are likened to "stars." This will become relevant as we look at other sanctuaries).

Finally, there is an altar of incense that is filled with the prayers of the saints (8:3). The fact that the church is found in this space means that we have moved a level up in gradation of holiness. This is not just common space, but a "Holy Place." It appears that those who have washed themselves in (pictured as standing beside) the sea of glass are allowed to move into this part of the sanctuary vicariously as Christ takes their prayers before the throne. This corresponds to the NT teaching on the church that we are a "royal priesthood, a holy nation" (1 Pet 2:9).

Most Holy Place (The Inner Sanctuary)

The final or third space is separated by an emerald rainbow that encircles the throne of God (4:3). Further making this change of space are "four living creatures" that are "around the throne" (4:6). This emerald rainbow is attended with other imagery of wealth in stone. The brilliance of the One seated on the throne is said to resemble "jasper and carnelian" (4:3). This makes a three-fold reference to brilliant stone. The fact that both the One seated and the rainbow are likened to precious stones is a possible demonstration that both (all three?) are God.

If so, the rainbow would be an image of the Holy Spirit.[70] For example, in Rev 10:1 the glorious Christ comes down from heaven, robed in a cloud and with a rainbow above his head. We have already seen that the cloud is a special illustration of the Holy Spirit. The accompanying rainbow appears to be the same thing.

The fact that only God and his very special attendants are found in this space shows that we have moved to the highest gradation of holiness. This is the Most Holy Place, the space where God's presence is fully manifest. This is confirmed later as the Lamb (Christ) is the only one who is able to enter the throne-room and stand in its center (5:6), because he has triumphed over death and evil. This is what we saw in Heb 9:24. Christ went into the heavenly sanctuary and now appears for us in God's presence.

---

[70] See note 69.

Conclusion

We have seen that the archetypal sanctuary has three levels of holiness: common, holy, and most holy. The numbers that are given are highly symbolic. Three is the number of God (i.e., the Trinity). Four is the number of creation, or the number that immediately follows God (3 + 1). Seven is the number of fullness or completion. 24 is the number of the eschatological church (12 + 12). The architecture is likewise symbolic of a host of things: sacrifice, baptism (death, resurrection, preparation for entering the sanctuary as priests [i.e., "initiation"]), service and many other things.

Perhaps the strangest thing of all about this archetypal sanctuary is that it is also the antitypal sanctuary, for it incorporates both physical and spiritual characteristics of the typical and antitypical sanctuaries (see below). Obviously, much of what we have seen here takes place *in history*. Prior to creation, when it was only God seated on his throne, the sanctuary was practically speaking in design phase. Yet, what this sanctuary says about God's holiness, his purity, his majesty and any other attributes has *always* been true.

But we can say more than this. Revelation gives us an insight into why it is proper to call this an archetypal sanctuary. First of all, it shows things that have not completely come to pass. Yet, it is still true in heaven. Second, dove-tailing off of this, we have the verses that speak about the death of Christ and the election of the saints as having been "from the foundation of the world" (Rev 13:8, 17:8). Thus, the archetypal sanctuary has always resided in invisible places. It serves as a pattern for all those types to come.

Section III: Baptism and Typical Sanctuaries

iscussions of typological sanctuaries are often limited to two: the Tabernacle and the Temple. Both were patterned according to the design of God that was impressed upon Moses and David. To Moses God said, "Exactly as I show you concerning the pattern of the tabernacle, and of all its furniture, so you shall make it" (Ex 25:9; cf. Heb 8:5, 9:23-24). David observed, "All this the LORD made me understand in writing by His hand upon me, all the details of this pattern [of the temple]" (1 Chron 28:19). Since these are the two that are usually thought of, we will spend some time discussing them. We want to look especially at the relation to the archetype of the previous chapter.

Tabernacle

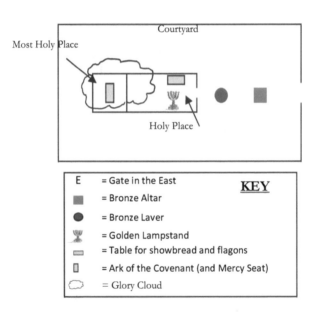

Above is a diagram of the tabernacle. You can immediately see a resemblance to the sanctuary of Revelation (as we go through each section of these sanctuaries, we will deliberately show as many repetitions of the archetypal sanctuary as possible, so that the parallels will impress upon you a strong biblical-theology of baptism). This diagram does not contain everything in the tabernacle, but only that which is most helpful to our discussion on baptism and in identifying other biblical sanctuaries. Therefore, this will not be an exhaustive treatment of the tabernacle, but it will contain information that is germane to furthering our purposes.

In the Archetypal sanctuary we saw a three-fold gradation of holiness. God makes this explicit in the creation of the tabernacle. There was the outer space (the courtyard; Ex 27:9-18), the holy place (Ex 26:33), and the most holy place (Ex 26:33).

Common Space

One first enters the courtyard from the east (Ex 27:13-15; cf. note 4). This courtyard is common space. Any Jew (including a Gentile convert) was allowed access to this. The primary purpose of coming here was ritual purity and cleansing. It was marked off by a series of curtains, which all had cherubs embroidered on them (Ex 26:1). This corresponds to the myriads of angels in the outer-regions of the archetypal sanctuary.

As you entered the gate you would come upon the bronze altar (Ex 27:1-7). Bronze is among the least precious of the metals used in the entire tabernacle construction. Upon this altar many kinds of animal sacrifices were offered. These were typical of the sacrifices of the saints in the sacrificial altar in the archetypal sanctuary.

The Laver and Baptism

After the altar you came to a bronze washing basin (Ex 30:18). The basin stood just outside of the entrance to the Holy Place, in the same general proximity of the sanctuary as the glassy sea in the archetypal sanctuary. Though we do not have exact dimensions, it was big enough that it needed its own separate stand (Ex 30:17), and a priest could wash his whole body with the water. Again, we will take some time to look at this since it relates most directly to our discussion of baptism.

What was the purpose of this washing basin? This is an important question. As the name suggests, the laver was created specifically for ceremonial washing. The Hebrew word used in the verses that describe the purpose of the basin is *rachats* (Ex 30:18; 40:30). Unless otherwise specified, this word describes a full-body washing, as in a bath (see 'Rachats,' BDB: 934). This is illustrated by the case of Bathsheba who was "*rachats-ing*" on her roof when David saw her – (2 Sam 11:2; see also Appendix 1).

It is significant that the LXX uses the rare word *niptō* in the translations of *rachats* in these verses. *Niptō* is not just an ordinary word for washing. It has *ceremonial* overtones. It is used in the NT on only two occasions; for foot-washing (John 13:5, 6, 15) and for hand washing (Matt 15:2).[71] What is quite related to our baptismal discussion is how the Matt 15:2 passage has a synoptic parallel in Mark 7:1ff. Mark does not use *niptō*, but instead uses the noun *baptismos* and the verb *baptizmō* to describe the same "washing" event that Matthew calls a *niptō*. The conclusion is that *baptismos, niptō*, and *rachats* are biblical synonyms.

This is a very specific explanation for why Hebrews calls legal OT rites "baptisms." In its legal form, the fount of baptism starts here—at the laver of the tabernacle.[72] The NT seems to make a correlation between baptism and the laver in another way. Scripture calls the washing of regeneration a baptism (Acts 1:5, 11:16). Titus 3:5 says, "Not by works of righteousness which we have done, but according to his mercy he saved us, by the *washing* of regeneration, and renewing of the Holy Ghost." The word for washing here is literally "lavering" (*loutron* is the verb, and *loutern* is the noun that translates washing basin), recalling the Tabernacle laver.

The basin was used by the priest. He was to wash his body (Ex 29:4; 40:12), parts of his body (Ex 30:19) and/or his clothes (probably Num 8:7, 21[73]) in the water prior to entering the Holy Place. This served two purposes. *Repeated* washings (Ex 30:20[74]) served the purpose of ceremonially cleansing him, since nothing unclean could enter the sanctuary. "They shall wash with water, so that they may not die. They shall wash their hands and their feet, so that they may not die" (Ex 30:20-21).

The other purpose specifically relates to the *Aaronic* priests (as opposed to the more general Levites[75]) in a *one-time* ceremony taking place at the beginning of his ministry. Ex 29:4 says, "You shall bring Aaron and his sons to the

---

[71] For the same use of the washing basin in the regular life of the priest, see Ex 30:18-21.

[72] Speaking on Exodus 40:30 Cyril of Jerusalem (313-386 A.D.) says, "The laver placed within the tent was a symbol of baptism." Origen (185-254 A.D.) wrote, "The word of the precept, truly, with the feet, orders the washing with internal water, announcing, figuratively, the sacrament of baptism." Clement of Alexandria (150-211 A.D.) says, "An image of this baptism was communicated to the poets, from Moses, thus – 'Having washed, and being clothed with clean vestments...'" (All three sources are found in Dale 1869: 175-176).

[73] The rite in Num 8:5ff concerns the Levites. Though most clothes washing commands take place outside the camp, this particular event takes place in front of the Tent of Meeting, and it therefore probably means they washed the clothes *in the washing basin*.

[74] The NIV seems to be correct in saying, "*whenever* they enter the Tent of Meeting," since what is in mind here is the regular work of service of the priest. In this case the infinitive construct of the verb *bô'* ("to come in") with the *bᵉ* prefix receives the temporal translation of "when" (see Kelley 1992: 182), and it also acts like the English gerund or Greek participle, indicating ongoing activity. Hence, the LXX inserts the word *hotan* ("whenever").

[75] For the distinction see Num 8:19, "I have given the Levites as a gift to Aaron and his sons from among the people of Israel, to do the service for the people of Israel at the tent of meeting..." We have noted how some paedobaptists have confused the two and in the process have misunderstood the application of baptism in the NT as a sprinkling rather than a washing/immersion (see paragraph surrounding note 20).

entrance of the tent of meeting and wash them with water." Immediately after this, the priest was clothed with his amazing garments, and in this way it says, "You shall ordain Aaron and his sons" (Ex 29:9).

The water portion of the priestly ordination ceremony is quite unlike the regular washings that took place after this one-time event. The *IVP Bible Background Commentary on the Old Testament* states, "It would not be appropriate for the new priests to clothe themselves in their new sacral garments without first taking a ritual bath. They were to be *fully immersed* as a part of the consecration ceremony. After this only their hands and feet had to be washed before performing their duties [emphasis added]."[76] Thus, the function of the one-time ceremony at the washing basin at the beginning of an Aaronic priest's ministry was not just to cleanse, but also to ordain (*mālē'*) and consecrate (*qādash*; see the fulfillment in Lev 8:6ff) him into service. Tremper Longman III agrees and adds some illuminating commentary,

> The first rite [of a priest] was washing with water, symbolizing cleansing as the potential priest moved from the realm of the common and every day to the sacred precincts of the temple. Thus, it is appropriate that the washing of Aaron and his sons took place at the entrance of the tent (Ex. 29:4). Next, Aaron was given new clothes to wear. This act of investiture again symbolized the priests' entrance into a new world. They did not wear the clothes they wore in their old world, but put on new ones that associated them with the tabernacle... One gets the feeling that the priests were part of the tabernacle structure itself. Thus at their ordination the priests were invested with the symbols that made them one with the sacred space where they would minister.
>
> (Longman 2001: 124-125)

In what seems like an obvious allusion to the ordination ceremony of the priest in Ex 29:1-9, Paul says, "For all of you who were baptized into Christ have clothed yourselves with Christ" (Gal 3:27). This is more evidence of the close relationship between NT baptism and the OT tabernacle laver.

This discussion solidifies our understanding that the glassy sea (which corresponds to the washing basin architecturally) is the place of baptism for the saints in the archetypal sanctuary. What is true of the tabernacle must be true of the archetypal sanctuary. The Puritan John Lightfoot was surely right then when he (commenting on Exodus 29) said, "This Laver fitly resembled the water of Baptism that admits us to sacred Mysteries, and chiefly the blood of Christ that cleanseth us from al filthinesse of flesh and spirit" (Lightfoot 1643: 52).

---

[76] *IVPBBCOT*, Exodus 29:4: Wash with Water.

Holy Place

After passing through the waters of the washing basin, the priest was allowed to enter through the east door of the tabernacle into the Holy Place. It is important to note that *only the priests* could enter the holy place. No common Israelite was allowed to approach or they would be put to death (Num 3:38). This was symbolized by the 24 elders who made of the wall of this part of the archetypal sanctuary.

Inside the holy place there were various items. Of concern to us are the lampstand, the table of showbread, and the altar of incense. A look at these items will help us identify other sanctuaries that are not as explicitly mentioned as such.

On the left of the entrance (the south wall) there was a lampstand. It was made of pure gold (Ex 25:31). The change from bronze to gold is a symbol that we have increased a degree in holiness. Gold is also a glimmering metal, reminding one of the stars of the visible heavens. This is further seen in the close relationship between the seven stars and the seven lampstands in Rev 1:20. We remember that in the archetypal sanctuary, the seven lamps represent the Church. On a related note, each of the seven letters to the churches in Revelation is addressed to the *angel* of that particular church.

The personification of stars occurs often (Gen 37:9; Num 24:17-19; Neh 9:23; Isa 14:12; Rev 22:16 [these last two designations are probably of Venus, which is the brightest "star" at night]). Sometimes Scripture identifies angels with the stars of the sky (Job 38:7; Isa 14:12; Rev 1:20, 12:4). Vern Poythress (Poythress 1991: 18-19), G.K. Beale (Beale 2004b) and others have argued that the seven lamps may also represent the seven main lights of the heaven (Sun, Mercury, Venus, Moon, Mars, Jupiter, and Saturn).

This "heavenly" imagery of the lampstand continues in the Most Holy Place (as we will see). This has caused many commentators to see a vertical ascension being symbolized in this very horizontal tabernacle. One goes from the earth outside in the courtyard to the visible heavens as one moves into the holy place.

There was one lampstand with seven lamps. This was fashioned in such a way that the lampstand was made to look like a tree. It is even said to have branches, buds, blossoms, and almond flowers (Ex 25:31-39). Here then we have the symbol of a tree in the holy place.

On the right (north wall) of the holy place there stood a golden table with the bread of the Presence and flagons (that is large bottles usually containing wine; Ex 25:23-30) for drink offerings (Num 4:7). This was covenant food, only to be taken by or given out by the priests (1 Sam 21:6; Matt 12:4).

At the back of the room, in front of the curtain separating the holy place from the most holy place there was an altar of incense (Ex 30:1-10). Its incense fires were to burn perpetually while unauthorized fires were absolutely prohibited (Ex 30:9; Lev 10:1). Once a year, atonement was made on its horns by the High Priest (Ex 30:10).

The smoke from this incense would have filled the air like a cloud. This incense represents God's very presence in the holy places (Lev 16:13). Here we can see the man-made effects that mimicked the Glory-cloud that descended upon the Tabernacle in the days of the Exodus (Ex 40:34-38). This also seems to parallel nicely the seven spirits of God in the holy place as well as the rainbow-cloud that surrounds the throne of the archetypal sanctuary.

Most Holy Place

Finally, through the curtain you would enter the Most Holy Place. The Most Holy Place was the place of God's special dwelling (Lev 16:2; 2 Cor 3:13). In here the main features are the Ark of the Covenant and the mercy seat. The Ark was also fashioned with pure gold. It contained a jar of manna (covenant food), Aaron's staff that budded (covenant tree?), and the Ten Commandments (covenant terms; see Heb 9:4).

God's presence is represented figuratively in the Mercy Seat (which covered the Ark) and in the curtains. The Seat is surrounded by cherubs (Ex 25:18). This seat was the place where the High Priest would enter once a year in order to make atonement for the people (Ex 30:10; Heb 9:7). This typological sacrifice is seen in the archetypal sanctuary when the Lamb goes to the center of the throne (see also Heb 9:11-12). Besides these cherubs, there were many others that were engraved in the curtains inside the Holy Place (Ex 26:1). These angelic creatures clearly are patterned after the Living Creatures that surround the throne of the archetypal sanctuary. The altar of incense also figured the presence of God as we have just seen.

This detailed look at the tabernacle helps us flesh out some of the less explained aspects of the archetypal sanctuary. It will also be of great benefit to us as we look at other typical sanctuaries in the OT. Before we get to those, we will look at the Temple.

Temple

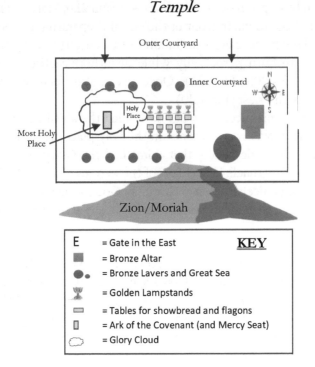

T   here were actually two temples in the OT. Solomon built a temple
     that was destroyed. The second temple was erected in its place
     and stood until it was destroyed in 70 A.D. The temple had an
outer ["great"] courtyard as well as an inner courtyard (1 Kgs 7:12). Solomon
oriented his temple east-west, so that the entrance was on the east (2 Chron
3:4; cf. 2 Chron 26:17; 29:4). This is identical to the tabernacle's positioning.
In fact, nearly everything was either identical to or an expansion of the
tabernacle because as *Wisdom* 9:8 says, "You have given command to build a
temple on your holy mountain... a copy of the holy tent that you prepared
from the beginning."

Common Space

The outer courtyard was the place for the Gentiles. This outer court
means a fourth level of holiness in the temple. This fourth element represents the universal scope that Jewish worship was eventually to encompass.
Perhaps it was pictured by the camp around the tabernacle, which clearly
had Gentiles in its midst (Ex 12:48-49; Lev 16:29 etc).

The inner courtyard was only permitted to Jews. This corresponds to the only courtyard in the tabernacle. There is no wall separating these two courts in the archetypal sanctuary, because in Christ, the wall of separation has been broken down (Eph 2:14).

Solomon fashioned cherubim into the walls of the temple (1 Kgs 6:29), corresponding to the angelic hosts wherever they flow in the archetypal sanctuary. He also put trees and flowers on the walls (6:29, 32), so that the entire complex was symbolically surrounded or made up of trees.

Like the tabernacle, furnishings were placed here. Many scholars see these furnishings as representing the visible earth and sea.[77] All of these furnishings functioned the same way in the temple as they did in the tabernacle. Sacrifices were offered here on the bronze altar (1 Kgs 8:64; 2 Chron 4:1). This is possibly symbolic of earth.

The Sea and Baptism

There was also something called the Great Sea (1 Kgs 7:23). It was made of bronze. The Great Sea was tremendously large; some seven feet high and fifteen feet in diameter, holding about 10,000 gallons of water and weighing between 25-30 tons when empty. As Beale notes, "Priests would have had to climb a ladder to wash in it." (Beale 2004b: 34, n. 11). There were also ten additional washing basins (1 Kgs 7:38) added to the temple for various washings. All of the lavers were surrounded by animal figures, further illustrating the earthly theme of this part of the temple.

These washings (especially in the Great Sea) were later called by the Jews "mikvehs." A mikveh is a ritual bath in a pool of fresh water. It is *necessarily* an immersion.[78] These baths have been practiced since before the times of Christ, and they are still practiced today. Josephus refers to his master Banus (an Essene) as ritually "bathing himself in cold water frequently by night and by day." (Josephus, *Vita* §2).

Jews refer to the baths of the priest into temple ministry (2 Chron 4:6) or tabernacle ministry (Ex 29:4) as mikvehs.[79] The ceremonial idea comes from

---

[77] See Beale 2004b: 32-34.

[78] See Adler, 'mikveh', *JE* at:
http://www.jewishencyclopedia.com/view.jsp?artid=608&letter=M.   Jewish immersions have direct bearing upon the mode of Christian baptism (see final chapter).

[79] One Jew writes, "In Temple times, the priests as well as each Jew who wished entry into the House of G-d had first to immerse in a mikvah. On Yom Kippur, the holiest of all days, the High Priest was allowed entrance into the Holy of Holies, the innermost chamber of the Temple, into which no other mortal could enter. This was the zenith of a day that involved an ascending order of services, each of which was preceded by immersion in the *mikvah*" (Slonim 1996: xiv).

Lev 15:13, "When the one with a discharge is cleansed of his discharge, then he shall count for himself seven days for his cleansing, and wash his clothes. And he shall *bathe his body in fresh water* and shall be clean." Fresh water could come from an ocean, a river, rain, snow, or a place created to hold any such fresh water.

Solomon had gigantic aqueducts and cisterns of water running right up to the temple so that all of the water could be *fresh* water, because this is what the law demanded. The *Letter of Aristeas* (2nd Century B.C.) apparently is an eye-witness report about this as it continued in the second temple,

> The whole foundation was decked with (precious) stones and had slopes leading to the appropriate places for carrying the water which is (needed) for the cleansing of the blood from the sacrifices... There is an uninterrupted supply not only of water, just as if there were a plentiful spring rising naturally from within, but also of indescribably wonderful underground reservoirs, which within a radius of five stades from the foundation of the Temple revealed innumerable channels for each of them, the streams joining together on each side.
>
> (*LetAris* 88-90)

The origin of *mikveh* is primordial. Gen 1:10 describes the gathering of the waters away from dry land. The word "gathering" is *mikveh*. This is salient because the previous verse also talks about a "gathering," but it uses a different word (*qavah*).

In Ex 7:19 and Isa 22:11, *mikveh* is used for a reservoir, which is a collection of fresh water. A curious play on *mikveh* occurs in Jer 17:13 where the word is translated "hope." "O LORD, the hope [*mikveh*] of Israel, all who forsake You will be put to shame. Those who turn away on earth will be written down, because they have forsaken the fountain of living water, even the LORD." Our Mikveh is the "Fountain of Living Water." This, of course, is fulfilled in Christ who gives us living water to drink (John 4:10).[80]

Jews who practice mikvahs recognize that the equivalent word in Greek and English is baptism. If true, then the immersion practice of baptism has Jewish and OT roots beginning right here in the Temple. If true, then we also have new evidence that original creation was a baptism.

---

[80] In this regard, the *Epistle of Barnabas* (circa 70-132 A.D.) notes seven OT passages which it says prefigure baptism. "But let us inquire whether the Lord took care to foreshadow the water and the cross. Now concerning the water [of baptism], it is written with reference to Israel that they would never accept the baptism [*baptisma*] that brings forgiveness of sins, but would create a substitute for themselves." (*Barn* 11:1, cf. vs. 2, 5-6). Five of these seven (in the order they appear in the Epistle: Jer 2:12-13; Isa 16:1-2; 33:16-18; Ps 1:3-6; and Ezek 47:1-12) show overt relationships to water. Apparently, someone very early on thought that it was correct to see baptism is very unfamiliar places to those of us living in contemporary America.

Holy Place

After passing through the waters of the Great Sea, the priest was allowed to enter through the east door into his own courtyard. This was the Holy Place. Again, only the priests could enter here, as we have seen in the tabernacle and archetypal sanctuary.

On the left and right there were ten lampstands made of gold (2 Chron 4:7), ten tables containing the showbread (2 Chron 4:8), and scores of jars and bowls for drink offerings. The same things we discovered in the tabernacle are true here. There is a symbolic movement upwards, into the visible heavens.

In the back there was another altar for incense (1 Kgs 9:25). As with the tabernacle, its smoke filled the air like a cloud. This was a perpetual symbol of the singular event when the Holy Spirit descended upon the Temple at the dedication and filled it with the Glory of God (1 Kgs 8:10-12).

Most Holy Place

Again, inside the Most Holy Place there was the Ark of the Covenant with the Law and the Mercy Seat. Besides the two cherubim on the Mercy Seat, Solomon created two cherubim that stood guard at the entrance of the Most Holy Place. The walls were also decked out with angelic figures. Everything that has been said about these in the tabernacle (and archetypal sanctuary) remains true in the temple. The temple is more than a permanent tabernacle. It is an extended tabernacle. It has an extra space. It has many extra items. And it has one extra important element: it was built by a king.

Heaven and Earth

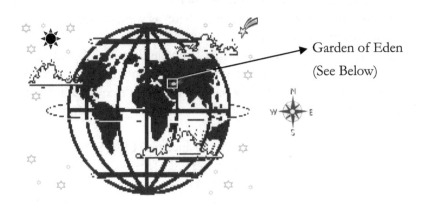

Garden of Eden
(See Below)

The tabernacle and temple were not the first typological sanctuaries in redemptive history.[81] They were simply the ones to be created entirely out of raw materials into architectural form at the hand of man by the command of God. These two sanctuaries came after a prototype (i.e. the first *created* sanctuary) was created by God. Ps 78:69 talks about the prototype, "He built his sanctuary like the high heavens, like the earth, which he has founded forever." So Meredith Kline says, "The heavens declare the glory of God in the special way that they are a copy of the archetypal Glory of God" (Kline 1999: 20ff). Philo wrote, "The whole universe must be regarded as the highest and, in truth, the holy temple of God" (Philo, *De spec. leg.* 1:66).

In a similar way Psalm 104:3 says, "He lays the beams of his chambers on the waters; he makes the clouds his chariot; he rides on the wings of the wind." The *Bible Background Commentary* explains that "the psalmist's attempt to express God's complete control over all creation includes a multistoried or many-chambered sanctuary or palace in the heavens. In the biblical and ancient Near Eastern view the cosmos was a temple and the temple was a mi-

---

[81] I say "redemptive history" to separate them out from "secular history." In secular history, obviously, there were many temples created by pagans. Baptism has always been a ritual practiced by the heathens (see below). They did this often in the context of their temples, which had many similar features to biblical sanctuaries, not because Israel was copying them, but because these pagans remembered in some twisted way, the original sanctuaries created by God. See Beale's fascinating discussion (Beale 2004b: Ch. 1).

crocosmos. The cosmos can therefore be described in architectural terms as a temple would be."[82]

It may be helpful here to discuss a curious but related fact about ancient pagan temple complexes. They are self-described "mirrors of heaven" on earth. The *Enuma Elish* (6.113) describes Marduk's temple, "He shall make on earth the counterpart of what he has brought to pass in heaven." Similarly, Pharaoh Ramses III (1195-1164) wrote about his god, "I made for thee an august house in Nubia... the likeness of the heavens." He also said, "I made for thee an august palace... like the great house of [the god] Atum which is in heaven."[83]

The structures in the complex at Angkor Thom (Cambodia) are ancient. They appear to form the exact shape of the constellation Draco (Hancock 1998: 193). The complex at Giza in Egypt is perhaps the most curious and famous temple complex (especially in light of Ramses' comments). The Great pyramid is well known for its almost impossible architecture. But its astronomical alignments are perhaps even more impressive. Perfectly aligned to the cardinal points and perfectly centered at the geographical center of earth it sits, waiting for us to discover its mysteries. Its height is exactly 1/43,000 the size of the earth. It is probable, therefore, that it is meant to be a replica of the earth. The complex is apparently a replica of the heavens. The Three Pyramids are the exact size and distance to one another so that they mimic Orion's belt as seen from earth. The Sphinx reminds one of the Constellation Leo (Hancock 1995: Ch. 48-49). And there are too many more things to discuss here.

Mirror's of Heaven and Baptism

As noted in the Introduction, baptism is found in all of these ancient religions. Baptism is also associated with their temples. Since, "The temple was... the cosmos in microcosm" (Shafer 1997: 5), it is striking that archaeologists have found the outer mud-brick walls were cut "to look like waves of the sea or lake water," along with ponds or small lakes "for ceremonial washing, representing primeval waters." (Beale 2004b: 54-55). Beale writes, "Temples were symbolically the 'embodiment of the cosmic mountain' representing the original hillock first emerging from the primordial waters at the beginning of creation; such waters themselves were symbolized in temples together with fertile trees receiving life from the waters... That the bronze

---

[82] *BBCOT*, Psalm 104:3: Cosmos as Temple.
[83] Cited in Beale 2004b: 51-52.

'sea' basin in the courtyard represented the cosmic seas is borne out by ancient New Eastern Temples that also have artificial replicas of seas symbolizing either the chaotic forces stilled by the god or the waters of life at the cosmic centre " (Beale 2004a: 195).[84]

The fact that pagans apparently built their temples as models of the heavens and replicas of creation shows the relationship between earthly temple-architecture and the created order. Apparently, the ancients had a universal belief that the original waters were baptismal waters. The problem is, the pagans had only a dim memory of the truth, and their worship became corrupted (or perhaps they knew full well what they were doing, but did what they did out of pure rebellion against the LORD).

It should not surprise us, therefore, when we see Israel's holy architecture replicating the cosmos that God (who designed the architecture in the first place) created. Gen 1:1 says, "In the beginning, God created the heavens and the earth." I suggest that Genesis 1 is the account of God's priestly-kingly work of temple building. After all, heaven is his throne and earth is his footstool (this is temple language).[85]

It is difficult to know with exact precision, however, the relationship between the various parts of the universe and the tiered gradation of holiness in the prototypical temple. Various theories have been presented, each probably having a measure of truth. The best suggestion is that the outer court was the habitable world (symbolized in bronze, animals, water, etc.), the holy place was the visible heavens and its light sources (symbolized by the shining gold, the lamps, the cloud etc.), the holy of holies was the invisible dimensions of the cosmos, where God and his heavenly hosts dwelt (symbolized by the angels around the Ark of God's presence etc.).[86] This seems to fit well with the architecture as we have already described it.

Heaven and earth are clearly vertical in relation to one another. The earth is lower than heaven. We have already seen the many allusions to both earth and heaven that were put into place in the building of the tabernacle and temple. In the tabernacle/temple framework, this movement from earth to heaven is a movement from common to holy to most holy.

---

[84] See also Lundquist (1984: 53-76) and his related sources.

[85] Read in this light, Ps 65 appears to be a song of praise for God's *temple building*. It begins by praising the God of Zion (65:1) for those he brings near to his courts and his temple (65:4). The scene immediately shifts to God's deeds in establishing the mountains (65:6), stilling the seas (65:7), watering the earth with the "river of God" (65:9-10), and crowning the year with bounty (65:11) in the overflow of the wilderness (65:12), the meadows and the flocks, and the valleys with grain (65:13).

[86] See Beale 2004b: 32ff.

One "enters" the prototypical sanctuary from the east. That is, the sun rises (or enters the day on the earth) in the east.[87] This is the probable reason for the eastern orientation of what we have seen so far. Pagan temples also followed this pattern. But the pagans have this strange problem with the eastern sun. Rather than seeing it as a symbol of God's invisible abode (i.e., God himself), thereby being led to worship God, they actually worship the sun (Ezek 8:16). This is a failure to see the invisible behind the visible.

Common Space and Creation and Baptism

Reading Genesis 1 as a description of the temple is an absorbing and exciting exercise. The "common space" is the earth. Here there is a clear description of water being "gathered" from the dry land. The word is *mikveh*. In temple architecture, this corresponds to the laver-sea and glassy sea. In fact, sea (*yam*; Gen 1:10) is the same word Solomon uses to describe his temple sea-baths (1 Kgs 7:23) and *thalassa* (LXX) is the word used to describe the sea in Genesis and in the archetypal sanctuary (Rev 4:6). In apocryphal literature, 2 Enoch 27:3 picks up on this idea of creation waters as a glassy sea, "And thus I made the solid waters, that is to say, the Bottomless, and I made a foundation of light around the water. And I created seven great circles inside it, and I gave them an appearance of crystal, wet and dry, that is to say glass and ice, and to the circuit for water and the other elements." Again, baptism is a chief symbol of this in temple architecture.

Thus, baptism is right here in creation.[88] As we have seen, Tertullian, Jerome, Anglicans, Roman Catholics, and even the early Jews considered this moment of creation a baptism. The creation of the world was patterned after the replica of the heavenly archetypal sanctuary. Here, the baptism is not to purify or cleanse from sin, because sin had not been introduced into the created order. Rather, the idea fits more the idea of a glory covering. Hab 2:14 says, "The earth will be filled with the knowledge of the glory of the Lord as the waters cover the sea." It is like the covering of water that protects the child in the womb before it comes out "dry." It is also a kind of initiation prior to the revealing of the sanctuary, like the priest underwent (Ex 29:4) prior to his entrance into the holy place, where he was not only washed, but covered in garments. Galatians 3:27 puts it together, "As many of you as were baptized into Christ have *put on* Christ."

---

[87] *1 Enoch* 72 is obsessed with understanding the astronomical movements of the heavens. Over and over again it refers to the "gates" through which the lights of the sky rise and set. It is apparent that this kind of language is derived from understanding that earth is a temple through which the sun "enters" through the "east" gate.

[88] We will deal more with this in Section 5.

One of the hang-ups that people have is the idea that baptism is only *for people*. While this is obviously true for the ceremonial purposes of God's priests, it is still true that the sanctuary *itself* is baptized. Though we are not prepared to understand the meaning of these things fully yet; Scripture talks about land being baptized every bit as much as people. Priests often sprinkled items in the sanctuary. The flood covered the "earth." Jesus talks about throwing "this" mountain (the Zion-temple) into the sea (Matt 21:21)[89], in preparation for the fuller sanctuary that will replace it: His body and the church (cf. John 4:20-34).

Holy Place

The holy place is the sky. In the sky are the winged creatures (birds etc.). These represent angelic beings, which are etched inside the holy place on curtains in the other temples. The sky is separated from the land on day two (Gen 1:6-7). Of course, in the sky there are clouds (Gen 2:6[90]), and this corresponds to the cloud filling the holy places. The sky is also up, lifting our eyes higher as we enter holier places.

God fills his earth-space with trees (symbolized in the lampstand and the walls of the temple; Gen 1:11), which are also said to be of use for food (symbolized in the showbread; Gen 1:29). God filled his temple with animals (which are found all over the tabernacle and temple) on the fifth day (Gen 1:20). Also, stars and the other lights of the heavens (symbolized in the lamps and the metal gold) filled the temple on the fourth day (Gen 1:14). They reflect the angelic host in invisible places. These things become the prototypical architecture of the first created sanctuary. In one form or another all of these are found in specific design, detail, and purpose in the tabernacle and temple.

Most Holy Place

The cosmic Archetypal temple gives us a good picture of what lies in the heavenly realm, since this temple seems to describe things that take place in

---

[89] This little story of Jesus cursing the fig tree is extraordinary when viewed from the perspective of "sanctuary." The "architecture" of the story is a tree, food, mountain, and sea. It takes place "outside of Jerusalem." This is easily read as sanctuary language. Throwing the mountain into the sea is a picture of baptism. I am indebted to Pastor Tony Jackson for pointing this story out to me.

[90] The common translation of the "cloud" (i.e. "God sent a *mist*") obscures this meaning. The two better options are "river" or "rain-cloud." As we show in the next section, the word for mist is *'ed*. It is used only one other time in Scripture. Kline (1958) and Futato (1998) both argue that the word should be translated as "rain-cloud." For, in Job 36:27 this is what it seems to mean. "He draws up the drops of water, which distill from the mist (*'ed*) as rain."

heaven. Therefore, in order to understand more about the Most Holy Place of this sanctuary, consult Part II, Section II.

Garden of Eden

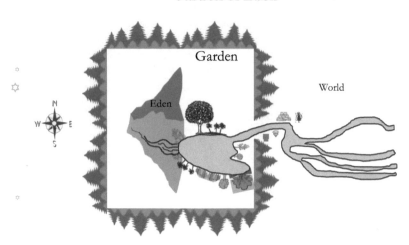

There is another angle to view the prototypical sanctuary. Previously we viewed it from the perspective of Genesis 1. Now we will look at it from the angle presented in Genesis 2. Ezekiel describes Eden as a sanctuary, "You were in Eden, the garden of God... the holy mountain of God... [yet] you profaned your *sanctuaries*" (Ezek 28:13, 14, 18).[91] Numbers 24:5-7 also compares the tabernacle to Eden, therefore calling Eden a sanctuary.[92]

The interpretation of Eden as a sanctuary can be traced back to the times before Christ. The book of *Jubilees* (2nd century B.C.) states, "When she had completed these eighty days we brought her into the garden of Eden, for it is holier than all the earth besides, and every tree that is planted in it is holy. Therefore, there was ordained regarding her who bears a male or a female child the statute of those days that she should touch no hallowed thing, nor enter into the sanctuary until these days for the male or female child are accomplished" (*Jub* 3:12-14). Later it calls Eden, "The holy of holies" (*Jub* 8:19) and compares the Garden with Mt. Sinai, Mount Zion, and "the Mount of the East" saying that "the Lord has four places on the earth... (which) will be

---

[91] The plural "sanctuaries" is used to describe the tabernacle (Lev 21:23) and the temple (Ezek 7:24).

[92] "How fair are your tents, o Jacob, Your dwellings, O Israel! Like palm trees that stretch out, Like gardens beside the river, Like aloes planted by the Lord, Like cedars beside the waters. Water shall flow from his buckets, And his seed shall be by many waters, And his king shall be higher than Agag, And his kingdom shall be exalted." For an exposition of this, see Beale 2004b: 162ff.

sanctified in the new creation" (*Jub* 4:26).[93]   As we will see, these other places are also to be understood as sanctuaries.

In addition to Jubilees, the Dead Sea Scrolls turned up a fragment that seems to describe Eden as a sanctuary. 4Q418 Frag. 81 tells us that the true "sons of Adam" will "walk" in an "eter[nal] plantation" (lines 13-14). They are to "honor" God "by consecrating yourself to him, in accordance to the fact that he has placed you as a holy of holiness [over all] the earth, and over all the angels" (line 4). Beale cites this Qumran fragment in his discussion with John's vision of the City-Temple (Rev 21). The community refers to itself as the "sanctuary of Adam" (Beale 2004a: 199). We will take note of John's inclusion of Eden later on. For now, we want to note Beale's comments. "John and Qumran are not dependent on one another, but rather are on parallel trajectories in interpreting the OT in this manner, though both may have been familiar with a common earlier tradition that interpreted the OT like this" (Beale 2007: 1155). The point is that Jews from before the time of Christ, as well as Christians like John (inspired by the Holy Spirit), understood the Garden of Eden as a temple-sanctuary that is like other sanctuaries we find in the Bible. Because of this, it is useful to identify the architectural features that make up the Garden of Eden temple.

The Garden-sanctuary contained three gradations of holiness: the world (heavens and earth), the Garden, and Eden.[94] First, there is a separation between the world and the Garden. Remembering the first Eden, Isaiah talks about eschatological Eden's *walls*, "foreigners will build up your walls" and "your gates will be opened continually" (Isaiah 60:10).[95] We have already noted how walls are an intricate part of other biblical temple ectypes. These walls were adorned with palms and other trees. Now we can answer why. They gave the appearance of the Garden of Eden.[96] "Garden" is regularly translated by the LXX as *paradeisos* (paradise). "Very similar to the Greek *paradeisos*, the Persian word '*pardez*,' originally denoted 'an enclosed garden,

---

[93] Hellerman (2003: 415-417) discusses the sacred and profane places of Jubilees.

[94] This follows Beale 2004b: 75 and Walton 2001: 167-168, 182-183. A slightly different idea is presented in Martin 2004. He sees the Most Holy Place as the "Garden Midst" (Gen 2:9); the Holy Place as the Garden; the Outer Court as Eden; and the land of Nod (east and outside of Eden) as the rest of the world. Because Gen 2:8 and 2:10 seem to make differing claims, we see this as a difficult decision. We slightly favor Beale and Walton.

[95] That Isaiah is talking about Eden is made clear in Isa 60:13 (Beale 2004b: 72; Stordalen 2000: 411-414, 435-436). Here, the prophet tells us that all kinds of trees will be in this heavenly place. Only in Eden are trees of every kind said to be present like this together and so we get the picture that Isaiah is seeing a sort of glorified Eden.

[96] 2 *Enoch* 30:1 discusses Eden as having walls. "I laid out paradise as a garden, and I enclosed it; and I placed armed guards, angels aflame with fire. And thus I created the renewal of the earth."

especially a royal part... planted with fruit trees, laid out regularly, and often stocked with animals of the chase.'" (Hemer 1986: 50).

But the Garden is also a separate space from Eden itself. Ancient near eastern temples were built in such a way that the garden adjoined the palace. This is also what Scripture tells us about the Garden. "A river flowed *out of Eden* to water *the garden*" (Gen 2:10). Obviously, these spaces are related but separate. With the source of the river being in Eden, this corresponds to the Most Holy Place, the place where God dwells. Other Scriptures that talk about the river having its source near the throne confirm this interpretation of Eden as the Most Holy Place (Ps 46:4; 65:9; Dan 7:10; Ezek 47:1; Rev 22:1). Thus, both the garden and the river belong to God (Isa 51:3; Ezek 28:13; Ps 65:9).

Common Space

So let us look at the common space just outside of the Garden. This space is to be found east of Eden. Not only was Eden planted "in the east" (Gen 2:8), but its gate or entrance was in the east (3:24; 4:7[97]). Even Cain, when he was exiled from Eden was sent east to the land of Nod (4:16). As we have seen, east is quite significant in temple architecture (especially as it corresponds to the rising of the sun in the heaven-earth sanctuary).

As noted a moment ago (see previous note 97), Cain and Abel offered sacrifices outside the Garden, but still in the region of Eden. So there is an altar here. This corresponds to the altar in the common space of previous sanctuaries. This altar becomes symbolic for the altar of slain saints in the archetypal temple. Hebrews says, "Jesus blood speaks a better word than the blood of Abel" (Heb 12:24).

It is also true that the Scripture mentions "the land of Havilah where there is gold." Of course, there was gold both inside and outside of the tabernacle and temple. A related comment on this can be found in *Pseudo-Philo* (pre-70 A.D.). It says that the Amorites pillaged the "land of Haviliah" of twelve precious stone—identical to those of the priestly garments (Ex 28)—and used them for idolatrous purposes, until they were taken by Israel and

---

[97] The idea in Gen 4:7 where is says "sin is crouching at the *door*" may not be entirely spiritual (i.e. "the door of your heart"). It appears that the door (*pethach*) may actually be the door of the Garden of Eden! *Pethach* is the same word used for the entrance of the tabernacle (Ex 29:4) and the entrance of the temple (Ezek 8:7). The angels were put on the eastern side of the garden in order to *guard* it. So apparently, the entrance to the Garden was in the east. If, as we are arguing here, the Garden of Eden is the holy/most holy place, the fact that Cain and Abel were offering sacrifices while apparently still in the region of Eden (4:16) is significant. This would put their sacrifice somewhere just outside the entrance of the Garden, exactly where we find the sacrifices of the temple, tabernacle, and archetypal temple taking place... in the region that corresponds to the world or the courtyard.

placed into the ark of the Temple. *Pseudo Philo* 25:10ff, though legendary in its history, provides a Jewish commentary on the land itself.

<u>Eden's River and Baptism</u>

Also as mentioned a moment ago, Genesis notes a curious geographical characteristic that is usually overlooked other than for its basic geographical information. Eden has a river that is said to water the garden, and eventually make its way to the four corners of the earth (Gen 2:10-14). The meaning of the word "Eden" is helpful here. It is related to the Akkadian word *edinu*, which is based on the Sumerian word *eden*, meaning "plain, steppe" (*TWOT*, #1568). A steppe is easily pictured by thinking of the terraced mountainous rice fields of the east (cf. Eden as mountain in Ezek 28:13-14). So John Walton describes it this way, "The word *Eden* refers to a well-watered place, suggesting a luxuriant park. The word translated "garden" does not typically refer to vegetable plots but to orchards or parks containing trees" (Walton 2000: CD ROM edition).

Besides "steppe," the word Eden can also means "to enrich, make abundant" (see Gen 13:10). In Ugaritic occurrences the idea is a "garden of abundance," specifically an abundance of *water supply* (Walton 2001: 167).[98] Again, water has significant importance to our study of baptism, so we will take some time to think about it.

Gen 2:6 says, "A mist was going up from the land and was watering the whole face of the ground." The mist is the source of the abundance of Eden. But what is this "mist"? There are two good options, with "mist" *not* being among them.

The word for mist is the Hebrew word *'ed*. It is used only one other time in Scripture. Kline (1958) and Futato (1998) both argue that the word should be translated as "rain-cloud." For, in Job 36:27 (the only other time the word is used) this is what it seems to mean. "He draws up the drops of water, which distill from the mist (*'ed*) as rain." Obviously, the rain comes from rain-clouds as the Scripture clearly teaches, "If the clouds are full of rain, they empty themselves on the earth" (Eccles 11:3).

The other option is that the *'ed* is a river. Some have argued that the word comes from the Akkadian *edû* or "onrush of water" (E. A. Speiser 195, 102-103), as in a river that floods. Édouard Dhorme was the first to connect *'ed* with the Sumerian *id* or "cosmic river" (Dhorme 1907, 274). *Id* was also the

---

[98] See also Tsumura 1996: 37-38 and Munday Jr. 1996: 135-136.

term used for the Akkadian cosmic river, and so McCarter concludes "the loan into Hebrew offers no linguistic difficulties" (McCarter 1973: 403). If the latter is true, Eden—as source of this water—is further enhanced as a copy of the cosmic temple of God.

If the *'ed* is a river, why use two different words in Gen 2 for river? (Gen 2:10-14 uses the word *nahar*). The answer could have theological significance. McCarter argues that Gen 2:6 is specifically calling our attention to the theme of the river *ordeal* and the use of the river as a cosmic judge (McCarter 1973: 403-412).

But the emphasis for the river text of Genesis is not on Eden or the Garden per se, but on its flowing out *into the world*. Here is the text,

> A river flowed out of Eden to water the garden, and there it divided and became four rivers. The name of the first is the Pishon. It is the one that flowed around the whole land of Havilah, where there is gold. And the gold of that land is good; bdellium and onyx stone are there. The name of the second river is the Gihon. It is the one that flowed around the whole land of Cush. And the name of the third river is the Tigris, which flows east of Assyria. And the fourth river is the Euphrates.

Notice how the majority of the passage talks about the divisions of the river and where they flow. It flows outside of the Garden. This happens to correspond to the placement of the glassy-fiery sea, the river of fire, the laver, the bronze sea, and the divided waters of the world. All of the seas are located in the literal or symbolic "world"—or common part—of the sanctuary, while Eden's river (and other future sanctuary-rivers) flows outwardly in that same direction.

Curious baptismal (and the connected judgment) legends have abounded regarding Adam (and Eve) in this—and other—rivers. Jews, with their keen awareness of the *mikveh* are especially prone to these speculations. As far back as the first century we have evidence of this. *The Life of Adam and Eve* (also called *Vita Adae at Evae*) discusses how Adam and Eve tried to repent and atone for their sin of eating the forbidden fruit.

> Adam said to Eve: "You cannot do as much as I, but do as much so that you might be saved. For I will do forty days of fasting. You, however, arise and go to the Tigris River and take a stone and stand upon it in the water up to your neck in the depth of the river. Let not a word go forth from your mouth since we are unworthy to ask of the Lord for our lips are unclean from the illicit and forbidden tree. Stand in the water of the river for thirty-seven days. I however, will do forty days in the water of the Jordan. Perhaps the Lord will have mercy on us." And Eve walked to the Tigris River and did as Adam had told her. Likewise, Adam walked to the Jordan River and stood upon a rock up to his neck in the water.
>
> (*VitaAE* 6:1-2, 7:1-2)

The Rabbis in the second century taught similar things in the Talmud. "[Adam] is described... (*Erub* 18b; Talmud tractate *Avoda Zarah*, 8a; *Ab. R. N. i.*; *Pirke de Rabbi Eliezer*) as undergoing a terrible ordeal while fasting, praying, and bathing in the river for seven and forty days."[99]

Nicholas Hannan-Stavroulakis comments, "Their purification took place through immersion in living water in the mikveh provided by the Jordan and Euphrates rivers" (Hannan-Stavroulakis 2002). Another writes, "Immersion in the mikvah has offered a gateway to purity ever since the creation of man" (Slonim 1996: xiv). Many more examples could be cited.

We note these things, not because we necessarily believe that Adam actually baptized himself in the River (this is speculation), but because it shows historical precedent for seeing this and other rivers as *baptismal* waters. The Epistle of Barnabas seems to concur when it says, "Then what does he [an unknown source] say? 'And there was a river flowing on the right hand, and beautiful trees rising from it, and whoever eats from them will live forever.' By this he means that while we descend into the water laden with sins and dirt, we rise up bearing fruit in our heart and with fear and hope in Jesus in our spirits" (*Barn* 11:10-11). The Edenic allusions are obvious, yet the whole context of this chapter is baptism. If our conclusion about the Garden as a sanctuary created by God after the pattern of other sanctuaries is proper, then the necessary conclusion is that Eden's river must be viewed as *baptismal* water, even if Adam never got a drop of its water on his skin.

One more interesting comment from the Scripture on the river is in order. John seems to have this river (or its eschatological antitype) in mind in Revelation 22. In this vision, John sees a city. In its center is the throne of God (22:1). The "river of the water of life, bright as crystal" flowed from the throne. (Its crystalline clarity is a clear reminder of the sea of glass that was before the throne in the archetypal sanctuary). Psalm 46:4 also talks about this, "There is a river whose streams make glad the city of God, the holy habitation of the most High."

How does John's river relate to the Eden-River? It waters the "tree of life" (Rev 22:2). This is a clear allusion to Gen 2:10 where the river waters the garden. A few verses later in Revelation the call goes out, "Blessed are those who *wash* their robes, so that they may have the right to the tree of life and that they may enter the city by the gates..." (Rev 22:14). It appears that washing one's robes in the river alone gives one the right to enter the city

---

[99] J. Frederic McCurdy, 'Adam', in *Jewish Encyclopedia* at:
http://www.jewishencyclopedia.com/view.jsp?artid=758&letter=A&search=adam#1859

and the holy place to eat from the tree of life. This is what baptism symbolizes as Peter says "Not as removal of dirt from the body, but as an appeal to God for a good conscience, through the resurrection of Jesus Christ" (1 Pet 3:21). A long time ago Christopher Wordsworth put this River to poetry,

> Thou art a port protected from storms round us rise;
> A garden intersected with streams of Paradise;
> Thou art a cooling fountain in life's dry, dreary sand;
> From thee, like Pisgah's mountain, we view our promised land.
> (Wordsworth, "O Day of Rest and Gladness")

Something significant took place the day Adam sinned. To protect the holy place, God put cherubim and a flaming sword on the eastern side of the Garden to guard the entrance. This is still common space. This parallels the station of the Levitical tribe that stood guard on the eastern side of the tabernacle and who were commanded to put anyone to death who tried to enter (Num 3:38, cf. 25:6-8). It is the later work of the Levitical priests to be temple guards (1 Chron 9:23; Ezek 40:45), to keep watch at the gates (Neh 11:19) so that no unclean person would enter (2 Chron 23:19). And we have already seen how the cherubim were fashioned on the walls of the Holy Place in earlier ectypal sanctuaries.

Holy Place

We know certain significant things that were present *inside* the garden. If we move past the cherubim, the significance of the Garden-architecture as "temple" architecture becomes apparent. There is a tree of life (Gen 2:9; Rev 22:2) here. This is what the Cherubim were guarding until Christ opened the way back to the tree (This shows how the tree has its antitype in Christ, as does everything else in these sanctuaries). The tabernacle and temple are recalling this when they fashion a lampstand in the shape of a tree. In this regard Vern Poythress notices,

> The tree reminds us of the Garden of Eden with its original tree of life. But now the true life of creation has been lost through sin. It is restored through God coming to be 'God with us.' The tabernacle is a renewed version of the Garden of Eden. But curtains with cherubim on them still bar the way into God's presence, just as cherubim barred the way into the original Garden of Eden after the Fall (Gen 3:24).
> (Poythress 1991: 19)

The trees were "good for food" (Gen 2:9; cf. 1:29-30). Especially the tree of life contains sacred holy food (3:22). The good fruit was sanctuary food, and like the tabernacle and temple, only those allowed inside the holy place were permitted to eat it (Gen 3:22). As we have seen in the ectypes of the tabernacle and temple, the holy place was where the showbread of God's presence was located.

The Garden and neighboring regions are specifically said to be rich with precious metals, specifically gold (2:11), bdellium, and onyx (2:12). Ezekiel adds, "Every precious stone was your covering: the ruby, the topaz, and the diamond; the beryl, the onyx, and the jasper; the lapis lazuli, the turquoise, and the emerald; and the gold, the workmanship of your settings and sockets, was in you" (Ezek 28:13). This is symbolized in the priestly clothing of the Levites, clothing that they would wear only when performing duties in the holy place (Ex 28:2-43). It is also symbolized in the gold and bronze of the man-made sanctuaries.

Bdellium is an interesting element to consider. It was an aromatic gum, much like myrrh (given to Christ at his birth), and it came from a tree. Perhaps this is why 4 Esdras 2:12 states, "The tree of life shall give them fragrant perfume, and they shall neither toil nor become weary." We have seen incense filling all of the sanctuaries so far. They symbolize God's presence in the cloud. Since Eden is patterned after the archetype, it is not surprising to find a veiled reference to it here.

Most Holy Place

What about the Most Holy Place? What do we know about Eden? As noted earlier, Eden is actually a mountain. Again, this provides the vertical dimension to the sanctuary that is prevalent in all of the sanctuaries we have looked at so far. Ascending upward is a symbol of reaching the heavens. The mountain theme will become important to keep in mind in identifying later ectypal sanctuaries, even as the vertical theme has been in those we have seen thus far.

Here on the mountain, there were cherubim that attended God (Ezek 28:13ff). We have seen how this had its origination in the arch-temple, and later, in the decorations inside the holy place(s) on the ark, in the walls, on the curtains, etc.

There was also a kind of cloud here. Ezekiel's "covering cherub" (Ezek 28:14) of Eden and Isaiah's creation (*bara'*) of a restored paradise under a new heavenly of divine Glory (Isa 4:5)[100] lead one commentator to say, "By virtue

---

[100] This verse also references the Exodus' "cloud by day" and "fire by night."

of the presence of this theophanic cloud-canopy, Eden had the character of a holy tabernacle, a microcosmic house of God" (Kline 1999: 36).

There is a priest-king whom God "puts" in the temple to "tend and care" for it (Gen 1:26-27, 2:15). We will have more to say about the priestly nature of this placement of man in Part III. To the man he gives his law (Gen 1:28), corresponding to the Law in the Ark of the Covenant. Specifically he was told, "You shall not eat from the tree of the knowledge of good and evil" (Gen 2:17). Gordon Wenham sees the Law of God (cf. Ps 19:8-9) as being patterned after this tree (Wenham 1994: 402-403; also Clines 1974). Greg Beale points out that touching both would result in death (Beale 2004a: 199). But other commandments were given to Adam as well (especially Gen 1:28).[101] The Ark of the Covenant, which was in the Most Holy Place, contained the Ten Commandments.

It also appears that a sacrifice of atonement occurred in Eden at the hand of God himself. Gen 3:21, "And the LORD God made garments of skins for the man and for his wife, and clothed them." Garments of skin do not occur without the shedding of blood. Since Adam and Eve did not deserve this grace, it is logical to conclude that this was a foreshadowing of the sacrifice of Christ on behalf of his people. Hebrews says Christ entered the Holy Place in order to offer this sacrifice (Heb 9:12).

The conclusion of the study of the Garden of Eden is obvious. As a host of commentators have begun to recognize, the Garden of Eden is the prototypical sanctuary. Not only is all of the architecture here, but the things which we have mentioned are the only things that Moses bothers to tell us about. We are not leaving things out in our description or picking out the things that only make it seems as if this were a sanctuary. God wrote the story this way so that we would see the sanctuary items of the Garden and begin to wonder. When we understand the Garden is a sanctuary, our study of other sanctuaries is enriched and our theology of baptism is deepened.

---

[101] The commands, "be fruitful," "multiply," "fill the earth," "subdue it," and "rule" each presuppose the moral 10 commandments are in place in order to do these things properly. It is unthinkable that God would allow a violation of any of these things, and the rest of Genesis demonstrates clearly that mankind understood the moral law before the receiving of it in the form of the Ten Commandments at Sinai.

Ararat-Ark Sanctuary

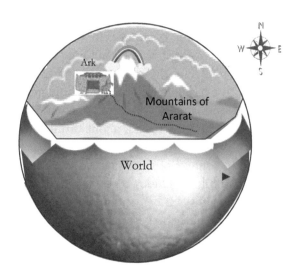

So far we have seen the archetypal sanctuary (Rev 4-5), two ectypal human sanctuaries designed at the command of God (tabernacle and temple), and the prototypical sanctuary as viewed from the perspectives of Genesis 1 and 2. Now we turn our attention to three more ectypal sanctuaries and two antitypical sanctuaries that will greatly strengthen our theology of baptism. All of these sanctuaries are like Eden in that they are created by the hand of God.

The first of these we wish to look at occurs immediately after the waters of the flood recede. Gen 8:4 says, "And in the seventh month, on the seventeenth day of the month, the ark came to rest on the mountains of Ararat."[102] Of all the sanctuaries that we are discussing, this is the only one not *explicitly* called a sanctuary. However, there are implicit references to it in a number of places.

---

[102] Note the words references to "seven" and "rest," which were earlier used at the ending of the creation of the prototypical sanctuary in Genesis 1-2. We could have talked much more about this Sabbath theme as it relates to sanctuaries. Here the theme helps us identify the Ararat-Ark as a sanctuary. "Noah" means rest. He took "seven" kinds of clean animals (Gen 7:2-3). The rains came "seven" days later (Gen 7:10). He waits "seven" days to send out the bird (Gen 8:10, 12). He offers a sabbatical sacrifice (Gen 8:21; a word play on the "Noah" takes place in Gen 8:21 when Noah builds an altar and sacrifices animals, creating a "rest-inducing" odor—where *hannihoah* is a Polel infinitive of the verb *nûach* or "rest" [see Hamilton 1990: 308]. "Seven" and "rest" are also associated with tabernacle and temple building and dedication/sanctification (Ex 29:30; 1 Kgs 6:37-38; 8:65).

First, Heb 11:7 and 1 Peter 3:20 talk about being "saved" through the Ark. This is similar to the language of God's salvation being (or being inside) a fortress, a stronghold, a house, or a temple (Ps 18:2; 62:2, 6; Luke 1:69). To be in God's presence is to be saved.

Second, Isaiah and Habakkuk combine temple and flood imagery. Isaiah says, "They shall not hurt or destroy in all my holy mountain; for the earth shall be full of the knowledge of the LORD as the waters cover the sea" (Isa 11:9; cf. Gen 7:19). As we have already seen, the holy mountain is a temple image. Habakkuk uses the same "waters cover the sea" language (Hab 2:14), but immediately after this begins to talk about drunkenness, gazing on nakedness (Hab 2:15) and beasts that terrify (Hab 2:17). Each of these are found in the immediate context of the Ararat-sanctuary story (see in order Gen 9:21 22, 2). Habakkuk concludes by saying, "The LORD is in his holy temple, let all the earth keep silent before him" (Hab 2:20).

Then there is the design of the Ark itself. This was not some creative ship invented by Noah. Instead, *God* told him exactly how to build it. Like other temples, it had a three tiered design (Gen 6:16). After discussing the Ark Meredith Kline (1996: 216) concludes, "Noah's ark was designed as a replica of the three-story universe, the cosmic city-temple of God (cf. Isa 66:1). Established in sabbatical rest on the Ararat mountaintop, the ark was a redemptive restoration of the mountain of God in Eden, itself a replica of the heavenly Zaphon."

The building of the Ark and Solomon's temple (also at the command of God) follows the same basic pattern. The Ark has first: measurements (Gen 6:15); second: a window (Gen 6:16a); third: a door (Gen 6:16b); fourth: three decks (Gen 6:16c). The Temple has measurements (1 Kgs 6:2); and entrance hall (1 Kgs 6:3); windows with recessed jambs (1 Kgs 6:44); and the side chambers with three layers (1 Kgs 6:5-6). Hence, the Temple seems to be a replica of Noah's Ark, thereby making the Ark a sanctuary.[103]

One final induction is worth mentioning, because we want it to be clear that Scripture indeed sees this place as a sanctuary. Noah comes out of the Ark on the first day of the first month (Gen 8:13) and offers his sacrifice.

---

[103] Gregory Beale (1999: 1075) has an interesting discussion on the Greek word *tetragōnos* (four-square). It is used to describe the heavenly city (Rev 21:16), which as we will see below is also a sanctuary. In Greek literature (Plato, Aristotle, Diogenes Laertius etc.), it is a symbol of perfection or completeness, particularly of a good man who is without reproach. The *LXX* uses the word to describe the "holy place and temple," the "altar," the "mercy seat," and the "heave offering" including the nation of Israel, the sanctuary, the priests, and the capital city (cf. Ezek 41:21; 43:16, 17; 48:20). Exodus uses it to describe the "altar" (Ex 27:1; 30:2) and the high priests' "breastpiece of judgment" (Ex 28:16; 36:16). The only other uses of the word occur in Gen 6:14 and 1 Kgs 7:42, describing parts of Noah's ark and Solomon's house respectively. One might reasonably conclude from this word alone that Noah's ark was indeed a temple.

This is the same day that Moses dedicated the tabernacle (Ex 40:17) and the day chosen to rededicate the temple (2 Chron 29:17). Not coincidently, this is the same day the third temple is cleansed (Ezek 45:18).

Now we are prepared to discuss the sanctuary itself. The most obvious feature of this place is that it was a mountainous region. This is identical to Eden. Note also that from the perspective of Israel, these mountains could be referred to as being in the east,[104] even as the descendants of Noah migrated "from the east" (Gen 11:2), giving us some reason to read the landing of the Ark as being in the east.

Common Space

When Noah opened the door of the Ark, the animals were dispersed back into the world (Gen 8:19) from which they came (6:19). If a sanctuary can be established at Ararat, the animal dispersion would correspond to the host of creatures in the visible realm (Rev 5:13) as well as all the creatures fashioned into the architecture of the temple, on the earth (Gen 1:24-25), and in the Garden (Gen 2:19).

The first explicit reference to an altar in the Bible occurs in Gen 8:20. Immediately after the animals left the Ark, "Noah built an altar to the LORD and took some of every clean animal and some of every clean bird and offered burnt offerings on the altar." This occurred because God made the waters of the flood subside (Gen 8:13).

The Flood and Baptism

The references to water in this sanctuary are aplenty: nineteen verses between Gen 6-9. Water is the dominate image of the story, which is why it is often called simply: The Flood. But water is not just a feature of the *story*. As with creation, it is an essential element of the *temple*. After the waters receded far away, the region ceased to be a temple.

In sanctuary architecture, these waters correspond to the sea of glass (mixed with fire), the river of fire, the lake of fire and other archetypical figures that mix water and fire together before God's throne. (This is undoubtedly some of the imagery behind John the Baptist's reference to baptism of water and fire in Matt 3:11-12, because John closes out his discussion on baptism by talking about judgment; i.e., "his winnowing fork is in his hand").

---

[104] Whether one locates this around today's Mt. Ararat in southeastern Turkey or in someplace like northern Iran, this is the *eastern* country from Israel's perspective (Job 1:3; Isa 46:11).

Meredith Kline offers some penetrating insight relating the structure of the Ark (as temple) and the waters of the flood (coming from the temple of the heaven/earth). The window of the Ark corresponds to the "window of heaven" (Gen 7:11). Kline remarks, "Appropriately, the window area is located along the top of the ark, as part of the upper (heavenly) story" (Kline 2006b: 226). The door at the bottom of the Ark corresponds to the "door that shuts up the depths of the sea, holding back its proud waves (see Job 38:8-11)." God shut the door of the ark (Gen 7:16) even as he opened the doors of the deep (Gen 7:11; Job 38:8). "Together, the window and door of the ark mirrored the two cosmic sources of the flood waters, the window of heaven, opened to unleash the torrents of the waters above the earth, and the door of the deep, unbarred to let the waters beneath the earth loose" (ibid). In this way there appears to be a relationship between the Ark as sanctuary and the prototypical temple.

Clearly, the flood waters were *baptismal* waters for both Noah and the world. We should remember, it is the water that is the type of Christian baptism (1 Pet 3:21). Heb 11:7 establishes the dual function of baptism when it says that Noah was *saved*—but the world was *destroyed*—through the same waters (see also 2 Pet 2:5, 3:5-7).

The difference between the two types of people that are baptized is that Noah was *saved* through the waters by God. The *Code of Hammurabi* may shed some light on the meaning of this. While regarding baptism as drowning (which we have seen with other ancient near-eastern literature), it adds a legal or legislative twist that we have not seen. The second law required the accused person to throw himself into the river of the deity.

> If a man has levied (a charge of) sorceries and then has not proved it, the one upon whom the charge of witchcraft has been laid shall go to the holy river, shall leap into the river, and if the river overwhelms him, his accuser shall carry off his house. If the river proves that man clear and he escapes safe, he who levied (the charge of) sorceries upon him shall be put to death, and he who leapt into the river shall carry off the house of his accuser.

Monte Python famously pokes fun of this kind of practice when Bedemir helps the townsfolk reason that witches are made of wood (which is why they burn). If you put her in water and she floats (like wood), then she must be made of wood and therefore she must be a witch. The backwards people believed that if she drowned, she was innocent. But of course by then she was already dead anyway. On a more serious note, Kline comments, "The concept was, therefore, that the accused was casting himself into the hands of the divine judge who would declare the verdict. Emergence from the divine waters of the ordeal would signify vindication" (Kline 1968: 55).

Thus, the idea that Peter develops is one of baptism as a legal declaration of innocence (i.e. "justification"). It isn't that Noah was sinless (just look at his life immediately after the flood), but that he had found grace in God's sight (Gen 6:8), and his safe passage through the waters was God's sign or pledge that he was blameless by a judicial decree. So, Peter says, "Baptism, which corresponds to this, now saves you, not as a removal of dirt from the body but as an appeal to God for a clear conscience, through the resurrection of Jesus Christ."

The conscience is a *legal* entity: now accusing, now defending (Rom 2:15). Baptism is "an appeal to God for a clear conscience," which like Noah can at times become dirty (1 Pet 3:16; cf. Gen 9:21ff). So, the idea isn't that baptism saves (as if Peter confuses the sign with the reality), but that it is our legal appeal combined with God's declaration that we are righteous by grace through faith in Christ alone. This "legal" aspect of baptism is another important point in furthering along our theology of baptism.

Holy Place

Ararat has other features that make it possible to identify it as a kind of ectypal sanctuary, which in turn supports our conclusion that the flood waters are sanctuary waters (since the archetypal sanctuary has water, all patterns of it must likewise have water). Recall the olive leaf, taken by the bird that comes back and tells Noah that the water had receded from the top of the mountains. This at least echoes the trees of Eden. God also provides food for Noah there on the side of the mountain (Gen 9:3).

The sacrifice that Noah makes is a burnt offering that becomes a "pleasing aroma" (8:20-21). Aromas remind us of the incense that always burns before the Lord in other temple holy places. There is also the first distinction between clean and unclean animals (7:2, 8), and this is language important to temple sacrifices (Gen 8:20; Lev 11:47; 20:25; Deut 12:15, 22).

Most Holy Place

Finally, we come to the Most Holy Place, the place of God's presence. This is established first in the rainbow and the clouds (Gen 9:13-16). The cloud is the place that fills the Most Holy Place. The rainbow occurs only in the archetypal sanctuary in Revelation where it surrounds the throne of God

(Rev 4:3).[105] Then there are the commands (especially to be fruitful, multiply, and fill the earth [Gen 9:1]; but also to eat food) that re-establish the commands given to Adam in Eden (the Most Holy Place). These commands parallel the Law being placed in the Ark of the Covenant.

Then, of course, on top of the mountain(s) there is the Ark: Noah's Ark. We have seen this vertical aspect of sanctuaries before. As mentioned a moment ago, the tabernacle and temple each had an ark in the midst of their Most Holy Place. Three points can to be made about Noah's Ark in this regard.

First, while Hebrew uses two different words for Ark, LXX uses the same word to describe both, as does the NT Greek (Heb 9:4; 11:7). The word is *kibōtos*. Comparing the two texts where the arks are commanded to be created yields several similarities. Ex 25:10, "Make an ark of acacia wood. Two cubits and a half shall be its length, a cubit and a half its breadth, and a cubit and a half its height." Gen 6:14-15, "Make yourself an ark of gopher wood... This is how you are to make it: the length of the ark 300 cubits, its breadth 50 cubits, and its height 30 cubits."

Second, comparing the two passages word order shows their similarity. They are both made of wood, each representing Eden.[106] Comparing the order of the dimensions (length, then breadth, then height) also shows similarity. (Note here: There are also the same patterns found in commands to

---

[105] *Sirach* 50:7 connects the rainbow and the temple saying, "Like the sun shining upon the temple of the Most High, and like the rainbow gleaming in glorious clouds."

[106] God tells Noah to make the Ark out of *gopher* wood (Gen 6:14). "Gopher" (גֹפֶר) is a transliteration of the Hebrew. The word is mentioned only here in the Bible. Though no one knows for sure, there are two basic options in understanding what gopher wood is. The first is to see the obvious word play that takes place in the text between the גֹפֶר (gopher) and כֹּפֶר (cover/atonement) and כֹּפֶר (pitch). Because of the similarity of these words (compare the Hebrew letters), some have understood the gopher to be a *process of making wood*, rather than the wood itself.

However, the Hebrew construct relationship between gopher and tree/wood make this option doubtful. A literal reading of the phrase is "a tree of gopher" (or gopher-wood), which seems to imply that gopher is a *type* of wood as nearly every English translation opts to translate it. A fairly typical idea is to identify gopher with the cypress tree. The NIV and NRS versions both translate "gopher" as cypress.

If the word "gopher" is used in this text as a word play, and it can legitimately be a type of cypress wood, then we have a problem understanding why the author would not use the normal word for cypress. This other word would not have made the point the way "gopher" does. What is clear is that this wood had to be durable and abounding, something that is quite true of the cypress in and around the Armenian mountains where Noah built his ark.

More than its practical value of keeping boats afloat, this wood was *Edenic* wood (Gen 2:9, cf. Isa 41:18-19, 60:13). This cypress wood would become for Noah, quite literally, his "tree of life." The very specific measurements of the ark were also more than just practical. The symmetry is symbolic of the perfect place (heaven) to house the living remnants of prediluvian earth. Into this ark would go the very items of creation, including two of each animal that Adam had named while he was alone in the Garden of Eden. Nearly every facet of this story takes us back to the first two chapters of Genesis.

Acacia wood (the Ark of the Covenant) is Edenic wood the only other time it is used outside of the Pentateuch in Isaiah's vision (Isa 41:19).

build other things in the tabernacle and Temple - Ex 25:17, 23, 26:2, 8, 16; 27:1; 28:16; 1 Kgs 6:2, 6; 7:2, 15:23, 27). God commands the exact dimension in both. This is followed by a completion formula that is identical when Noah finishes the Ark and Israel finishes the tabernacle (cf. Gen 6:22, Ex 39:42).[107]

Finally, there is a geometric relationship that exists between the two arks. 1.5 is twenty times less than 30. 2.5 is twenty times less than 50. 1.5 is two hundred times less than 300. Putting it another way, you could fit exactly 80,000 Arks of the Covenant into Noah's Ark. This cannot be a coincidence. For whatever reason, God wanted them both built upon the same ratio of 3 to 5. The Ark of the Covenant is patterned upon the dimensions of Noah's Ark.

Establishing the Ararat-Ark sanctuary helps us understand why Peter calls the flood a baptism. For, as in the archetypal sanctuary, baptism must be present. What is true about the flood is also true about the next sanctuary we will discuss: Mt. Sinai.[108]

---

[107] Joshua 21:8 has the same formula, except this time it pertains to the settlement and possession of the promised Land. This is useful information to keep in mind when we talk about the Promised Land Sanctuary.

[108] For a fascinating article on the Ark as a Sanctuary, see Holloway 1991.

Sinai Sanctuary

Though not the next sanctuary to be discussed in Scripture after the Ark, Sinai resembles Ararat so much that it seems appropriate to talk about it here. The "mountain of God" (Ex 3:1) becomes yet another ectypal sanctuary in the OT. Scripture calls it a sanctuary made by the hand of God (Ex 15:17; Ps 68:17). Like the rest, it has three gradations of holiness. Peter Leithart notes this and sees a direct relationship to the tabernacle saying, "The tent became a 'portable Sinai'" (Leithart 2003: 84).[109]

Common Space

The base of the mountain, where all the people camped, was the common ground (Ex 19:2, 17). They could walk here, but they were not allowed to even touch the mountain or they would die (19:12). They even had to put markers around the mountain (Ex 19:12). The thought is parallel to the tabernacle, where no common Israelite was allowed to approach the walled-off holy place, or they would be put to death (Num 3:38). It seems as if the same is true in the arch-temple in heaven, for there we see no people in the immediate presence of God and his throne.

In this common ground at the foot of the mountain, Moses built an altar (Ex 24:4; 32:5-6). Though the mountain faces no particular direction, the "eastern" direction is prominent in the story leading to Sinai: in the east-

---

[109] See Also Fretheim 1991:274.

wind that blew across the Red Sea (Ex 10:13). Because the Red Sea is a baptism, it is striking to note the direction associated with its opening.

Water from the Rock and Baptism

In this common space, the people had to wash their clothes and be consecrated before God would approach them with his covenant law: the Ten Commandments (Ex 19:10). This is a kind of formal baptism of Israel prior to receiving the Law. We need to take a look at this baptism.

First, this was the final (and only ceremonial) washing in a line of water events that immediately preceded (the baptismal Red-Sea baptism in Ex 14:16-30, the waters at Marah in Ex 15:22-27, and the water from the rock in Ex 17:1-6). Christian baptism obviously differs from this because we only undergo the rite a single time due to the once-for-all cleansing of Christ on our behalf. There is one Lord, one Faith, *one baptism* (Eph 4:5).

The water from the rock episode is particularly interesting. The people were in a place called Rephidim (Ex 17:1). They grew thirsty and began to test the Lord (17:2). God grew angry (because they were testing him, since he had already proven himself a giver of the gift of water two chapters earlier) and did not give them water there in Rephidim. Rather, he told Moses to go to Horeb (that is Sinai), strike the rock, and water would come gushing out (17:6).

The Psalms give us a commentary on this water. "He struck the rock so that water gushed out and streams overflowed" (Ps 78:20; cf. Neh 9:15; Isa 48:21). "He turns the rock into a pool of water" (Ps 114:8). "He opened the rock, and water gushed out; it flowed through the desert like a river." (Ps 105:41). The river obviously reminds us of the Garden River (and though we have not seen it yet, the Jordan River). It is this river that supplied the "living water" in which the Israelites bathed. (This is obviously what causes Jewish writers to see a mikveh take place here. One writes, "In the desert, the famed 'well of Miriam' served as a mikvah. And Aaron and his sons' induction into the priesthood was marked by immersion in the mikvah." Slonim 1996: xiv).

Isaiah talks about the "new thing" that God will do through Messiah. The new thing is likened to this water event. "Thus says the LORD, who makes a way in the sea, a path in the mighty waters [i.e., the Red Sea baptism]... I am doing a new thing... I will make a way in the wilderness and rivers in the desert... I give water in the wilderness, rivers in the desert, to give drink to my chosen people (Isa 43:16, 19-20). God's making a way in the Red Sea was a baptism. Hence, the parallel making a way in the desert with a river would likewise be a kind of baptismal event. The *Legends of the Jews* has an interesting take on this. One reads,

> Just as one who is admitted to Judaism must first submit to the three ceremonies of circumcision, baptism, and sacrifice, so Israel did not receive the Torah until they had performed these three ceremonies. They had already undergone circumcision in Egypt. Baptism was imposed upon them two days before the revelation on Mount Sinai. On the day preceding the revelation Moses recorded in a book the covenant between Israel and their God, and on the morning of the day of the revelation, sacrifices were offered as a strengthening of the covenant.
>
> (Ginzberg, *Legends of the Jews* 192, 3:88)

Why was it necessary for Israel to be baptized there at Sinai? It was for ceremonial reasons. This parallels the washing of the priest prior to his tabernacle ministry. First, Israel has just been pronounced a kingdom of priests (Ex 19:6). Just four verses later we read, "The LORD said to Moses, 'Go to the people and consecrate them today and tomorrow, and let them wash their garments'" (Ex 19:10). The LORD was about ready to come into their presence. Though this is a baptism for clothing, it is clear that it takes place before the holy mountain on the common space. Comparing the verse to later priestly washing ceremonies (Ex 29:4; 30:20; Lev 8:6; Num 8:5-7), it is difficult to see how this is not the direct predecessor to at least some of these later bodily baptisms. Therefore, it again seems appropriate to call this Sinai washing a baptism of sorts.

This Sinai-River gives us a couple of thoughts to pursue regarding our theology of baptism. First, baptism is a cleansing. What could be more appropriately pictured when a bunch of hot sweaty dirty people wandering around an arid desert are told to wash their clothes in the river (and are we really to assume that given all that water, that these people would only wash their cloths and not also their bodies given this condition)? Also, the baptismal river supplied water to their inner-self. They drank it and were filled. Though we do not drink water when we are baptized (unless accidentally), surely the very element itself teaches us that God is a fountain of living water who keeps our souls from thirsting.

Holy Place

Supporting this view of baptism here on Sinai is the rest of the Sinai sanctuary architecture which, not coincidently, follows the same basic pattern as all of the other sanctuaries. The mid to lower part of Mt. Sinai was the Holy place. This was seen earlier when Moses approached this part of the mountain, "The place where you are standing is holy ground" (Ex 3:5).

"Inside" this holy place there is the covenant meal "table." God told Moses, Aaron, Nadab, Abihu, and seventy of the elders of Israel to "come up to the LORD" (Ex 24:1), but only Moses was allowed to come "near" the LORD (Ex 24:2). So the seventy came up to mid-mountain where they beheld God and "ate and drank" (Ex 24:11). Here they saw God and "under his feet as it were a pavement of sapphire stone, like the very heaven for clearness" (Ex 24:10), reminding us of the heavenly sanctuary.

There is also a burning lamp or tree on this part of the mountain. Moses knew that this was holy ground because a voice from the midst of a burning bush told him so. The burning bush corresponds to the lampstand-trees found in all of the holy places of God's sanctuaries.

Most Holy Place

Only Moses was permitted on the top of the mountain. This was the Most Holy Place, and the exclusive privilege of one man to come here corresponds to the tabernacle and temple Most Holy Place. On top of the mountain there was smoke, cloud, thunder, and lightning (Ex 19:18; 20:18). We have seen this as far back as the archetypal sanctuary beheld by Isaiah, John, and others. The same theme continues all the way through each of the sanctuaries.

Finally, Moses received the Law in this place. This corresponds to the Ark of the Covenant being placed in the Most Holy Place, with the tablets of Law safely inside. When we begin to see that all of the architecture of the sanctuaries is the same, we understand better that baptism has a unique place throughout the Bible. This is why we are taking the time to discuss more than baptism when we look at these sanctuaries. We are making a sort of cumulative-case argument, to help our biblical theology of baptism be unimpeachable.

Promised Land Sanctuary

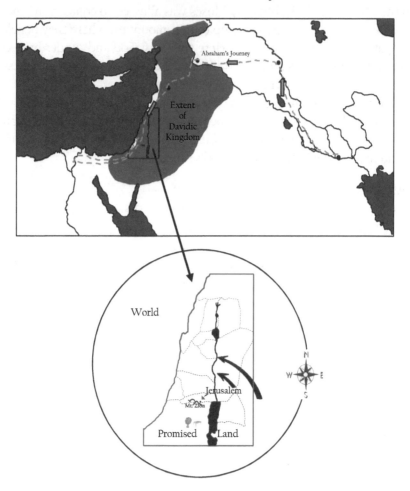

The last ectypal sanctuary we will look at is the land of Canaan. This is rarely discussed as a sanctuary, yet it has all of the same basic "architecture" as the other sanctuaries. It is even called a sanctuary in the Psalms. "Judah became his sanctuary, Israel his dominion" (Ps 114:2). This is talking about the physical land of Canaan. This is where God came and dwelt. God's very special presence was in Salem/Jerusalem (Ps 76:2; Ezra 7:15).

The three-tiered structure of this sanctuary appears to be the world, Canaan, and Salem/Jerusalem. The promise of this sanctuary was first given to

Abraham, "To your offspring I give this land, from the river of Egypt to the great river, the river Euphrates" (Gen 15:18; cf, Josh 1:4). Though we do not normally think of the Promised Land as extending this far, the possession of all the land was actually fulfilled in the Davidic dynasty (2 Sam 8:3; cf. Josh 21:44).

Common Space

Abram was a man from the east, having come from a place called Ur of the Chaldeans. The promise given to him was that he would be the father of many nations, and so his name was changed to Abraham (Gen 17:5). This shows that the whole world is important to God and should be considered the outermost (or common space) part of this sanctuary.

But it was the Promised Land itself that was the Holy Place. It was "walled off" by the boundaries set up by God. God told Abram to go into the land of Canaan, and he did so from the city of Heron (Gen 12:5), which was probably named after his uncle (Gen 11:26).[110] At the entrance to the land it says Abram built an altar (Gen 12:7), then he went into the land, up to a mountain (12:8), and pitched his tent (an early kind of tabernacle; Ex 27:21 etc.). Clearly, Canaan is being pictured even here as a sanctuary.[111]

The Rivers of the Promised Land and Baptism

In order for Abram to get from the common space to the Holy Land, he had to cross a river. This is the "Great River", the Euphrates, which also happens to be the *eastern* boundary of the land. Did God have baptism in mind when he later told Isaac and Jacob to go back to the land of their fathers (east of the Euphrates), only to return to the Promised Land by crossing the River *prior* to the reconfirming of the covenant with them? (see Gen 24:38, 25:11; Gen 31:21). Joshua 24:3 records this east to west movement with a particular emphasis on Abraham's river-crossing. It says, "I took your father Abraham from beyond the River and led him through all the land of Canaan" (Joshua 24:3). This has significance for baptism.

---

[110] From Bethel, Jacob travels to the "eastern" peoples (actually it is much more north—in today's modern Turkey—than east, but it is the eastern theme that matters most in the story) near Haran. It is merely a coincidence that the entire episode in Genesis 29 is set around a *watering* well?

[111] A particularly striking way of thinking about this is Jacob's famous dream at Bethel (the 'house of God') as opposed to Jerusalem. We normally call what he saw "Jacob's Ladder," but it could also be translated as a staircase. This has a pagan counterpart in the Ziggurat – those religious mountainous centers like the Tower of Babel, the Pyramids, and other ancient structures (Kline, 2006a: 109-111). When Jesus says "You will see the angels of God ascending and descending on the Son of Man" (John 1:51), he is making reference to this dream, thereby calling himself the antitypical temple.

Joshua is the only author who notes the Euphrates as an important feature in Abraham's journey. Why? It is probably because Joshua himself has just experienced a great river crossing at the banks of the Jordan. This was the way God would have Israel enter the Land, "You are to cross over the Jordan to go in to take possession of the land that the LORD your God is giving you" (Deut 11:31).

This crossing was a miracle akin to the Red Sea baptism, "As soon as [the priests bearing the ark of the covenant] had come as far as the Jordan, their feet were dipped in the brink of the water... the waters coming down from above stood and rose up in a heap very far away, completely cut off. And the people passed over opposite Jericho... on dry ground in the midst of the Jordan" (Josh 3:14-17). The language of crossing over on dry ground is identical to the Red Sea; the two are connected as identical miracles (Josh 4:23), and so if the one is a baptism, it appears that the other must be also. This is part of the reason for establishing each of these sanctuaries as models of the archetype. What is true of one must be true for all the rest, since they are each built upon the One.

Once more, crossing a river is how someone takes possession of the Land. This is significant because rather than coming up the short and easy route along the Mediterranean Sea from the south-west, they entered the land from the *east* (Josh 2:10; 5:1). Having lived through several baptisms, Joshua understood the importance of the water for entering the *sanctuary*. That is why he alone mentions Abraham and the Euphrates together, because this was the eastern boundary of the land promised to him. Though Abraham's crossing was not a miracle, it symbolically serves the same function for entering the sanctuary as all of the water baptisms that we have seen.

Besides the Euphrates, there is the Jordan River. The name Jordan (Yareden) means "the descender" or "the watering-place."[112] It reminded Lot of the Garden of Eden. "Lot looked up and saw that the whole plain of the Jordan was well watered, like the garden of the LORD ... (this was before the LORD destroyed Sodom and Gomorrah)" (Gen 13:10). In the course of time, the Jordan found itself square in the center of the Promised Land, just like the River of Eden was in the Garden.

The Jordan is of course significant for two of the baptisms we saw in Chapter 1. Jesus was baptized in this river (Matt 3:13), and Naaman was also baptized here (2 Kgs 5:10-14). It is probable that two more baptisms took place in the Jordan. 2 Kgs 2:6-14 record the final moments of Elijah. Elijah

---

[112] 'Jordan River', in *EBD*, http://bible.crosswalk.com/Dictionaries/EastonBibleDictionary/ebd.cgi?number=T2112

says to Elisha, "'Please stay here, for the LORD has sent me to the Jordan.' But [Elisha] said, 'As the LORD lives, and as you yourself live, I will not leave you.' So the two of them went on [while fifty men stood watching from afar]... As they were both standing by the Jordan Elijah took his cloak and rolled it up and struck the water, and the water was parted to the one side and to the other, till the two of them could go over on dry ground." Then it says, "They crossed over." Elijah is taken up by a whirlwind and chariots of fire into heaven. Elisha took up Elijah's cloak and it says, "He struck the water, the water parted to the one side and to the other, and Elisha went over." Seeing how this is once more identical language to the Red Sea crossing, it is probable that this is a baptism, which may even foreshadow Jesus' own baptism.[113]

But Israel's crossing of the Jordan is also significant, not the least because this crossing is a parallel miracle to the Red Sea Crossing (Josh 3:14-17). This makes yet another baptism in the OT. It is recorded that it was necessary to cross the River in order to posses the Land. "For I [Moses] shall die in this land, I shall not cross the Jordan, but you shall cross and take possession of this good land" (Deut 4:22; cf. Josh 1:2). The thing is, God didn't have to take the people east of Canaan, unless he wanted them to cross the River. We believe this is exactly what he wanted, because it was only after going through the water that the priests could take possession of this particular OT sanctuary.

This event helps establish more of why Jesus was baptized in the Jordan. Not only is he representing Israel, who crossed through the Jordan; but he comes in the power and spirit of Elijah (Mal 4:5; Matt 11:14) and Elisha. When the religious washing of Naaman is added (also in the Jordan), we see Jesus identifying himself with the whole world, symbolically entering into a judgment-ordeal with his Father at the entrance of the Promised Land.[114]

Holy Place

The Jordan River becomes the center of the Promised Land as we know it today, but not until after Israel crossed it in the days of Joshua (Josh 1:12ff). Its location in the center of the sanctuary reminds us of the Garden of Eden and the gushing river of Sinai. Lot even compares the Jordan to Eden saying,

---

[113] In this regard it must be noticed that Jesus calls himself the greater Elijah (Matt 11:14; 17:12) as is typified in Elijah's "double portion of the Spirit" (2 Kgs 2:9). Elijah had come in the power of John the Baptist. Jesus is the predecessor, like Elisha. See the helpful discussion in Dillard 1999: 86-87.

[114] For more on the Jordan as judgment ordeal see Kline 1999: 55-56.

"The Jordan Valley was well watered everywhere like the garden of the LORD" (Gen 13:10).

It is significant that two and a half tribes (Reuben, Gad, and half of Manasseh) decide to take the land east of the Jordan. This symbolically places the tribes around the Most Holy Place, inside the holy land. This recalls the archetypal sanctuary where the 24 elders (half of which are the 12 tribes of Israel?) encircle the throne of God. It is also similar to the encampment of the 12 tribes around the tabernacle (Obviously, one couldn't fit 2,000,000 people into the holy place of the tabernacle). But the priest did bear the tribes upon his breast when he entered the holy place (Ex 28:29). This demonstrates that the encampment was more than for protection of the Ark. It was to show the people that they were his treasured possession, even being allowed to enter symbolically through the priest into holy places.

The holy land itself has something prominently reported that is related to all sanctuaries. There are important trees mentioned throughout Genesis, though never outside of Canaan. One is the great Oak of Moreh (Gen 12:6; Deut 11:30). It is here that God first appears to Abram (Gen 12:5-6). Another is the Tamarisk tree in Beersheba, planted by Abraham as a covenant-tree between him and Abimelech (Gen 21:29). Then there is the great oak in the grove at Mamre (Gen 18:1-8). This tree is significant because it is here that Abraham eats a covenant meal with the angel of the LORD. Each tree is in the Holy Place.

Perhaps one other tree should be mentioned, though we do not read about it until the NT. This is the tree upon which Jesus was hanged (Gal 3:13; Deut 21:22-23). It does not appear to be accidental that the crucifixion took place "outside the city" (Jerusalem; Heb 13:12), for this would take it out of the Most Holy Place, putting it squarely in the Holy Place, just like all other sanctuary trees.

There is a law that describes a certain situation where, "When you come into the land and plant any kind of tree for food, then you shall regard its fruit as forbidden. Three years it shall be forbidden to you; it must not be eaten" (Lev 19:23). The language is obviously an echo of the Garden of Eden. As we saw, fruit was the food of choice (or not of choice, depending upon the tree) in the Garden sanctuary.

The meal Abraham eats with the LORD is also significant for how it reminds us of the other "tables" spread out in the Holy place. Besides this meal, Abraham goes out to meet the mysterious Melchizedek in the Valley of the Kings. Here they have a meal of "bread and wine" (Gen 14:17-18). Melchizedek, of course, prefigures Christ who comes in the "order of Melchize-dek" (Heb 7:1-3).

A striking sacrifice takes place in the holy land, outside of Jerusalem (although it occurs in a vision). This is the great covenant cutting ceremony where God swears an unconditional oath to give Abram all he has been promised. We read, "A smoking fire pot and a flaming torch passed between these pieces" (Gen 15:17). What would a sanctuary be without the burning smoke?

<u>Most Holy Place</u>

Christ's sacrifice is prefigured in Abraham's day by the near sacrifice of Isaac. The placement of this sacrifice is as important as the typology between Isaac and Christ. It takes place "in the land of Moriah... on one of the mountains that God will show to Abraham" (Gen 22:2). Moriah becomes the place where the temple will later be built (2 Chron 3:1). This sacrifice also seems to prefigure the action of the High Priest who would enter "inside the veil" once a year to make atonement for Israel (Lev 16:15-18).

Later, when the temple is built, the Ark of the Covenant finds its home in Jerusalem (1 Kgs 3:15; 1 Chron 15:3; Jer 3:17). The Ark of course is where the Law of God was placed. Thus, we can say that the Law resided in Jerusalem, the Most Holy Place.

Section IV: Baptism and Antitypical Sanctuaries

What is the Antitypical Sanctuary?

It is important to understand that ectypal sanctuaries have antitypical correspondence. Thus, whatever features are found in the ectypes will also be found in the antitype, just as they are in the archetype. What is the antitype? It is Jesus Christ and his Church (both of which are called temples; cf. John 2:21; Eph 2:21).

There are explicit references to this as well as implicit. We will only look at the explicit here.[115] The OT predicted that God would become a sanctuary for Israel. Isaiah 8:14 read, "He will become[116] a sanctuary and a stone of offense and a rock of stumbling to both houses of Israel." Peter (1 Pet 2:8) and Paul (Rom 9:32-33) make it clear that this stone is Christ.

What is extremely compelling for baptism about this particular Isaiah passage is what precedes it. It appears that in order for this new sanctuary to be built, the old type must first be destroyed. Specifically, the destruction described by Isaiah is a *baptism*. Isaiah predicts, "Because this people have refused the *waters of Shiloah* that flow gently... behold, the Lord is bringing up against them the waters of the River [Euphrates], mighty and many, the king of Assyria and all his glory. And it will rise over all its channels and go over all its banks, and it will sweep on into Judah, it will overflow and pass on, reaching even to the neck, and its outspread wings will fill the breadth of your land, O Immanuel" (Isa 8:6-8).

This imagery clearly harkens back to Noah's flood and the Red Sea, which were baptisms. Here, the baptism is metaphorical but no less real. The king of Assyria (who comes from the east) would *flood* into the Land and *drown* most of the people in his wrath. It is curious that only after this water-ordeal floods and recedes will the Lord *then* become the Sanctuary. (Read this in light of Ezek 11:16 where God says, "Though I removed them far off among the nations, and though I scattered them among the countries, yet I have

---

[115] Implicitly, we can infer that Christ is the New Heavens and Earth (Matt 28:18), the New Eden (Rev 22), the New Ark (1 Pet 3:20-21), the New Land (Rom 4:13), and the New Sinai (Matt 5-7), temple (John 1:51); but we will not develop these things any further here.

[116] This is a *perfect* tense verb. Kelley's Grammar states, "A perfect prefixed with *vav* conjunction will usually be translated in the future tense" (Kelley 1992: 86). This perfect verb is prefixed with the *vav* and the context of the stone of stumbling (who is Christ) makes it clear that this is something that will happen, but in the future.

been a sanctuary to them for a while in the countries where they have gone." God would first destroy the typological sanctuary–for a time–in order to teach Israel that He would be their temple).[117]   A baptismal destruction of the temple is exactly what we find Jesus predicting when we combine his teaching of his body (Matt 26:61; Mark 14:58; John 2:19) and his second baptism (Mark 10:38; Luke 12:50).

The idea of Christ as antitypical sanctuary is clear in the NT as well. Revelation 21:22 concludes, "I saw no temple in the city, for its temple is the Lord God the Almighty and the Lamb." This fulfills Christ's own prediction when he talks about destroying the temple of his body (John 2:19, 21). When Jesus first came down from heaven it says, "The Word become flesh and *dwelt* among us" (John 1:14). The word for "dwelt" is the verb *skenoō*. It literally means to spread a tent. The tabernacle is often called the "tent of meeting." LXX translates this as the noun *skene*. So, it is not improper to say that Christ "tabernacled" among us.

Christ is also called the "cornerstone" (Eph 2:20; 1 Pet 2:6-7). What kind of a cornerstone? One around which a *temple* is built. This is why Paul says that in him the whole structure is being joined together, growing into a holy temple in the Lord (Eph 2:21). In the Church, the temple of God will be built all over the earth, even as it was throughout the holy land with the Israelites. As we are united to Christ, all in the church are said to be the temple (1 Cor 3:16-17; 6:19; 2 Cor 6:16; Eph 2:21; 1 Pet 2:5; Rev 3:12). How do we enter this temple? Through baptism! Perhaps this is why Augustine would say, "Would you know the Holy Ghost, that He is God? Be baptized, and you will be His temple" (Augustine, *On the Creed*, 1.13).

---

[117] Destruction by flood was also the judgment through which Israel must pass. Because she rejected her Messiah, her final baptism would result in a flood to destroy the temple (Dan 9:26).

Antitypical Sanctuary in Ezekiel

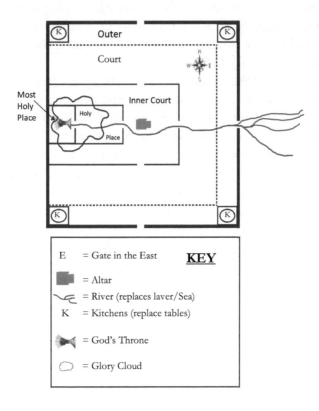

The antitypical sanctuary is symbolized for us in Ezekiel 40-48. These chapters contain very specific blueprints for a new temple. To think that this temple is a future physical temple like Solomon's is to make the fatal mistake that Christ is not the true temple (as if another building needs to be built to replace him). It is to go back to types and shadows.

That this temple is not literal is easily seen by the fact that there is a mighty river (which echoes the Eden River in 47:6-12) that has its source under the threshold of the temple (Ezek 47:1; cf. Joel 3:18; Zech 14:8). Unless men can somehow create rivers, there is no way that this temple can be literal. Furthermore, Christopher Wright points out, "That this river requires supernatural maintenance is underscored by realizing that the salinity of the Dead Sea does not affect the fresh water's purity, but rather the reverse" (C. J. H. Wright 2002: 356).

This temple says in the most unclear terms what we have learned about all mountain-temples. "This is the law of the temple: the whole territory round about upon the top of the mountain shall be most holy. Behold, this is the law of the temple" (Ezek 43:12). Thus, the three-tiered structure of temples and the three-tiered level of mountains correspond to one another.

As with all sanctuaries, this one faces east (Ezek 47:1). Though it has three entrances (east, south, and north) to the courtyard, "The glory of the LORD entered the temple through the gate facing east" (Ezek 43:4). Since the other features of the temple are not significantly different from elements described in the tabernacle and temple (this temple has an outer court [40:17], an inner court [40:23], a court for priests [40:7], and a sanctuary [41:1-2]; the sanctuary is divided into a holy place and a most holy place [41:3-4]; there is an altar in the priest's court [43:13-17]; there are also kitchens, ovens, priest's rooms, and other miscellaneous items that we do not need to detail here), we will skip a detailed look at most of them with the exception of this curious river.

Ezekiel's Temple and Baptism

A main feature that changes drastically from tabernacle and temple to Ezekiel's sanctuary is that there is no laver or sea—created out of bronze or any other type of metal—here. Instead, the *river* replaces the man-made furnishing. This River begins under the threshold of the temple and runs to the east. As it makes its way into the priestly court, it passes south of the altar (this is also where the laver and sea were located).

It runs outside of the temple complex (much like Eden's river runs outside the Garden). The water is measured for width and depth every thousand cubits (that's approx. 1700 ft.). At first it is ankle deep. Then it becomes knee-deep. Then it becomes waist deep. After 1 ½ miles, it becomes "a river that I could not cross, because the water had risen and was deep enough to swim" (Ezek 47:5).

At this point it says, "I saw a great number of trees on each side of the river" (Ezek 47:7). This is important to note because there are no lampstand furnishings inside the holy place to adorn the temple in this vision. This adornment now exits the temple, making that which was common holy again, as it did prior to sin when God created the heavens and the earth. It also says, "This water flows toward the eastern region and goes down into the Arabah (that is the Jordan Valley), where it enters the Sea." This is striking, because it makes the temple's River a tributary to the Jordan. Perhaps all three rivers then (Eden River, Jordan, and Ezekiel's Temple-River) are in mind when the Psalmist says, "There is a river whose streams make glad the city of God, the holy dwelling places of the Most High" (Ps 46:4).

Next Ezekiel reads, "When the water flows into the sea, the water will become fresh. And wherever the river goes, every living creature that swarms will live, and there will be very many fish. For this water goes there, that the waters of the sea may become fresh; so that everything will live where the river goes" (Ezek 47:8-9). This is obviously a "River of Life." (Zechariah 14:8 says a little more about the river here, "On that day living waters shall flow out from Jerusalem, half of them to the eastern sea and half of them to the western sea. It shall continue in summer and in winter").

Ezekiel continues, "But its swamps and marshes will not become fresh; they are to be left for salt." Salt acts as a burning agent when spread over land like this. We suggest that this is another way of talking about the sea of glass mixed with fire or the Lake of fire or the river of fire (all burning images). Some things, even this River will not heal.

Finally we read, "On the banks, on both sides of the river, there will grow all kinds of trees for food. Their leaves will not wither, nor their fruit fail, but they will bear fresh fruit every month, because the water for them flows from the *sanctuary*. Their fruit will be for food, and their leaves for healing" (Ezek 47:12).

Antitypical Sanctuary in Revelation

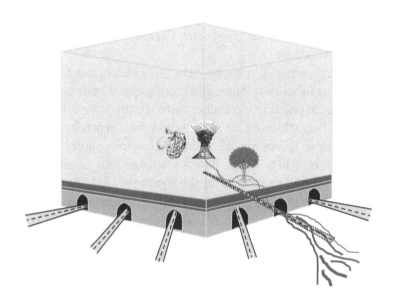

This last comment on the sanctuary by Ezekiel helps us understand one final sanctuary at which we will look. John gives us another way of viewing the antitypical sanctuary. Rather than a temple, he calls it a city. The city is a "bride come down out of heaven" (Rev 21:2). This is the language of God's Church. The important part for our study is the similarities between the city's river and the Ezekiel temple-river.

Revelation 22 begins by talking about "the river of the water of life, bright as crystal, flowing from the throne of God and of the Lamb" (Rev 22:1). Notice the emphasis on the river *of life*. Notice that it looks like *crystal*. The glassy sea was "like crystal" (Rev 4:6). Finally, notice that this river flows from the throne of God and the Lamb. The Lamb makes this an antitypical river. But as of now, it appears as if it is a temple-structure that is in mind.

But the next verse clarifies: "Through the middle of the street of the *city*." It is a city that is in view, the same city described in Chapter 21 that has several features reminding us of OT sanctuaries.[118] Psalm 46:4 has this river in mind, "There is a river whose streams make glad the city of God, the holy

---

[118] For example, there are walls and angels and the names of the twelve tribes inscribed, three on each of four different walls (Rev 21:13). There were twelve gems, similar to the stones on the priest's breastplate (Rev 21:19-20) etc.

habitation of the Most High." Revelation continues, "On either side of the river, the tree of life with its twelve kinds of fruit, yielding its fruit each month. The leaves of the tree were for the healing of the nations" (Rev 22:2-3). This language clearly has the Garden of Eden in mind (i.e., the tree of life). But it is nearly word for word with Ezekiel's description of the river that flows from his temple.

This demonstrates that all three have the same idea in mind. What is true of one is true of the other two. Since all sanctuaries are built upon the archetype, what is true for one is true for all of them. In this way, it is curious that John says a little later, "Blessed are those who wash their robes, so that they may have the right to the tree of life and that they may enter the city by the gates" (Rev 22:14; cf. 7:14). As we have seen (especially at Sinai), washing one's garments prepared the people for the coming of God. As Hebrews tells us, these kinds of washings are *baptisms*. This particular baptism takes place outside the holy place (as usual), and allows entrance into that space, including its tree of life.

There is an obvious return to Eden (only better) that Christ gives to believers. He alone grants that people may eat of the tree of life, in the paradise of God (Rev 2:7). That the city so emulates the Garden of Eden is a sign that the antitypical sanctuaries are in fact copies of the Garden, which in turn is a copy of the archetype in heaven. In other words, all of the sanctuaries in the Bible have the same basic pattern and meaning.

Summary

This lengthy section of the book has served two purposes. The first regards the sanctuaries as a whole. Scripture gives us *explicit* mention that all of these places discussed here are sanctuaries (The tent in heaven – Rev 15:5; heaven and earth along with Eden – Ps 78:69; Ezek 28:28; Canaan – Ps 114:2; Sinai – Ex 15:17; Tabernacle – Ex 25:8; Temple – 1 Chron 22:19; and even Ararat and the Ark – Hab 2). Biblical verses show that several of these were patterned specifically upon a single heavenly archetype (Gen 6:14-15; Ex 25:9; 1 Chron 28:19; Heb 8:5, 9:23-24 etc.). Repetition shows that all of God's sanctuaries are built upon the same basic pattern, and so therefore, what is true for one sanctuary must be true for all others.

Each of the elements of the sanctuary could be a book unto themselves. But the purpose of *this* book is to study baptism. There is the same water element in the same portion of each of the sanctuaries. From looking at the various sanctuaries, our theology of baptism is greatly enriched. It has elements of judgment, death (for unbelievers), resurrection (for believers), initiation, covering, cleansing, washing, and other things.

Having completed this survey of the sanctuary and specifically its water element, we will next turn our attention to comparing several of these sanctuaries *exegetically*. Specifically we will look at how Moses integrates several of the sanctuaries with literary and linguistic ties, and how the Gospels rely upon those themes in developing the story of Christ's baptism.

Section V: New Creation - Baptisms Compared

Comparing the Flood, Red Sea, & Jesus' baptism to Original Creation

It can be an exciting adventure, discovering baptism and learning about its various shades of meaning by studying its use in the sanctuaries of Scripture. But it is important to do everything that we can to ensure that our discoveries are on the right track. Typology is one avenue that brings us to the destination of baptism in the Old Testament. Comparing the various *stories* in which baptism occurs is another.

In this chapter we are going to evaluate the texts of Jesus' water baptism with three OT baptismal stories (see chart 2 for a quick reference guide to the content of this chapter). In doing so, it will become absolutely certain that it is correct to tie sanctuary typology together, as we have done in the previous chapter, thereby enhancing our theology of baptism by looking at both the New *and the* Old Testaments. In the process, we will also add a further meaning to baptism. This meaning is the idea that baptism is the ordination ceremony for a new creation.

The accounts of Christ's baptism in the River Jordan contain several events that find near or exact parallels in at least three baptismal stories of the OT. These stories are: the Red Sea, the Flood, and original creation. We will demonstrate that there is such an overwhelming number of literary links between the four stories, that we must conclude that not only is original creation a *baptism*, but the other three stories are kinds of new *creations*. The parallelism works both ways.

Wilderness

Let us look at the linguistic similarities between the stories of the flood (i.e., what Peter calls a baptism), the Red Sea (i.e., what Paul calls a baptism), Jesus' baptism, and original creation by starting at the beginning. Having already looked at Jesus' baptism (Part I), we will use this as the starting point for our comparisons. The first thing of notice in the story of Christ's baptism is where it takes place. It says, "In those days John the Baptist came preaching *in the wilderness*" (Matt 3:1). Why mention this fact? Perhaps a clue lies in the stories of creation and the Exodus, wherein the wilderness takes a prominent position in both stories.

Gen 1:1-2 says, "In the beginning God created the heavens and the earth. The earth was *without form* and *void*, and darkness was over the face of the deep. And the Spirit of God was hovering over the face of the waters." The Hebrew words *tohu* and *bohu* are the "formless void" of Gen 1:2. Isaiah comments directly upon Gen 1:2 saying, "For thus says the LORD, who created the heavens (He is the God who formed the earth and made it, He established it and did not create it a waste place [*tohu*], but formed it to be inhabited), 'I am the LORD, and there is none else'" (Isa 45:18). In this case, the waste place is put in apposition to habitation. (For more see Young 1961).

The two words are found together elsewhere only in Jer 4:23, "I looked on the earth, and behold, it was formless [*tohu*] and void [*bohu*]; And to the heavens, and they had no light." Jeremiah is describing the coming captivity in poetic terms like the existence of the world prior to Day One. As we continue reading we find that the "formless void" is like mountains quaking (4:24), uninhabited (4:25), where a fruitful land becomes *a desert*, with towns in ruins because of God's great anger (4:26).

This is arresting in light of Deut 32:10, the only other place where either word is used by Moses. It says, "He found him in a desert land, and in the howling waste [*tohu*] of the wilderness." The "him" being referred to here is Israel/Jacob. In this case, *tohu* is being linked directly to "desert" and "wilderness" (Hamilton 1990:109). So, the wilderness theme is prominent in the Exodus story and apparently in the Genesis story as well. Though the exact words are not used, it will become apparent that this is a major theme developed in the flood story of Noah.

Judgment

The next thing to notice is found in John's prediction of Jesus' future ministry. "He will baptize you with the Holy Spirit and with fire. His winnowing fork is in his hand, and he will clear his threshing floor and gather his wheat into the barn, but the chaff he will burn with unquenchable fire" (Matt 3:11-12). Though the "baptism of the Holy Spirit" and "baptism with fire" are themes of salvation (Isa 32:15; 44:3; Ezek 36:26-27, 39:29; Joel 2:28-32; Acts 1:5, 2:3-4, 2:38, 8:16, 10:47, 11:16; 1 Cor 12:13; 1 Thess 5:19), it is clear from this passage that judgment also accompanies this baptism.[119] This is the function of Matt 3:12. In other words, that which saves one person will be the very same thing that destroys another.

---

[119] Fire is often used of the judgment of Christ (2 Thess 1:7; Heb 10:27, 12:29; 2 Pet 3:7-12; Jude 1:7; Rev 1:14, 19:12). The Spirit too is seen as an Agent of judgment and fire (Ex 24:17; Isa 4:4).

Judgment is a theme we have already explored as it relates to baptism. Ex 15:1 was the song of Moses immediately after the Red Sea collapsed upon Pharaoh. Moses sang, "The horse and rider he has thrown into the sea." We have also seen how this same song is sung in John's vision of the heavenly temple (cf. Rev 15:2-3) as the people stood beside the temple's baptismal sea.

Judgment is also a major theme taken up in the flood, "And all flesh died that moved on the earth, birds, livestock, beasts, all swarming creatures that swarm on the earth, and all mankind [from the flood]" (Gen 7:21). Then we have Jeremiah relating God's judgment upon Israel directly to the conditions of Gen 1:2 in the only other place where *tohu* and *bohu* come together in Scripture. This theme then becomes a second major link connecting various baptismal stories.

<u>Baptism</u>

Probably the most obvious of the parallels comes with the baptisms themselves. Matt 3:16 records, "Jesus was baptized." How so? Here (and because of the various other similarities being discussed in this chapter) we want to offer what we believe are obvious parallels in each of the OT baptismal stories. Ex 15:10 records that, "The sea covered them." Gen 7:19 offers, "The waters prevailed so mightily on the earth that all the high mountains under the whole heaven were covered." Gen 1:2 says, "And darkness was over the face of the deep." Here, darkness is the covering, or better yet, the *water* is covering the land.

If Matthew is recording an immersion (something obviously questioned by some Christians, but which fits well with the kind of ritual commanded by the priests at their ordination), then the parallel is that Jesus was "covered" by the water. In this sense, baptism is a judgment undergone by Christ on behalf of sinners like us. The very mode would become a fulfillment of the death-baptisms of the OT. In this respect Meredith Kline (himself a paedo-baptist) writes,

> [Though] no exclusive claims can be made for the mode of immersion, it would nevertheless appear that the symbolic aptness of that mode remains unimpaired by the interpretation of baptism as a sign of judgment. Baptism by immersion will surely impress many as a most eloquent way of portraying the great judgment of God, while the familiar imposition of moistened finger tips which is generously called sprinkling must seem to many to project quite inadequately the threatening power and crisis of the ultimate ordeal. Is it not time for Reformed liturgists to address themselves to the task of finding a form for the baptismal sign which, while suitable for the very young

and the frail, will capture and convey something of the decisive encounter which baptism signifies?[120]

(Kline 1968: 83)

Along these same lines we read in Matthew that, "He went up from the water" (Matt 3:16). The most natural way to read this is that he went up because he was *under* the water. Most recognize that "up" (*anabainō*) means something like, "to go up, come up, ascend... or arise" (UBS Lexicon).

Paedobaptists sometimes say that what Jesus came up from is the *River*, not the water (see Adams 1975: 42). The idea is that he was down in the River, but that John sprinkled a little water on his head. Together, they came up from the River and back to dry land. The main problem with this is that it says he came up from "the water" (*hudor*) not "the River" (*potamos*; cf. Matt 3:6). Perhaps this is why we read in John 3:23, "John also was baptizing at the Aenon near Salim, because *water was plentiful there*, and people were coming and being baptized." When the cumulative force of OT baptisms is allowed to speak, we don't have to mess around with the simplest explanation for "plentiful water" (lit., "many waters"). John needed a lot of water, because a lot of water is needed to immerse. The same can hardly be true of sprinkling or pouring.

Heavens Opened

Yet another statement pertaining to Christ's water baptism finds parallel in the OT baptismal stories. It says, "The heavens were opened to him" (Matt 3:16). Admittedly, this one is not as explicit as the others. Nevertheless, we do read about the heavens in two Genesis baptismal stories. "In the beginning, God created the heavens and the earth" (Gen 1:1). "The windows of the heavens were opened" (Gen 7:11). This is one half of the way God sent the flood waters to destroy the earth.

Spirit of God

The "heavens" are vital to note because of what comes down *out of heaven* in Jesus' baptism. "He saw the Spirit of God descending like a dove" (Matt 3:16). Here is where the stories all converge in an extraordinary way.[121]

---

[120] Kline adds in a footnote, "Since the idea of qualification in the specific form of cleansing is included in the import of baptism (cd., e.g., Eph 5:26; Tit 3:5; Acts 22:16) it might seem desirable to practice a mode of baptism suggestive of washing as well as ordeal."

[121] Rev 12:14-15 provides a stirring poetic commentary on Jesus' baptism—Including an image of the Spirit as a bird, the waters, and the children that Christ gives birth to.

Most translations of Gen 1:2 talk about the "Spirit hovering" over the waters of creation (on the difficulty of this translation see below). If this is the proper translation, it has parallels in the flood, the Red Sea, and as we have seen in Jesus' baptism. Noah releases a bird over the water (compare Gen 1:2 with 8:8 and Gen 1:9 with 8:11). This bird was a dove. This is the same bird-image that the Holy Spirit takes when he hovers over the waters of the Jordan in Christ's *baptism*. In the early church [circa 254-56], an anonymous author connects the Spirit, the dove (of Noah), and baptism. He writes,

> That dove signifies to us a double type. Formerly, that is, from the beginning of the divine administration, it suggests its own figure, the first indeed and chief – that is, the figure of the Spirit. And by its mouth the sacrament of baptism... Moreover, three times sent forth from the ark, flying about through the air over the water, it already signified the sacraments of our Church.
>
> (Anonymous, TAHN, 3)

Moses uses the same figure of a bird to describe God's own presiding over Israel during the exodus-event (which includes the Red Sea).[122] The "hovering" of the Spirit in Gen 1:2 is the key to seeing this. The Hebrew word is *rachaph*. Some English Bible's translate it as "move" (NAS, ASV, KJV, RSV). Many more go with "hover" (YLT, ESV, NKJ, NIV). Which is better? This word is rare, used only one other time by Moses in Deut 32:11 where it reads, "Like an eagle that stirs up its nest; that *hovers* over its young." (Note: We have just seen the verse preceding this when we discussed the "wilderness" above). The idea is clearly of a bird flapping her wings with maternal tenderness while hovering over her chicks in an effort to teach them how to fly (see the important inspired commentary on this in Isa 63:9-11). The singular repetition of *tohu* and *rachaph* in this story as well as the likening of God to a bird hovering over Israel (cf. Matt 22:37) helps us decide that the more common interpretation of *ruach* in Gen 1:2 is the Spirit (which is then being personified as a bird).

But "Spirit" is not the only way to translate *ruach* in Gen 1:2. It could be translated as a "wind sweeping" over the face of the waters (NRS). Markedly, this also has parallels in the flood and Red Sea narratives. Gen 8:1 says, "God made a wind blow over the earth, and the waters subsided." Ex

---

[122] We are referring to Moses' song at the end of Deuteronomy. It is difficult to decide if Moses picks up the story of Israel in this song as they are traveling through the desert towards the Red Sea and their baptism (Ex 13:18), or as they are leaving their baptism and entering the wilderness of Shur (Ex 15:22). Either way, the Red Sea baptism is not far from the song, which helps solidify the interpretation of original creation waters as the prototypical baptismal waters.

14:21a says, "The LORD drove the sea back by a strong east wind all night." This wind is what makes the dry land appear in the flood ("The face of the ground was dry," Gen 8:13; "And made the sea dry land," Ex 14:21b). This is what we see happening at original creation when God said, "Let the dry land appear" (Gen 1:9).

(Jesus makes a related comment to Nicodemus in this regard. Anyone who wants to see the kingdom of God has to be "born of water and the Spirit" (John 3:5). He then gives an example of the work of the Spirit. He moves around like "the wind" (John 3:8). Here again the Spirit, the wind, and the water all converge, showing how intimately related the idea of baptism and the Spirit actually are).

Comparing the language of the stories and using typology, it is possible to see Jesus as "the land" which comes up out of the water at his baptism (Matt 3:16b). The close association between the flood and the creation narrative continues as the dove comes back with a freshly plucked olive leaf in its mouth (Gen 8:11). This reminds us of God's command, "Let the earth sprout vegetation" (Gen 1:11).

Voice from Heaven

Another element of Christ's baptism was that the heavens were opened. It says, "A voice from heaven said, 'This is my beloved Son'" (Matt 3:17). The significance of this has to do with the "sons" that link the OT baptismal stories to Christ. Ex 4:22 tells us why God did all of these things for Israel (including baptizing him in the Red Sea). "Thus says the LORD, Israel is my firstborn son." This language creates an exact literary (and typological) parallel between Christ and Israel at the baptism.

But it should not be forgotten that the genealogy given by Luke *immediately* after Christ's baptism tells us both that Noah is the son of God (Luke 3:36; cf. Matt 24:37 and the relationship between Noah and the "Son of Man"), and that Adam is the son of God (Luke 3:38; cf. Gen 1:26-27, 28-30). This puts their "sonship" in direct relation to Christ's, so that all four stories talk about a beloved son. [123]

---

[123] There are various relationships between Noah and Adam in the Genesis narratives which lead us to conclude that Noah is a kind of second Adam (though not like Christ who is "The" second Adam [Rom 5:12-21; 1 Cor 5:20-22], or, more biblically, the "last Adam" [1 Cor 15:45]). These include the command to "be fruitful and multiply and fill the earth"(Gen 1:28 and 9:1), the command to eat food (Gen 2:16 and 9:3), the restating of the image of God (Gen 1:26-27 and 9:6), God bringing animals coming to the men (Gen 2:19 and 7:8-9, 9:2), and the fall of both men (Gen 3:1 and 9:20-24) including the nakedness (Gen 3:7 and 9:21), a need for covering (Gen 3:21; 9:23), and the means of the fall taking place through fruit (Gen 3:6 and Gen 9:20-21. In this regard, it is curious that the ancient Jews often talked about the Tree of the Knowledge of Good and Evil as if it were a grape-vine! Cf. 1 Enoch 32:4; Bab. Talmud, *Berakoth* 40a; *Sanhedrin* 70a; *Midrash Rabbah*, Gen 15:7, 19:5. Also Brown 1969: 150, 170).

The Multiplying/Gathering

There are still more parallels in the stories. At the baptism of the Lord Jesus Christ it says, "Jerusalem and all Judea and all the region about the Jordan were going out to him" (Mat 3:5). Here we believe two kinds of statements made in the OT stories converge to draw out the parallel. Gen 1:20, 24 says, "Let the waters swarm with swarms of living creatures, and let birds fly above the earth... Let the earth bring forth living creatures according to their kinds – livestock and creeping things and beasts of the earth according to their kinds." After it becomes safe for Noah to leave the ark God said, "Bring out with you every living thing that is with you of all flesh – birds and animals and every creeping thing that creeps on the earth – that they may swarm on the earth" (Gen 8:17). At the Exodus we also read, "A mixed multitude also went up with them, and very much livestock, both flocks and herds" (Ex 12:38).

The command comes to the animal world at creation, "Be fruitful and multiply" (Gen 1:22). It is then repeated *word for word* after the flood (Gen 8:17). The Exodus is prefaced by similar language, "The people of Israel were fruitful and increased greatly; they multiplied and grew exceedingly strong" (Ex 1:7). Obviously, the story of Christ's baptism is telling us about the historical event by adding that many people came to the wilderness. But this does not contradict the possibility that this occurred in conjunction with typological fulfillment of earlier baptismal events in order to make Christ's baptism the great antitype of all others.

Resting

Finally, our ninth parallel describes the dove as "coming to rest on [Christ]" (Matt 3:16). This Sabbath idea is prominent in all of the OT baptismal stories that we are looking at in this chapter. After creation we read that God "finished his work that he had done, and he *rested* on the seventh day" (Gen 2:2). On the seventh month the ark comes to *rest* on the mountains of Ararat (Gen 8:4). After his baptism, Israel *rests* on the seventh day (Ex 16:30).

Conclusion

These parallels are important textual clues that these stories are to be related theologically. There are far too many relationships in relatively brief narratives for this to all be coincidental. Moses is intentionally relating one story to the next. Matthew, Mark, and Luke pick up on these themes to various degrees, because they see Christ's baptism as intimately related to all of these earlier baptisms.

We have explicit proof from Scripture that the Red Sea and the Flood are baptisms. Creation is different. There is nothing explicit about this being a baptism. This chapter helps us understand two related things. First, original creation may be understood as a baptism. Second, these later baptisms are kinds of new creations.

Each new creation begins in a baptism. Each has a representative, a new kind of Adam. Jesus' baptism is the climactic antitype of it all, especially as the final Adam who fulfills everything where the earlier types failed. If this is true, it means our baptism into Christ symbolically begins our life as new creations in Christ. 2 Cor 5:17 says, "Therefore, if anyone is in Christ, he is a new creation; the old has gone, the new has come."

Significantly for our paedobaptist brothers, circumcision has *nothing* to do with this. "Neither circumcision nor uncircumcision means anything; what counts is a new creation" (Gal 5:16). Baptism has *always* been the symbol of a new creation, way before the advent of circumcision. This is why even the priest was baptized at the start of his earthly ministry. He was becoming a "new creation" of sorts. But it is nothing like the priestly ministry now given to believers, who do not serve before God in a man-made temple. Rather, we serve him with our whole lives wherever we go in anticipation of the day when God will make the temple-heavens and earth new and eternal.

Part III – Baptism and the Priesthood

A further way to develop the baptismal links already established in this book is to look at the priestly tasks performed by those we might not otherwise think of as priests. We have already seen quite a bit about how Christ acted as a priest after his baptism. But what about those men associated with Old Testament baptismal stories? Were they priests—or at least quasi-priests—too? How do the various acts of building altars, offering sacrifices, protecting sanctuaries, paying tithes, and imparting blessings play into this?

Baptism is a ceremonial rite of the sanctuary. We have seen this in great detail earlier in the book. It is logical to assume that if there is a sanctuary, then there must also be a priest to attend it. As we will see in this chapter, God sends priests to carry out cultic duties so that his sanctuaries might be kept pure and holy. Baptism is the rite that initiates the priest for his priestly duty. In looking at this topic it will become increasingly clear what it means to say that baptism is a rite that initiates someone into the priesthood of the believer.

Adam

The Garden of Eden was the prototypical temple built by God himself. Adam was his high priest. "Then the LORD God took the man and put him into the Garden of Eden to cultivate it and keep it" (Gen 2:15). We are also told in Gen 2:5 that there was no man yet to "work the ground." Adam was given the responsibility of working, but what sort of work was it to be? Was it merely that God wanted Adam to be a gardener and a farmer? Is this the extent of the work he was to do? The word for "cultivate" (also "till" or "tend") has the idea of serving. The word is `ābad, and it is usually translated "to serve." Moses gets this idea across when he orders the *priesthood* to service (`ābad) in the tabernacle-sanctuary in Numbers 4 (Num 4:23, 24, 30, 35, 39, 43, 47).

The idea that Adam was to serve as a priest (rather than merely cultivate as a farmer) is strengthened by the next word: "keep" the garden. This word is *shāmar*, and can also be translated "guard." In fact this should be the translation of it here (as the YLT has it). This word occurs only twice in this Genesis narrative. The other time it is used is in Genesis 3:24, when the

cherubim are said to *guard* the way to the tree of life (Gen 3:24).[124] Greg
Beale explains the significance of these two words when they are used
together,

> When these two words occur together later in the OT, without exception they have
> this meaning and refer either to Israelites 'serving and guarding/obeying' God's word
> (about 10 times) or, more often to priests who 'serve' God in the temple and 'guard' the
> temple from unclean things entering it (Num 3:7-8; 8:25-26; 18:5-6; 1 Chron 23:32; Ezek
> 44:14).
>
> (Beale 2005: 8)

Meredith Kline agrees and concludes,

> Here *shāmar* unmistakably signifies the maintenance of the sanctity of the garden...
> Elsewhere in the Bible, especially in passages dealing with the functions of the priests
> and Levites in Israel, the verb *shāmar* occurs frequently in the sense of guarding the
> holiness of God's sanctuary against profanation by unauthorized 'strangers' (cf., e.g.,
> Num 1:53; 3:8, 10, 32; 8:26; 18:3ff.; 31:30, 47; 1 Sam 7:1; 2 Kgs 12:9; 1 Chr 23:32; 2 Chr 34:9;
> Ezek 44:15ff., 48:11)... The conclusion appears warranted, therefore, that Genesis 2:15
> contains an explicit reference to the entrusting of man in his priestly office with the
> task of defending the Edenic sanctuary against the intrusion of anything that would be
> alien to the holiness of the God of the garden or hostile to his name.
>
> (Kline 2006b:86)

What was Adam's vocational failure? Was it that he was not doing
enough hoeing and planting of flowers and this made God angry? Of course
not. Rather, Adam's failure was a lapse of his priestly duty. He failed to
keep sin from corrupting and profaning the Garden-temple. He did not
guard the Edenic-tabernacle, the holy tree in the holy place. He allowed
something unclean to remain in the Garden (i.e., the serpent and sin). Furthermore, he himself became profane while in the holy place. Therefore, he
lost his privilege to serve as a priest in God's Garden sanctuary.

Because Eden is a sanctuary, we should take note that in the narrative,
Adam was not created in the Garden. He was *put* there sometime after his
original creation. Genesis says God "put" (*sîm*) Adam in the Garden *after* he
was fully formed (Gen 2:8).[125] In the context of a sanctuary, the word carries
with it a connotation of *ceremonial appointing*. Each of the instruments in the
tabernacle were carefully "put" (*sîm*) or placed according to the design of
God (see for example Ex 24:6; 28:12; 39:19; Lev 8:8-9; Deut 10:2 etc.).

---

[124] *Jubilees* 3:16 says, "And he was naked, but he neither knew it nor was he ashamed. And he was guarding the
garden from the birds and beasts and cattle."

[125] *Jubilees* 3:9 shows how old this interpretation is when it says, "And after forty days were completed for Adam
in the land where he was created, we *brought him* into the garden of Eden so that he might work it and guard it."

Sam Meier writes, "To put or place an already existing object or person implies that the person or object is removed from one sphere of reality in order to be transported to another." (Meier, 'sîm', *NIDOTTE* 3:384). Thus, Adam was in essence taken out of the ordinary sphere of life, and put into a life of sacred, holy service. Adam was sanctified or consecrated by God through his placement into the Garden of Eden. The location (Eden), the act of placing, and the commands to serve and to guard demonstrate that God is calling his son to faithfully serve in the capacity of a priest.[126]

Before the fall, the priest did not have the duty to offer sacrifices for sin. The obvious reason is that sin had not yet contaminated him. But after the fall, this changed. God himself comes to Adam to show him the need for this new duty. While still in the Garden, the Lord comes to Adam and Eve and dresses them in the clothing of animal skins. "The LORD God made garments of skin for Adam and his wife and clothed them" (Gen 3:21). Here, God shows *himself* to be the Great High Priest.[127] Even the mighty Adam is not permitted to cover his sin by himself. That this is a sacrifice for sin is unquestioned by the certain death of an animal and its subsequent shedding of blood that is necessitated by "clothing of animal skins."

Abel

The priestly theme is continued in the next chapter of Genesis. Here are two brothers: Cain and Abel. There is a particular irony in what is said about each. Abel is said to be a "keeper" (*ra'ah*) of flocks while Cain is said to be a "worker" (*`ābad*) of the ground. The irony is that Cain seems to be doing exactly what the mandate called for in Genesis 3:15. He was *working* the ground.

While some English translations might lead us to think that Abel was doing the other command (keeping), he was actually doing something else. The Hebrew words are different. Abel was pasturing, something not spoken of previously.[128] Therefore, it is Cain who (so far) is carrying out the priestly mandate of creation. At the beginning of this story, the reader is lead to

---

[126] This is one more reason to understand why the Jews created myths that Adam and Eve were baptized in the River. Except under this kind of speculation, Adam would have been baptized prior to sinning, to initiate him into the priesthood. The idea would be that God did not beam Adam into the Garden like Scotty would beam Kirk and Spock onto the Enterprise. Rather, God led Adam into the Garden through the eastern gate, passing through the River thereby initiating him into the priesthood.

[127] It is probable that Adam was clothed by *Christ* in a Christophany, since no man may see the Father and live. Christ is, of course, the Great High Priest of Scripture.

[128] This does not make Abel's work disobedient. Instead, Abel is acting out the "cultural mandate" given to Adam and Eve in Genesis 1. His shepherding (an early type of Christ), was his secular vocation in the world.

think that Cain—the older obedient brother—is the good brother, while Abel the younger and novel brother is the antagonist.

Next we read that both are taking time to bring sacrifices to God. These sacrifices were to cover their sin. "In the course of time Cain brought some of the fruits of the soil as an offering to the LORD. But Abel brought fat portions from some of the firstborn of his flock. The LORD looked with favor on Abel and his offering, but on Cain and his offering he did not look with favor... sin is crouching at your door; it desires to have you, but you must master it" (Gen 4:2-5, 7).

The close proximity of this story to the clothing of Adam and Eve (a mere four verses), and the fact that the story presents this as an event that they did not wonder about, demonstrates that Cain and Abel knew all about the requirements of sacrifices. They knew that they were to offer sacrifices *as priests*, whatever their "secular" vocation may have been. It is also clear that both knew that they were to offer *animal* sacrifices here, because God accepted Abel's sacrifice, but the sacrifice of Cain he did not look upon with favor (vs. 5). This improper sacrifice by Cain was a sin that must be mastered (vs. 7).[129] Undoubtedly, they learned this knowledge from God himself or from their parents, who were the beneficiaries of God's kind sacrifice towards them.

The story of Abel closes as God says to Cain, "The voice of your brother's blood is crying to Me from the ground" (Gen 4:10). Abel's blood in this way prefigures Christ's own blood. "Jesus [is] the mediator of a new covenant, and... [his] sprinkled blood speaks better than the blood of Abel" (Heb 12:24). Abel's sacrifice is a type of Christ's sacrifice. His sacrifice reminds us of the necessity that a holy (perfect) man must die for the sins of the people. This was prefigured in the sacrifice of animal skins in the Garden.

After the Garden is forsaken and men are left to tread outside of God's sanctuary, human priests have a new task, which becomes as important as the older task (to serve and to guard). These priests are to take over the *sacrificial* job originally taken up by God. In the sacrifice of Abel we see the same picture that is presented to us in the tabernacle. Outside of the Holy Place, in the courtyard stands the altar. Here, the common Israelite— together with the priest—offers a sacrifice for his sins. Abel, standing

---

[129] This is the same word that is used in Gen 3:16, "Your desire will be for your husband, and he will *rule* over you."

outside of Eden "at the door"[130] and in the courtyard of the earth, offers a sacrifice for his own sins in priestly fashion. The fact that Cain was doing the original requirement, yet not faithfully acting upon this second requirement shows that God requires obedience to all his commands, not just some of them.

Seth

After Abel is murdered, God replaces him with Seth. Seth means "appointed one." This is an appropriate name for the one from whom the promise (Gen 3:15) will come, as well as for one whose line "calls upon the name of the LORD" (Gen 4:26). To call upon the name of the LORD is, among other things, to worship God. To be the appointed one is to take the place of Abel the priest, whose own blood became a pre-figurement of the death of Christ our High Priest. In these early times, the priesthood was not confined to a special class of people. Rather, it seems that men who followed in the line of Seth became priests before God Most High.

Noah

This is made clear in the creation story of Noah. The first recorded thing that Noah set his mind to do upon leaving the ark—that brought him safely through the water—was to offer a sacrifice. "So Noah went out, and his sons and his wife and his sons' wives with him... Then Noah built an altar to the LORD, and took of every clean animal and of every clean bird and offered burnt offerings on the altar. And the LORD smelled the soothing aroma" (Gen 8:18, 20-21). It is the soothing aroma of animal sacrifice that comes to God's nostrils throughout the institution of the Levitical priesthood (Ex 29:18, 25, 41; Lev 1:9, 13, 17; 2:2, 9, 12; etc.). Noah offered his priestly sacrifice on top of the mountains of Ararat *after his baptism* through the flood. This repeats the feat of Yahweh as he made animal skins for Adam and Eve atop

---

[130] Martin (2004) offers an interesting interpretation of Gen 4:7 from that which is normally given. Taking the temple motif and applying it to the sacrifice he suggests that the phrase, "sin is crouching *at your door*" (NIV) is not as much metaphorical (i.e "the door of your heart") as it is literal. It is better to understand "sin" as a "sin-offering" (Young's Literal) that "lies" (as dead) in front of *the entrance* (door) to the holy place. In other words, this verse is a gracious offering to Cain even after his evil sacrifice is presented. The next words, "[Sin] desires to have you, but you must master it" (NIV) harkens back to Gen 3:16 where the wife's desire will be for her husband, but he will rule over her. In this context here it means, "Cain would have a sin-offering provided for him that would allow him to rule over 'sin'... Cain would gain mastery over sin — over his mistakes — by an offering provided by God. (Genesis 4:7). This was a noble gesture of grace on God's part. Yet in spite of this act of mercy, Cain did not obtain the proper animal, nor did he accept God's grace of supplying a sin-offering for him to master sin. He responded with something very bad and in no way in accordance with the divine command. He offered up his own brother."

that lofty Garden sanctuary of Eden. In this Noah's sacrifice symbolizes faithfulness that Adam never had.

Melchizedek and Jethro

At least two other Yahweh priests are mentioned before the institution of the Levitical priesthood of Aaron. One is Melchizedek. He is the High Priest of Salem (later Jerusalem), the city of God. He is so mighty that even Abraham offers him a tenth of all he owns. Moses' father-in-law is the other priest. This peculiar man was the priest of Midian—the home of Sinai—and the place where Moses saw the form of God (the Angel of the LORD surrounded by Holy-Spirit fire) in a non-combustible fiery bush.

Abraham

We do not really know how the idea of having one priest for a group of people was established. Melchizedek, in the days of Abraham, is the first and only person who is called priest of God most high (he was also the king of Salem, showing an intimate connection between the priest, the king, and the Holy of Holies as Salem is *Jerusalem*). He provides a very early pattern of the established priesthood that is to come in Israel.

But it is important to see something else regarding Abraham. Because of the story with Melchizedek, it is quite common to think that only he was a priest. In an "official capacity" this is perhaps true. Nevertheless, when God asks Abraham to sacrifice his only son, he is asking Abraham to act *as a priest*. Probably not coincidentally, this takes place after Abraham enters the Promised Land by passing through the waters of the Euphrates River.

The fact that we do not usually think of "priest Abraham" does not mean that it was wrong for Abraham to act in this capacity. Such a thing was not confined to the descendants of Levi until the establishment of the Levitical priesthood within the nation of Israel. Indeed, until the establishment of the priesthood in Israel, with the exception of Melchizedek, we have every reason to believe that God permitted any of his people (at least the men) to act in some priestly capacities.

Israel

It is important to point out that before the Levites served in this capacity, the title of priest was originally given to *all* of the people who lived in the nation. After the nation of people are baptized into the Red Sea (1 Cor 10:2) they are told, "Now then, if you will indeed obey My voice and keep My covenant, then you shall be My own possession among all the peoples, for all the earth is Mine; and you shall be to Me a *kingdom of priests* and a holy *nation*.' These are the words that you shall speak to the *sons of Israel*" (Ex 19:5-6). We have already mentioned how Israel was to "wash," a mere four verses after this statement was made.

Levites

Probably because Israel broke the covenant established in Ex 19:5; God in his foreknowledge provided a gracious promise. It would ensure that the people could always come before God. God ensured that one of the tribes of Israel, the Levites, would serve forever before Him as priests and temple servants. This promise was unlike the promise of the priesthood to the nation; for this promise was not based on their works, but on God's grace.

We must note how truly gracious this promise to the Levites was. Levi was the son of Jacob. Together with his brother Simeon, he devised a scheme to kill an entire town for the sins of one man (Shechem who had raped their sister Dinah; cf. Gen 34:2ff). The plan was to circumcise all of the males of the town and then murder them three days later. The plan succeeded and Jacob took note of it on the day of his death as he blessed/cursed his twelve sons.

The text reads, "Simeon and Levi are brothers– their swords are weapons of violence. Let me not enter their council, let me not join their assembly, for they have killed men in their anger and hamstrung oxen as they pleased. Cursed be their anger, so fierce, and their fury, so cruel. I will scatter them in Jacob and disperse them in Israel" (Gen 49:5-7).

Though Jacob had cursed Levi, God turns this curse into a mighty blessing (but not without a little sense of humor). Levi is indeed dispersed and scattered throughout Israel. But this is done graciously, because God has ordained that Levi should serve as priests before God. The Levites were not to be given an inheritance of territory, because they must be scattered throughout Israel in order to perform their duties for the people. (The ironic humor of this "calling" is that Levi—who circumcised this town with the purpose of killing them—must now be forced to remember this act forever, as the only tribe who will perform circumcision from this point on. This is probably not exactly the sort of "calling" that you would particularly pray to God to have if the choice were up to you.)

The calling of Levi to the priesthood is ratified through his descendant Aaron. In Ex 19 God had said, "Bring near to yourself Aaron your brother, and his sons with him, from among the sons of Israel, to minister as priest to Me—Aaron, Nadab and Abihu, Eleazar and Ithamar, Aaron's sons" (Ex 28:1). Among the duties of these priests were the perpetual offering up of sacrifices before God, the moving, cleansing, and serving of the tabernacle, and the ritual washing of the people and themselves in the bronze laver.

Sons of Aaron

The first priests in the Aaronic order were Aaron's two eldest: Nadab and Abihu. But they were killed by God for offering "strange fire" in the tabernacle (Lev 10:1-3). The reason seems to be that they defied the Law in Lev 16:13 which reads, "He is to put the incense on the fire before the LORD, and the smoke of the incense will conceal the atonement cover above the Testimony, so that he will not die." Their "strange fire" was an autonomous attempt to mimic the Spirit Glory-cloud that was represented only in the manner prescribed by God (see Part II, Section III).

Out of this debacle, the grandson of Aaron rises like a shining star at night. Phinehas was zealous for the LORD and was rewarded out of grace,

> The LORD spoke to Moses, saying, "Phinehas the son of Eleazar, the son of Aaron the priest, has turned away My wrath from the sons of Israel, in that he was jealous with My jealousy among them, so that I did not destroy the sons of Israel in My jealousy. "Therefore say, "Behold, I give him My covenant of peace; and it shall be for him and his descendants after him, a covenant of a perpetual priesthood, because he was jealous for his God, and made atonement for the sons of Israel.
>
> (Num 25:10-13)

This "covenant of peace" is so critical to a proper understanding of baptism that we will look at it in great detail in the next section.

Joshua, Priests, and the Jordan Crossing

Christ was baptized in the Jordan River. There are several episodes in the OT that seem to foreshadow this. One is considerable in light of our discussion about the priests of the OT. In Joshua we read,

> Joshua said to the people, "Consecrate yourselves, for tomorrow the LORD will do wonders among you." And Joshua spoke to the priests, saying, "Take up the ark of the covenant and cross over ahead of the people... When you come to the edge of the waters of the Jordan, you shall stand still in the Jordan... it shall come about when the soles of the feet of the priests who carry the ark of the LORD, the Lord of all the earth, shall rest in the waters of the Jordan, the waters of the Jordan shall be cut off, and the waters which are flowing down from above shall stand in one heap... And the priests who car-

ried the ark of the covenant of the LORD stood firm on dry ground in the middle of the Jordan while all Israel crossed on dry ground, until all the nation had finished crossing the Jordan

(Josh 3:5, 8, 13, 17)

Here we see the importance of the priesthood in conducting the ceremony of baptism for the people. We also see in the Ark of the Covenant that God's very presence goes in front of people, even before they enter the waters. In this way, both act to baptize a new generation in a new River prior to entering the sanctuary of the Promised Land.

Naaman

We have discussed the baptism of Naaman. He too demonstrates how baptism and the priesthood go together. *Immediately* after he is cleansed in the Jordan, Naaman takes this vow, "your servant will no more offer burnt offering nor will he sacrifice to other gods, *but to the* LORD" (2 Kings 5:17). Though Naaman was a Gentile—an Aramean—he desires to sacrifice offerings to the LORD. The text never condemns him for this desire and promise, though he is not an Aaronic-Levitical Jew. In this way, he foreshadows what is to come when Gentiles who are baptized into Christ become priests in the new covenant.

Conclusion

This discussion on the priests of the OT helps confirm our view of baptism in the OT while illuminating more of what it means to be baptized into the priesthood of the believer. The theme of *the covenant* has been raised several times in this chapter. We need to take a look at this in the next chapter, because arguments for baptism often center upon this important topic. This is only natural since baptism is the initiatory sign of the *new* covenant.

Part IV - Baptism and the Covenant

The idea of covenant is closely tied to baptism. Baptists and paedo-baptists have recognized this. Unfortunately (in our opinion), the *Abrahamic* covenant—with its sign of circumcision—has become the battle field upon which paedobaptist arguments have been waged. In response to this, Baptists have switched the playing field to Jeremiah's "new covenant." This is also unfortunate, because while the new covenant does tells us about the practice of baptism, it does not by itself—because of Jesus' own "fulfillment" of baptism from the OT—tell us about *how the practice came to be that way.*

In this chapter, we will show that covenants always take place in the context of sanctuaries, where as we have seen, baptism is never far away. A brief survey of various covenants will turn into a rather detailed look at one covenant not usually discussed in baptismal debates. This covenant is the priestly covenant (called by Scripture the "Levitical covenant") that is made within the context of the tabernacle-sanctuary. We feel that both sides of the baptismal divide would do well to come to a better understanding of this covenant. If we are correct, this covenant is the proper fountain out of which covenantal, sacramental arguments for baptism should flow.[131]

Baptism as Sacrament

We have just used the word "sacrament" to describe baptism. A short study of sacramental theology will serve as a useful diving point for our broader discussion of the covenant, because sacraments and covenants go together. Covenants always have *signs* attached to them.[132]

---

[131] If the two sides could agree upon a single covenant as the source of the sacramental institution of baptism, then perhaps baptism itself could finally become the issue around which we center our discussions. As of now, this is not the case. It is also apparent that baptism is presently one of several other issues that work together to foster disagreement. Central to these "other" issues is the debate over "covenant membership." The paedobaptist says that infants belong to the covenant and should therefore receive its sign (ala, the covenant with Abraham), while Baptists say that only *spiritual* infants (i.e. those "born again") belong to the new covenant. Only they should receive its sign. One simply cannot find a book on baptism that is not filled to the brim with arguments of who is in the covenant. Related to this are discussions on Abraham, circumcision, household baptisms, "holy children," and questions of who is "sanctified" by in the new covenant. We believe that a proper understanding of baptism—in its correct OT covenantal roots—will show that the question of covenant membership is, while still important, not logically or biblically tied to the question of baptism.

[132] There are many signs in the OT (cf. Gen 28:12; Num 16:38; 17:10; 26:10; 21:7-8; Josh 2:12, 15; Josh 4:6; Jdg 6:17ff; 2 Kgs 20:8-9; Isa 7:14; Matt 12:39), and sometimes a covenant will have more than one. In the Garden of Eden there were the two trees along with their fruit. Then there was the sacrifice provided for Adam and Eve. In the flood there was the rainbow. In the Abrahamic covenant there was circumcision. The Mosaic covenant had

We instinctively understand what a sign is. In the physical realm, signs are those things that point towards a particular destination; they explain where an artifact might be purchased or describe why a product ought to be acquired. Signs are both signifiers and informers. A sign is itself not the destination. It is a *pointer* that guides us towards the destination. Once the destination is reached, or the product is purchased, there is no more need for a sign. The function of the sign ceases having meaningful value.

In the spiritual realm, a sign is a pointer that God gives to direct a person's faith toward an unfulfilled eschatological[133] reality. These signs are posted on historic mileage markers on the road of redemption. They tell us exactly where we are on the journey, where we have come from, and where we are going.

Biblical signs are not empty of meaning. They are not gravestones that cause us merely to remember only the past. They are not memorials to some golden age. They are alive with meaning *today*. While they do point backwards, they also fix our spiritual eyes upward (to a heavenly reality) and forward (to an historical climax).[134]

Do not confuse a sign with a *sacrament*. Some things may be both signs and sacraments. But signs are not identical to sacraments. For instance, we may talk about Christian baptism as both a sign and a sacrament. Original creation, the Flood, and the Red Sea are signs—not sacraments—because they were miraculous events done *one time* by the hand of God Almighty. They help inform the meaning of baptism, but they cannot inform its practice, because the *sacrament* of baptism comes from an OT *sacrament*, not a sign.

Sacraments are signs that are codified into Law so that they become repeatable, institutional, visible rites to signify and seal the promises of the covenant in the heart of the covenant participant. John Calvin taught,

> The sacraments themselves were also diverse, in keeping with the times, according to the dispensation by which the Lord was pleased to reveal himself in various ways to men. For circumcision was enjoined upon Abraham and his descendants. To it were afterward added purifications, sacrifices, and other rites from the law of Moses. These were the sacraments of the Jews until the coming of Christ.
>
> (Calvin, *Institutes* 4.14.20)

---

many signs including the Sabbath and many of the ceremonial laws. For a helpful discussion, see Horton 2002: 96, 98, 118, 122).

[133] We should understand eschatology as the study of "last things." This is different from popular Christianity's understanding of eschatology which is the study of the *future*. Something may be eschatological in Scripture while not necessarily being future to a twentieth century reader. For example, Hebrews 1:2 says the "last days" are here now.

[134] See John Murray's, "Structural Strands in New Testament Eschatology," http://www.kerux.com/documents/KeruxV6N3A2.asp

Notice that circumcision was not the only sacrament in the OT, according to Calvin. Sacrifices, purifications (of both blood and water), and other rites were sacraments for the Jews as well. This will have significance when we study practical implications in the final chapter.

Since the time of the Church Fathers, baptism has been understood as an outward sign of an inward grace. As the Reformers saw it, baptism was one of two continuing sacraments of the church. The other is the Lord's Supper.

The term "sacrament" scares many in our day. Some automatically default to Roman Catholicism, where sacraments are said to work *ex opere operato* (literally, "by the very fact of the action's being performed"). Under this definition, faith is not at all necessary for a sacrament to do its work. Protestants kept sacramental language, but without accepting the magic that is said to work in them apart from faith. Others are uncomfortable with the term because it is not used in the Bible. In and of itself, this should not be of great concern. "Trinity" is not a biblical term either, yet it is very much a biblical idea.

"Sacrament" comes from the Latin, and the Bible was not written originally in Latin. The biblical word "mystery" (*mystērion*) is the Greek equivalent of the Latin *sacramentum*. "Mystery" appears many times in the Bible. The Latin Vulgate often translated "*mystērion*" as *sacramentum* (Eph 3:3, 9, 5:32; Col 1:27; 1 Tim 3:16; Rev 1:20, 17:7). For example, Ephesians 1:9 says, "He made known to us the mystery [*sacramentum*] of his will." Whenever Paul uses the Greek term, he is talking about the gospel (Rom 11:25; 16:25; 1 Cor 15:51; Eph 1:9; 3:3-9; 5:32; 6:11; Col 1:26-27; 2:2; 3:16; 4:3).

Originally "sacrament" was a military term describing the oath of allegiance and obedience that a soldier solemnly pledged to his commander (Vander Zee 2004: 28). Later it came to mean anything that is sacred or consecrated (Horton 1994: 221). Tertullian (ca. 155-230 A.D.) was among the first Fathers to apply it to baptism.

Calvin provides a good working definition of a sacrament, "It is an outward sign by which the Lord seals on our consciences the promises of his good will towards us in order to sustain the weakness of our faith" (Calvin 1960: 4.14.1). Notice that when the sacrament is administered, faith is (as far as humanly possible to see) *already present* in the application of the sacrament.[135] Four hundred years before Calvin, Hugh of St. Victor (ca. 1096-1141

---

[135] An infant Baptist like Abaham Kuyper would "presuppose" faith in the infant, though there is no visible evidence of it to the world. This is the doctrine of "presumptive regeneration," which was upheld by the Christian Reformed Church in 1905 in the *Conclusions* of the Synod of Utrecht as being a faithful interpretation of the Infant Baptist Reformed Confessions.

A.D.) asked, "Why is a sacrament called a sacred thing? Because by a visible reality seen externally, another invisible, interior reality is signified" (cited in Lawler 1987: 33).

Hugh is following the lead of the Fathers. From the time of Augustine, it was noted that a sign must bear some relation to the thing that is signified. "If sacraments did not bear some resemblance to the things of which they are the sacraments, they would not be sacraments at all" (cited in McGrath 2007: 421).

The Bible refers to the "inward grace" sealed by baptism as the Baptism of the Holy Spirit (Matt 3:11; Mark 1:8; Luke 3:16; John 1:33; Acts 1:5; 11:16; 1 Cor 12:13). To be baptized with the Holy Spirit is to receive the Holy Spirit (remembering that repentance and faith are the prerequisite for baptism). During the first Christian sermon Peter said, "Repent and be baptized every one of you in the name of Jesus Christ for the forgiveness of your sins, and you will receive the gift of the Holy Spirit" (Acts 2:38).[136]

It is because physical baptism and spirit baptism resemble each other that the Scripture links the two so closely. Peter demonstrates this close relationship when he writes, "Baptism, which corresponds to [the flood] now saves you, not as a removal of dirt from the body but as an appeal to God for a good conscience, through the resurrection of Jesus Christ" (1 Pet 3:21). Paul uses similar language, "Do you not know that all of us who have been baptized into Christ Jesus were baptized into his death? We were therefore buried with him by baptism into death, in order that, just as Christ was raised from the dead by the glory of the Father, we too might walk in newness of life" (Rom 6:3-4). In a mysterious way then, baptism symbolizes and seals the newness of life that we have been given by the Holy Spirit.

Baptism and Covenant

Establishing baptism as a sacrament has importance as we consider its *sacramental* roots in the OT. While it is necessary to see Christian baptism as the sign of the new covenant, it is helpful to see its *covenantal* origins in the

---

[136] The baptism of the Holy Spirit is therefore not a "second blessing" given to *spiritual* Christians. He is the seal given to all Christians. Eph 1:13-14 says, "In him you also, when you heard the word of truth, the gospel of your salvation, and believed in him, were sealed with the promised Holy Spirit, who is the guarantee of our inheritance until we acquire possession of it." 2 Cor 1:21-22 seems to combine the idea of baptism, the Spirit, and sealing when it says, "God has anointed us, and has also put his seal on us and given us his Spirit in our hearts as a guarantee."

OT. Sadly for the paedobaptist, this does not occur in the Abrahamic administration of the covenant of grace.[137]

What is not often noticed is that each sanctuary (described in Part II, Sections 1-2) has a covenant that belongs to it.[138] While still in the Garden of Eden, God comes to Adam and Eve to give the great promise that becomes the foundation of all later covenant promises, "I will put enmity between you and the woman, and between your seed and her seed; he shall bruise your head, and you shall bruise his heel" (Gen 3:15). The sign of this covenant seems to have been the garments of skin given to Adam and Eve immediately after the promise (Gen 3:22), for in this act, God is showing forth his gracious pledge (i.e., a sign) to cover sin with the skin of the sacrificial animal. It is probable, then, that sacrifices also became the sacrament of this covenant (cf. Gen 4:3-7).

The first explicit mention of "covenant" (*berith*) occurs in Gen 6:18, "I will establish my covenant with you [Noah], and you will enter the ark— you and your sons and your wife and your sons' wives with you." We believe this same covenant is reconfirmed[139] on the side of Mt. Ararat after the flood when it says, "I now establish my covenant with you and with your descendants after you and with every living creature that was with you" (Gen 9:9-10). The sign of this covenant was the rainbow (Gen 9:16-17).

Several times it records that God gave Abraham, Isaac, and Jacob a covenant (Gen 15:18; 17:2ff; 17:21; 26:3-5, 24; 27:28-29; 28:14-15; Ex 2:24 etc.). These are not three different covenants, but the same covenant reconfirmed to each Patriarch as the line is narrowed down. Thus, the Scripture speaks about the covenant (singular) that was given to Abraham, Isaac, and Jacob (Ex 2:24; Lev 26:42; Deut 4:31; 7:12; 8:18; 2 Kgs 13:23; 1 Chr 16:16-17; Ps 105:9-10; Acts 3:25).

Always involved with this covenant is the Promised Land, which they always happen to be living in at that moment the covenant is cut. For instance, "On that day the LORD made a covenant with Abram and said, 'To

---

[137] By "covenant of grace" we mean the overarching covenantal rubric under which each particular historical OT covenantal administration may be subsumed. We will not get into a detailed discussion of this in this book.

[138] We will not look in this book at the covenant which belongs to the archetypal sanctuary, which we believe is the same thing that theologians often call the "Covenant of Redemption" or "Counsel of Peace" or "*Pactum Salutis.*" Biblical support for this covenant may be found in places like Ps 110:1; Prov 8:22-23; Zech 6:12-13; John 6:39, 17:4; Eph 1:4, 2:10; 2 Tim 1:9; Titus 1:2; Heb 4:3, 7:20-21; 1 Pet 1:20; Rev 13:8; and especially Luke 22:29-30 (cf. Kline 2006: 72). Neither will we look at the covenant which belongs to the creation sanctuary of heaven/earth/Eden which we believe is the same thing that theologians often call the "Covenant of Works" or "Covenant of Creation." Biblical support for this covenant may be found in places like Gen 2:16; Isa 24:5; Jer 33:20-35; Hos 6:7; Rom 5:12ff.

your descendants I give *this* land, from the river of Egypt to the great river, the Euphrates' (Genesis 15:18). The *sign* of the Abrahamic covenant was the land, but its *sacrament* (i.e., "sign and seal") was circumcision (Gen 17:11; cf. Rom 4:11).

On God's Mountain—also known as Mt. Sinai or Mt. Horeb—God made a covenant with Israel (Ex 19:5). The Ten Commandments are the covenant words that God spoke to Moses on the mountain. While there were many signs given to the people during the Exodus, one stands out in particular as the sign that "sealed the deal" on Horeb. It is the Sabbath, which is said to be the sign of the covenant (Ex 31:13; 17). The version of the Ten Commandments in Deut 5 just so happens to tie the reason for this sign into the exodus events themselves (Deut 5:12-15).

God also makes a covenant that becomes closely associated with the temple. Remembering the events told in 2 Samuel 7:11-16, David says, "You said, 'I have made a covenant with my chosen one, I have sworn to David my servant, I will establish your line forever and make your throne firm through all generations'" (Ps 89:3-4). The events of 2 Samuel 7 tell us that David had it in his mind to build God a temple. Therefore, the temple and the covenant are closely related to one another.

Levitical Covenant Established for a Covenantal Baptismal Argument

These are the OT covenants usually discussed with Covenant Theology.[140] We have also given their accompanying sanctuaries. However, there is one final sanctuary and one final covenant that belong together. Hywel Jones describes it as a "Forgotten Covenant" (Jones 1999:1).[141] But though the covenant is often forgotten, certainly its sanctuary is not. The sanctuary in mind here is the tabernacle, and it is intimately associated with the Levitical priesthood. In our judgment, the initiatory sacrament attached to this covenant is baptism. But let us first try to understand this covenant.

Is there a covenant with the priesthood that might be linked with the tabernacle? Scripture repeatedly confirms that there is. But is this covenant significant enough to mention along side of the other giant covenants of the Old Testament? Many today do not think so. O. Palmer Robertson tells us that this covenant "does not possess the same epoch-making character as the

---

[139] Theologians differ as to whether or not the covenant with Noah is a single covenant or dual covenants. If it is dual covenants, then the sanctuary of the first is the Ark while the sanctuary of the second is the Mountain.

[140] The "new covenant" is a prophetic rather than historical covenant in the OT, so I have not considered it here.

[141] Carnagey (1998: 24) calls it the "Phinehasic Covenant," and says it is "almost totally unrecognized." Our research concludes that this is a bit of a hyperbole.

ones noted above [Noah, Abraham, Moses, David, and the new covenant]" (Robertson 1980: 27, n. 1).

We are absolutely convinced that Robertson has not thought carefully enough about the covenant that God made with the priests. This is the same problem that many other systematicions (both paedobaptist and Baptist alike) have had as well.[142] But it *is* attested in varying degrees in several systematic treatments of OT covenants.[143] Even more so, as we will see shortly, it is *well* attested in the commentaries on the Scriptures that deal explicitly with this covenant. These commentaries range from very ancient (pre-Christian and early Christian) to modern.

Explicit passages from the Bible include Numbers 18 (especially vs. 19-20); Numbers 25:6-13 (especially vs. 12-13), Malachi 2:5-6, 8, Jeremiah 33:17-22, and Nehemiah 13:29. Implicit OT passages include but are probably not limited to Gen 49:7; Ex 32:25-29; Deut 10:8; 18:1-2; 33:8-11; Josh 18:7; 1 Sam 2:28; 1 Kgs 2:35; Isa 56:3-8, 66:19-21; Ezek 44:15-16, 48:11. It follows that any fulfillment of these particular passages in the NT would also be referring to this covenant too (cf. Matt 21:13-14; 1 Pet 2:9; or any passage that refers to the Levitical fulfillment of Christ or priestly duty of the believer). There are also apocryphal passages that discuss implicitly or explicitly this covenant: *1 Esdras* 5:5[144]; 8:63[145]; *4 Esdras* 1:1-3[146]; *1 Maccabees* 2:26, 50[147]; *Jubilees* 30:18-20[148];

---

[142] The reason why paedobaptists would not treat this covenant systematically seems obvious. If they did, their whole association of baptism with circumcision would completely unravel. The reason why Baptists do not usually treat this covenant systematically is less obvious. Maybe they have just followed the paedobaptists and therefore have unwittingly missed it. However, it is also probable that many simply assume, like Robertson who offers no significant argument for his assertion, that this covenant is to be subsumed under the Mosaic covenant and that therefore it is not worthy of being given such a lofty place in a systematic treatment of biblical covenants. As we will see, this assumption cannot be supported by the biblical data.

[143] For example Baugh 2000: 22; Boston 1848: 1:328; Busenitz 1999: 180, 186-89; Iannelli-Smith 2004; Hahn 1995: 213-304; Henry n.d.: 512-513; Mayhue 1996: 255; Mclean 1994; Packer 1990: 16; van der Wall 2003: 39; Williamson 2000).

[144] "The priests, the sons of Phinehas, son of Aaron; Jeshua the son of Jozadak, son of Seraiah, and Joakim the son of Zerubbabel, son of Shealtiel, of the house of David, of the lineage of Phares, of the tribe of Judah" (*1 Esd* 5:5).

[145] "And with him was Eleazar the son of Phinehas, and with them were Jozabad the son of Jeshua and Moeth the son of Binnui, the Levites" (*1 Esd* 8:63).

[146] "The second book of the prophet Ezra the son of Seraiah, son of Azariah, son of Hilkiah, son of Shallum, son of Zadok, son of Ahitub, ² son of Ahijah, son of Phinehas, son of Eli, son of Amariah, son of Azariah, son of Meraioth, son of Arna, son of Uzzi, son of Borith, son of Abishua, son of Phinehas, son of Eleazar, ³ son of Aaron, of the tribe of Levi" (*4 Esd* 1:1-3). The genealogies traced in these three passages expose the line of the priesthood through Phinehas and Aaron according to the priestly covenant in the same way that genealogies of kings expose the line of the kings according to the covenant of David. This is why we include them. The genealogies imply a covenant.

[147] "Thus he burned with zeal for the law, as Phinehas did against Zimri the son of Salu... Now, my children, show zeal for the law, and give your lives for the covenant of our fathers." (*1 Mac* 2:26, 50). Cf., *2 Mac* 4:23-50 where the very negative commentary of one Menelaus is given the priesthood by Antiochus IV Epiphanes as a supreme act of blasphemy against God's Law.

Sirach 45:6-7, 15, 23-24;[149] *TSim* 3:10-11[150]; *TJud* 4:1-2[151]). The importance of these works is that they are ancient reflections on this covenant. It is time we recovered what the ancients understood.

Malachi is probably the best place to start this study, because he is an inspired, biblical writer, and he gives the most detail to the events surrounding the establishment of this "forgotten covenant." Malachi says,

> My covenant with him was one of life and peace, and I gave them to him. It was a covenant of fear, and he feared me. He stood in awe of my name. True instruction was in his mouth and no wrong was found on his lips. He walked with me in peace and uprightness, and turned many from iniquity... But you have turned aside from the way. You have caused many to stumble by your instruction; you have corrupted the covenant of Levi."[152]

(Mal 2:5-6, 8)

What is Malachi predicting? Hywel Jones gives one answer,

> It was not Nehemiah's return to Jerusalem that Malachi was looking for as a validation of the covenant, or even for a prophet like Elijah (4:5). He was looking for the coming of the greatest Levite, *the messenger of the covenant* (3:1) who would bring into existence purged and consecrated Levites, that is, gospel preachers (3:2). The magnificent words which Malachi used therefore describe the Lord Jesus Christ and his servants who proclaim the truth of God. They are, perhaps, the most wonderful description in

---

[148] "And the seed of Levi was chosen for the priesthood and Levitical (orders) to minster before the LORD always just as we do. And Levi and his sons will be blessed forever because he was zealous to do righteousness and judgment and vengeance against all who rose up against Israel. And thus a blessing and righteousness will be written (on high) as a testimony for him in the heavenly tablets before the God of all. And we will remember for a thousand generations the righteousness which a man did during his life in all of the (appointed) times of the year. And (it) will be written (on high) and it will come to him and his descendants after him. And he will be written down as a friend and a righteous one in the heavenly tablets" (*Jub* 30:18-20).

[149] "He exalted Aaron, the brother of Moses, a holy man like him, of the tribe of Levi. He made an everlasting covenant with him, and gave him the priesthood of the people... Moses ordained him, and anointed him with holy oil; it was an everlasting covenant for him and for his descendants all the days of heaven, to minister to the Lord and serve as priest and bless his people in his name... Phinehas the son of Eleazar is the third in glory, for he was zealous in the fear of the Lord, and stood fast, when the people turned away, in the ready goodness of his soul, and made atonement for Israel. Therefore a covenant of peace was established with him, that he should be leader of the sanctuary and of his people, that he and his descendants should have the dignity of the priesthood for ever. Just as a covenant was established with David son of Jesse of the tribe of Judah, that the king's heritage passes only from son to son, so the heritage of Aaron is for his descendants alone" (*Sir* 45:6-7, 15, 23-25).

[150] "And now, my children, obey Levi and Judah, and be not lifted up against these two tribes, for from them shall arise unto you the salvation of God. For the Lord shall raise up from Levi as it were a High Priest, and from Judah as it were a King, God and man, He shall save all the Gentiles and the race of Israel" (*TSim* 3:10-11).

[151] "And now, my children, I command you, love Levi, that ye may abide, and exalt not yourselves against him, lest ye be utterly destroyed. For to me the Lord gave the kingdom, and to him the priesthood, and He set the kingdom beneath the priesthood" (*TJud* 4:1-2).

[152] It is possible that the phrase to the Levites, "You have corrupted the covenant of Levi" is a reflection of Deut 33:9 where the opposite is true. There the priests, "observed your word and kept your covenant" (See Adamson 1970: 807, van der Waal 2003: 39). Stuart (1998: 1316) gives a detailed exegetical treatment of the similarities between Num 25:11-13; Deut 33:8-11, and Mal 1:6-2:9. If this is true, then Deut 33:9 refers to the covenant of Levi rather than the Mosaic covenant.

the Bible of the preacher of God's good news, even though they are found in the Old Testament [emphasis added].

(Jones 1999)

Jones' insight into Malachi's description of the Lord Jesus Christ as "the greatest Levite" is the same theme taken up by a good portion of the book of Hebrews. The addition of Christ "and his servants" by Jones has significance *for baptism*, as we will see as we move deeper into this discussion. But for now, we want to look at what Malachi means by the "covenant with Levi." Where does this idea originate? Malachi is rather cryptic and it is not entirely clear what historical episode he refers to (though the commentaries are almost entirely in agreement that we can narrow it down to a select and related handful of texts, texts which we will demonstrate are all related to one another *covenantally*).

<u>Levi</u>

Malachi's language is reminiscent of the zeal of Levi, the third son of Jacob. Levi and his brother Simeon went into Shechem and murdered all the men, in revenge for the rape of their sister Dinah (Gen 34). Because of this, God sends a curse upon them (later turned into a blessing for Levi, but apparently not Simeon[153]) via Jacob, "I will scatter them in Jacob and disperse them in Israel" (Gen 49:7).

This is all that we know with certainty about Levi's relationship to this covenant. However, it is clear that pre-Christian Jews were wrestling with the same question that we are here. The book of *Jubilees* (3rd-2nd Cent. B.C.) attempts to answer the question through either speculation or historical information now lost to us. Either way, it is important to read what it says about Levi. It begins this way,

> And the seed of Levi was chosen for the priesthood and Levitical (orders) to minister before the LORD always just as we [angelic hosts] do. And Levi and his sons will be blessed forever because he was zealous to do righteousness and judgment and vengeance against all who rose up against Israel.

(Jub 30:18)

Next we read about the special blessing that Jacob had Isaac grant to two of his sons: Judah and Levi. And it reads,

---

[153] Simeon is absorbed into the tribe of Judah (Josh 19:9), and is not mentioned in the tribal blessings of Deut 33. This shows that there was no permanent covenantal separation attached to Simeon as there was to Levi (cf. Taylor 2004: 297).

And they drew near to him [Isaac] and he turned and kissed them and embraced the both of them together. And a spirit of prophecy came down upon his mouth. And he took Levi in his right hand and Judah in his left hand. And he turned to Levi first and he began to bless him first, and he said to him, "May the God of all, i.e. the LORD of all ages, bless you and your sons in all ages. May the LORD give you and your seed very great honor. May he draw you and your seed near to him from all flesh to serve in his sanctuary as the angels of the presence and the holy ones. May your sons' seed be like them with respect to honor and greatness and sanctification. And may he make them great in every age. And they will become judges and rulers and leaders for all the seed of the sons of Jacob."

(Jub 31:11-15)

Next comes a section that can appropriately be summarized as *covenantal* in its essence:

The word of the LORD they will speak righteously,
And all of his judgments they will execute righteously.
And they will tell my ways to Jacob,
And my paths to Israel.
The blessing of the LORD shall be placed in their mouth,
So that they might bless all of the seed of the beloved.
(As for) you, your mother has named you 'Levi,'
And truly she has named you.
You will be joined to the LORD
And be the companion of all the sons of Jacob.
His table will belong to you,
And you and your sons will eat (from) it,
And in all generations your table will be full,
And your food will not be lacking in any age.
And all who hate you will fall before you,
And all your enemies will be uprooted and perish,
And whoever blesses you will be blessed,
And any nation which curses you will be cursed.

(Jub 31:15-17)

After the blessing of Isaac we read that "Levi dreamed that he had been appointed and ordained priest of the Most High God, he and his sons forever" (Jub 32:1). Then on the day that Benjamin was born, Jacob began counting his sons and the lot fell to Levi. "And his father put garments of the priesthood upon him and he filled his hands... and Levi served as priest in Bethel before Jacob, his father, (apart) from his ten brothers. And he was a priest there" (Jub 32:3, 9).

It is obvious that someone was trying to figure out how Malachi and others could refer to a "covenant with Levi." As Richard Taylor (2004: 297) notes, this is an ancient tradition that sees Levi as being elevated to the priestly office. It goes back to at least the 3rd century B.C. This explains in part why Levi is so prominent in these ancient books. He is singled out like this in *Jubilees*, *Aramaic Levi*, *The Testament of Twelve Patriarchs*, *Joseph and Asenath*, *Ascension of Moses* and many others. The Puritan William Sclater appears to recognize these traditions when he speaks of "Levi's behavior in the Covenant" (Sclater 1650: 64, 66, 67). Whether the Jews knew something about this man that we do not or they were just speculating is beside the point. There is a covenant here that they were trying to understand.

Aaron

From Genesis alone, it is difficult to root the covenant in Levi himself. So, we need to move forward in time. As we do this, we find that Levi's curse becomes the basis for the Le*vites* disinheritance of the land. Instead of land, the LORD would be their inheritance (Num 18:19-26). It is important to remember that God gave an unconditional promise to Abraham that his descendants would inherit the land. Levi was one of those descendants. Yet, God—in his providence—did not let the Levites inherit the land. They would inherit something else. This "something else" is God himself, and the promise of Himself came to the Levites in the form of a covenant.

Importantly, God—as the Levite's inheritance—puts the spectacular promise this way. Num 18:20 reads, "The LORD said to Aaron, 'You will have no inheritance in their land, nor will you have any share among them; I am your share and your inheritance among the Israelites'" (cf. Deut 18:1-2; Josh 18:7).

Importantly, this "I am your..." language is *covenantal* language. It reminds us very much of the covenant promise that God gave to Abram, "Fear not, Abram, *I am your* shield; your reward shall be very great" (Gen 15:1). Genesis continues by saying, "*On that day* the LORD made a *covenant* with Abram" (Gen 15:18).

In an almost identical way, Num 18:19 also uses the term "covenant" to speak about what God is giving to Aaron, "All the Holy contributions that the people of Israel present to the LORD I give to you, and to your sons and daughters with you, as a perpetual due. It is a covenant of salt forever before the LORD for you and for your offspring with you." (Note: vs. 19 immediately precedes the "I am your..." language of vs. 20). C. van der Wall writes,

In Num. 18:19 the guaranteed income of the priests is mentioned. This provision consisted of a salt covenant of (the) age before the LORD, that had to be observed by Israel and his offspring. So the care and the service of the Levites had been included in the great covenant between Israel and the LORD. Aaron however, as representative of Levi, was given a special covenant promise: 'I am your portion and your inheritance among the people of Israel (18:20).

(van der Waal 2003: 39; cf. Mayhue 1996: 255)

Van der Waal's insight demonstrates a reasonable probability that the promise in Gen 49:7 is indeed the conception of the Levitical covenant (cf. Taylor 2004: 298).

Levites

Now, the action of Levi and Simeon is never identified in the Bible as one of "peace, uprightness, and turning many away from sin." What they did was clearly wicked. This is why God cursed them both. Yet, it must be acknowledged that God turned the curse into a blessing, at least for Levi. However, since Scripture does not explicitly refer to their actions as being the time of the cutting of a priestly covenant, Malachi may instead be referring to the episode of the golden calf when the Levitical *tribe* stood up as one in zeal for the LORD,

> Then Moses stood in the gate of the camp and said, "Who is on the LORD's side? Come to me." And all the sons of Levi gathered around him. And he said to them, "Thus says the LORD God of Israel, 'Put your sword on your side each of you, and go to and fro from gate to gate throughout the camp, and each of you kill his brother and his companion and his neighbor.'" And the sons of Levi did according to the word of Moses. And that day about three thousand men of the people fell. And Moses said, "Today you have been ordained for the service of the LORD, each one at the cost of his son and of his brother, so that he might bestow a blessing upon you this day."[154]

(Ex 32:26-29)

If this story is in Malachi's mind, then the "him" (third person *singular*) that God gave the covenant to would be the whole tribe of Levi. But it is equally possible that Malachi is referring here to the zeal of one particular Levite, Phinehas the grandson of Aaron, and to the covenant God made with him.[155]

Phinehas

Numbers 25 tells about a horrific sight that begins to unfold at the entrance to the Tent of Meeting (i.e., the tabernacle; Num 25:6). It occurs after the men of Israel begin having relations with Moabite women who then entice them into sacrificing to, eating the covenant meals of, and bowing

---

[154] Cf. Brown (1996: 197) and Taylor (2004: 297) suggest that this is at least part of what Malachi has in mind.

[155] See Pohlig 1998: 78, where the "he" and "him" in the passage "refer to Phinehas (Num. 25:10-13; cf. Ps. 106:30-31)."

down to foreign gods. In this way, Israel began worshipping the Baal of Peor (25:1-3). The LORD takes great offence at this, and commands that each man and his family be killed on the spot. Aaron's grandson, Phinehas the son of Eleazar, takes his spear and begins obeying the command of the LORD. For this, God rewards Phinehas with a great covenant promise, "Tell him I am making my covenant of peace with him. He and his descendants will have a covenant of a lasting priesthood" (Num 25:12-13). Psalm 106:30-31 is a commentary on this passage. "But Phinehas stood up and intervened, and the plague was checked. This was credited to him as righteousness for endless generations to come." VanderKam (2002: 471) comments on *Jubilees* saying, "It appears that the Levi of Genesis 34 and the Phinehas of Numbers 25 were sufficiently parallel to one another for the author of Jubilees to associate the description of the latter with the former."

Why is it so rare to read about this covenant in the Systematics? Jones (1999: 1) asserts that most do not highlight the "covenant with Levi" (as Malachi puts it) because the episodes with the Levites and Phinehas (the two "most probable occasions when this covenant with Levi was made") are "connected with the Sinaitic covenant which is so prominent in the Old Testament, not to mention the new." But this begs the point. What if those episodes are not connected to the Mosaic covenant, but to the Levitical covenant?[156] God did not make this covenant with Moses, but with Aaron. If we presuppose that these episodes are linked to the Mosaic covenant, then we will run into all sorts of problems when trying to identify the beginning of the Levitical covenant. Even if Malachi and others happen to tell us when that occurred, we simply won't be able to hear what they are saying.

But Malachi is telling us that God gave the covenant to someone *when* he "revered me and stood in awe of my name," when "he walked with me in peace and uprightness, and turned many from sin." The KJV reads like this, "My covenant was with him of life and peace; and I gave them to him for the fear wherewith he feared me, and was afraid before my name." Some specific episode(s) of fearing God was the occasion of covenant ratification. If we can identify when this occurred (and perhaps it is on more than one occasion with more than one person), then we can know with certainty when God made (and/or re-established) the covenant with Levi.

---

[156] At this point we should remember that *all of the covenants are connected* to each other. Connection doesn't rule out individuality. Abraham's covenant didn't come out of thin air, but was in line with the promises that God gave to Noah (which were themselves in line with the promise of Gen 3:15), and confirmed to his son Shem. In Genesis 6:18, God makes a covenant with Noah and his family. In Genesis 9:26-27 the promise (i.e., "covenant") is narrowed through the line of Shem. This is why Genesis goes to pains to tell us that Abram comes from the line of Shem!

All three stories (Levi, the golden calf, and Phinehas) show significant zeal for the Lord, if not also fear (though, again, Levi does not seem to ever be praised for his actions in the Bible). But Phinehas is particularly interesting in light of Malachi. The "peace" and "righteousness" surrounding the episode with Phinehas is identical to what Malachi says (cf. Num 25:15; Ps 106:20; Mal 2:5-6). Furthermore, as Beth Glazier-McDonald in her dissertation on *Malachi* explains, the events surrounding the story of Phinehas and the setting of Malachi are identical. "It is interesting to note that in Num 25:1f., Phinehas is commended for combating idolatrous practices: illicit sexual relationships and worship of other gods. It is precisely these two practices that Malachi condemns in the next oracle unit, 2:10-16" (Glazier-McDonald 1987: 80, n. 159). It seems highly probable that Malachi does in fact have at least the episode with Phinehas in mind. We are not alone in drawing this conclusion.

Edward Pococke—professor of Hebrew at Oxford in the late 17th century—wrote,

> With him, i.e., with him that is here meant by Levi, that whole Tribe; or more particularly Aaron and his prosperity, to whom the Priesthood was appropriated, among whom Phinehas was eminent for his zeal towards God and his worship, and who, some think, is here particularly pointed out.
>
> (Pococke 1692: 23; cf. Stock 1641: 29)

The "some" who agree with Pococke include Abraham ben Meir ibn Ezra (Aben Ezra - 1092-1167), the medieval Jewish theologian. Pococke says,

> He concludes that both [Aaron and Phinehas] are here meant, and not only they, but as many of their posterity as were holy priests, as they ought all to be, they are all comprehended under the common name of Levi their Father, and so spoken of as but one person, all meeting in the same stock, all separated to one holy function; and so as many as were such as he here describes are together the Levi of God.

Calvin seems to take a similar position in his commentary on Malachi when he refers to God covenanting with "Levi their father, that is, with the tribe itself." The editor of Calvin's Commentary on Malachi felt it necessary to add this informative footnote to Calvin's words,

> That we may understand these terms we must have recourse to the case evidently alluded to, that of Phinehas, in Num. 25:12, 13. God promised to him the covenant of peace and of perpetual priesthood – of peace, that is, of reconcilement, because God through the zeal displayed by Phinehas became reconciled to the children of Israel – and of perpetuity as to the priesthood, signified here by life or 'lives,' as the word is plural.
>
> (Owen 1848: 522, n. 1)

An interesting passage from the more famous John Owen (1616-1683) surfaces in his work on the *Perseverance of the Saints*. He says,

> There was a twofold engagement made to the house of Aaron about that office, - one in general to him and his sons, the other in particular to Phinehas and his posterity the latter to Phinehas is far more expressive and significant than the other.

After quoting Numbers 25:11-13 he continues,

> Here is a promise indeed, and no condition in terms expressed; - but yet being made and granted upon the condition of obedience, which is clearly expressed once and again, that the continuance of it was also suspended on that condition, as to the glory and beauty of that office, the thing principally intended, cannot be doubted; yea, it is sufficiently pressed in the occasion of the promise and fountain thereof this; was not that promise wherein Eli's was particularly concerned. Indeed, his posterity was rejected in order to the accomplishment of this promise, the seed of Phinehas returning to their dignity, from whence they fell by the interposition of the house of Ithamar"
>
> (Owen 2004: 237-238)

Though Owen doesn't use the word "covenant," it certainly seems like the perfect word to summarize his language of "office," "promise," "condition," "posterity," and "seed."

In fact, the majority of commentaries on Malachi reference the story of Phinehas, and the covenant that God gave to him, as being highly influential in Malachi's development of the covenant with Levi.[157] Scott Hahn in his dissertation (which must surely be the most detailed exposition of the Levitical covenant to date) writes that it "seems to establish a line of priestly succession from Aaron through Phinehas and his descendants. At the same time, it serves to purify, preserve, and strengthen the Levitical covenant of priesthood" (Hahn 1995: 266).

Turning now to the systematic treatment of this covenant we find Stephen Baugh citing it along side of the Noahic, Abrahamic, and Davidic

---

[157] Cf., Barrick 1999: 214, 217 n. 20; Brown 1996: 197; Busenitz 1999: 188; Carnagey 1998: 24; Day 2003: 105; Feinberg 1982: 236; Henry n.d.: 512-513; Keown 1995: 174; Glazier-McDonald 1987: 80; Jordan 1984: 86; Kaiser 1988: 59-60; Merrill 1994; Pohlig 1998: 78; Scalise 1987: 411; Stuart 1998: 1316-1318; Taylor 2004: 297; Weyde 2000: 194. Ralph Smith is among the minority who note the relationship between Malachi and Numbers 25, and yet conclude that Malachi does *not* have Phinehas in mind. In fact, he goes so far as to say that the covenant with Phinehas "was not made with the Levites as a whole. Most writers believe the reference here is to Moses' blessing of Levi (Deut 33:8-11)" (Smith 1984: 317). While we found Deut 33:8-11 often mentioned in relation to Malachi 2, we also found the covenant with Phinehas mentioned in the same breath. This is because most writers in fact believe that *both* texts refer to the same covenant. The reason why Smith cannot connect the "Phinehasian" covenant to Malachi (even though he realizes the close linguistic connections) is because though he recognizes that not all Levities are priests (Num 8:19; cf. Rehm 1992: 303-304; Glazier-McDonald 1987: 73-80), all priests are still Levites. Therefore, it is acceptable to call the covenant that God gave to the priests the covenant of Levi. There are not two different covenants, one given to the priests and one given to the Levites (cf. Block 1995: 124 and Tate 1987: 400 who makes that mistake).

covenants. All four are "manifestations of the covenant of grace under the Old Testament," and particular attention is given to the covenant with Phinehas because of the similar language of justification both here and in the covenant with Abraham (Baugh 2000: 22).

J. I. Packer, in his introduction on covenant theology in the 2 volume set of Herman Witsius' *Economy of the Covenants between God and Man*, places Phinehas along side of Noah, Abraham, the Israelites, Aaron, and David where each man "directs us to covenantal thinking by the *specific parallel between Christ and Adam* [where]... one person stand[s] for a group" (Packer: 1990: IV). This is a critical insight, because it shows how Phinehas and Aaron did not represent merely themselves, but also those who would come after them in their covenant.

Thomas Boston is probably the most detailed on this that we have found. He is worth quoting at length.

> Covenants typical of the covenant of grace were made with persons representing their seed. The covenant of royalty, a type of this covenant, was made with David, as representative of his seed; therefore the covenant of grace typified by it was made with Christ, as the representative of his seed. Hence in our first text the party covenanted with and sworn to is called David, which is one of the names of Christ typified by David, Hos. 3:5 for which cause the mercies of the covenant are called 'the sure mercies of David,' Isa. 55:3. And this David is God's servant having a seed comprehended with him in the covenant, Psal. 89:4. To the same purpose it may be observed, that Phinehas' covenant of priesthood was a type of the covenant of grace; and in it Phinehas stood as representative of his seed, typifying Jesus Christ representing his spiritual seed in the covenant of grace, Numb. 25:12, 13. This is evident from Psal. 90:4. where the everlasting priesthood promised to Phinehas has had its full accomplishment in Jesus Christ. Hereto may be added, that the covenant made with Noah and his sons was made with them as the heads of the new world, and representatives of their seed, Gen. 9:9, 11. And that this covenant was a type of the covenant of grace, and Noah therein a type of Christ, is clear from its being established on a sacrifice, Gen. 8:20, 21.; from the nature of that covenant, viz. that there should not be another deluge, chap. 9:11.; typical of the wrath of God against the elect, Isa. 54:9, 10. confirmed by the rainbow about the throne, Rev. 4:3. Wherefore, since in the covenant of royalty, by which the covenant of grace is typified in our text, and in other covenants typical thereof, the parties with whom they were made stood as heads, public persons and representatives of their seed, it is evident, that the covenant of grace typified by these was made with Christ as the head and representative of his spiritual seed : for whatever is attributed to any person or thing as a type, hath its accomplishment really and chiefly in the person or thing typified.
>
> (Boston 1848: 1:328-329)

Boston places two well-attested OT covenants (Noah and David) side by side with the covenant that God gave to the priests—particularly as it came to Phinehas—and then refers to all of them as "covenants typical of the covenant of grace." There is no hint that Phinehas' covenant is viewed by

Boston as some peculiar, dissimilar covenant to the others. There is no hint that he sees it as given only to a single man, but actually just the opposite. And there is no hint that it is viewed as a subordinate covenant to David or Noah (he also cites the covenant in Gen 3:15 prior to this as being in the same category as these). In fact, Phinehas is representative of Christ, just as David and Noah are. Surely, what we are proposing here is not novel. It is attested time and again in the Systematics, and especially in the commentaries of the Church.

But if Malachi is referring to the covenant given to Phinehas, why does he call it the covenant with *Levi*? The answer to this important question is found in understanding that God gave the *same covenant* to Levi as he gave to Aaron, Phinehas, and (later) Zadok. This is very much like what God did with Isaac and Jacob.

God reconfirmed the Abrahamic covenant with Isaac and Jacob, because he was narrowing the promise through their seed. In the same way, this covenant with Phinehas is not some isolated, personal, yet insignificant covenant. It is an extension of the Levitical covenant through this specific man. Matthew Henry says,

> This covenant was made with the whole tribe of Levi when they were distinguished from the rest of the tribes, were not numbered with them, but were *taken from among* them and *appointed over the tabernacle of testimony* (Num 1:49, 50), by virtue of which appointment God says (Num 3:12), *The Levites shall be mine.* It was made with Aaron when he and his sons were taken to *minister unto the Lord in the priest's office,* Ex 28:1. Aaron is therefore called *the saint of the LORD*, Ps 106:16. It was made with Phinehas and his family, a branch of Aaron's, upon a particular occasion, Num 25:12-13. And there the covenant of priesthood is called, as here, the covenant of peace, because by it peace was made and kept between God and Israel. These great blessings of life and peace contained in that covenant, God gave to him, to Levi, to Aaron, to Phinehas.
>
> (Henry 1960: 1196)[158]

Along the same lines, Glazier-McDonald (1987: 80) writes, "That Malachi calls this covenant Levitical rather than Aaronic (via Phinehas) stems from the aforementioned subordination of the priesthood to the house of Levi."

The covenant with Aaron is remembered by Eli when he said to Samuel, "Did I choose him [Aaron] out of all the tribes of Israel to be my priest, to go

---

[158] Henry says basically the same thing in his "A Treatise on Baptism" (p. 512-513). The discussion concerns the "seed" that is so important in most of the OT covenants between God and man. The Levitical covenant is no exception. Here he discusses the covenant of works (with Adam and his seed), the covenant with Noah (and his seed), and the covenant of grace which includes the Abrahamic (and his seed), the Mosaic (which he says is not strictly speaking part of the covenant of grace), "the covenant of the priesthood made with Phinehas" (and his seed), and the covenant of royalty made with David (and his seed).

up to my altar, to burn incense, to wear an ephod before me? I gave to the house of your father all my offerings by fire from the people of Israel" (1 Sam 2:28).[159]

The story at this point picks up the covenant with the priesthood as it was passed on through Phinehas. Though Eli made this wonderful covenantal connection with *Aaron*, he had forgotten about the promise of *Phinehas*, a line from which he was himself not personally descended.

Eli was a priest from the line of Ithamar (1 Kgs 2:27; 1 Chron 24:6), the brother of Eleazar, and uncle of Phinehas (Ex 6:25). But once the covenant came to Phinehas, the priestly line of Ithamar was doomed. So, the lineage of Eli becomes the focus of the story. And it will soon come to pass that only the sons of Eleazar-Phinehas will be able to serve God as priests.

Because of Eli and his sons' wickedness, God chooses this as the time to cut the line of Ithamar off completely from the priesthood, in order to fulfill his covenant given to Phinehas. This first begins to manifest itself a few verses after Eli speaks to Samuel. "The time is coming when I will cut short your strength and the strength of your father's [that is Ithamar's] house... And what happens to [Eli's] two sons, Hophni and Phinehas, will be a sign to him – they will both die on the same day. I will raise up for myself a faithful priest, who will do according to what is in my heart and mind. I will firmly establish his house, and he will minister before my anointed one always" (1 Sam 2:31, 34-35).

Though the context might lead the reader to believe that *Samuel* is the "faithful priest" (i.e., Eli was training the young Samuel who was serving before God in the temple), this cannot be the case because Samuel comes from the line of Korah (1 Chr 6:16, 22-28). John Gill correctly writes, "And I will raise up a faithful priest,... Not Samuel, as some, for he was not of the seed of Aaron, and of the priestly race" (Gill n.d.). Therefore, the *perpetual* priesthood could not go through Samuel. This is why the Scripture never refers to Samuel as a priest, even though he was trained by Eli, and as a Levite is said to serve (*sharath*) God in the temple (1 Sam 2:11, 18; 3:1, cf. 1 Chr 6:17; 1 Chr 16:4, and 37).[160]

Thus, this prophecy would be fulfilled in another way, as promised: through the line of Phinehas. The priestly covenant given to Levi and Aaron

---

[159] Stock connects 1 Sam 2:28 with Num 18:13-14 ("And you shall set the Levites before Aaron and his sons, and shall offer them as a wave offering to the LORD. Thus you shall separate the Levites from among the people of Israel, and the Levites shall be mine") and Mal 2:4 (Stock 1641: 24-25). See also Day (2003: 105, n. 46).

[160] Here the distinction between the Levites and the priests (of Aaron's line) must be strictly maintained (cf. Num 8:19; 16:10).

and his sons must finally be funnelled down through Phinehas, because it is through *him* that the covenant of a "perpetual priesthood" is given. Until now, this covenant was no more special to Phinehas than it was to his cousins through Ithamar his uncle. This is where the priest Zadok and the continuation of the priesthood through his seed comes sharply into focus (cf. 1 Kgs 2:35; Ezek 44:15-16, 48:11).

<u>Zadok</u>

Zadok was a contemporary of David and Solomon. He was a descendant of *Phinehas* son of Eleazar (1 Chr 6:3-15). Through him, the line of Phinehas would continue forever.[161] It is also in Zadok's day that the promise to Eli comes to pass. (This is why Barrick [1999: 214 n. 7] refers to the priestly covenant, or Levitical covenant, also as the "Zadokite Covenant").

Things had gone astray when Abiathar, a descendant of Eli and Ithamar (Ex 6:23; 1 Chr 6:3-15), became priest. After a long story, we read the conclusion, "[Solomon]... replaced Abiathar with Zadok the priest" (1 Kings 2:35). We learn why, "Solomon removed Abiathar from the priesthood of the LORD, fulfilling the word the LORD had spoken at Shiloh about the house of Eli" (1 Kings 2:27). But it was also clearly done to fulfill the covenant given to Phinehas as well. In this way, of the four sons of Aaron who originally served before the LORD as his priests (Nadab, Abihu, Eleazar, and Ithamar), only the descendants of Eleazar (who had only Phinehas as a son) remained as those who could legitimately serve God as his priests (cf. Neale and Littledale 1871: 377).

The importance of the Zakokian-Phinehasian line was confirmed again in the days of Ezekiel when it says, "This will be for the consecrated priests, the Zadokites, who were faithful in serving me and did not go astray as the Levites did when the Israelites went astray" (Ezek 48:11). And again, "But the priests, who are Levites and descendants of Zadok and who faithfully carried out the duties of my sanctuary when the Israelites went astray from me, are to come near to minister before me; they are to stand before me to offer sacrifices of fat and blood, declares the Sovereign LORD. They alone are to enter my sanctuary; they alone are to come near my table to minister before me and perform my service" (Ezek 44:15-16).[162]

---

[161] It continues today through the *spiritual* descendants of Zadok, in the new covenant Levitical priesthood of the church (see below, especially the discussion on Isaiah's treatment of the Levitical covenant).

[162] Cf. Rivkin 2003: 58.

The magnitude of the correct line continues to come to the surface in the Apocrypha and other inter-testamental sources. For instance 1 Mac 2:50, 54 says, "Now, my children, show zeal for the law, and give your lives for the covenant of our fathers... Phinehas our father, because he was deeply zealous, received the covenant of everlasting priesthood." Williamson (2000) traces the one "priestly covenant" history and line from the ordination of Aaron (Ex 28-29) to the "covenant of salt" (Num 18:19) to Phinehas (Num 25:10-13) to Zadok (1 Chr 6:3-15) and finally into the Maccabean priesthood (1 Mac 2:54). The genealogy is tracing out the *same* covenant. This is why we noted earlier several of these inter-testamental lineages as being implicit references to the Levitical covenant.

Another apocryphal book, *Sirach* (45:6-24), has so much to say about the covenant with the priests that several commentators have shown that it is viewed as *superior to the Davidic covenant* (!) by Ben Sira, the author of Sirach. Martha Himmelfarb gives us this important evaluation of this Jewish take on the covenant God made with the priests,

> Ben Sira notes that Aaron and his descendants are parties to a covenant that will endure 'as the days of heaven' (*Sir* 45:1). The source of the phrase is Psalm 9, a poem mourning the loss of the Davidic king: 'I will establish his line for ever / and his throne as the days of heaven' (Ps 89:30[29])... After Aaron, ben Sira turns to Phinehas and his zealous violence against idolatry at Baal Peor (Num 25:12-13). Ben Sira's focus is the covenant Phinehas receives as a reward for his zeal rather than the nature of the deed he performs (*Sir* 45:23-24). He notes the eternity of this covenant too and compares it to the covenant with David (*Sir* 45:24-25). The details of the comparison, which differ significantly in Greek and Hebrew, are not clear, but there can be no doubt about the point, the superiority of the priestly covenant to the Davidic covenant. (Cf. Skehan and Di Lella 1980: 510; Goodblatt 2006 102, n. 70).
>
> (Himmelfarb 2006: 35)

It makes perfect sense that this would be important to the inter-testamental Jews, because a major reason for going into captivity was the forsaking of this priestly covenant. That was Malachi's very point. In these ways, we see the covenant to Levi, and then to Aaron, and then to Phinehas confirmed and reconfirmed to their particular descendants through the line of Zadok. This all goes to show how long-lasting and epochal the Levitical covenant actually is.

Malachi is not alone in referring to the covenant of Levi in the Bible. Jeremiah (Jer 33:17-22[163]) and Nehemiah (Neh 13:29[164]) also talk about the

---

[163] "For this is what the LORD says: 'David will never fail to have a man to sit on the throne of the house of Israel, nor will the priests, who are Levites, ever fail to have a man to stand before me continually to offer burnt offerings, to burn grain offerings and to present sacrifices... If you can break my covenant with the day and my

"covenant with Levi." Jeremiah is especially decisive in helping us under-stand the stand-alone quality of this covenant, because he places the cove-nant of Levi side by side with the Davidic covenant, showing that in his mind both are equal yet separate epochal covenants.

The Davidic and Levitic covenants are related to one another as "cove-nants of salt" (cf. Lev 2:13 and Num 18:19 with 2 Chron 13:5). Van der Waal explains the meaning of a covenant of salt, "This is a perpetual institution, without which the covenant could not function. Therefore it is called a salt covenant. Compare Lev 2:13 ("salt of the covenant") in connection with the salt of the offerings; and 2 Chron 13:5 in connection with the covenant with David" (van der Waal 2003: 39).

Regarding the Levitical covenant as being separate and epochal from other OT covenants, Busenitz says, "The language of Jer 33:20-21 places its permanence alongside the Davidic Covenant, contending that it remains in force as long as the cycle of day and night remains" (Busenitz 1999: 188).

As a Premillennialist, Busenitz makes an even stronger claim about the Levitical covenant being a stand-alone covenant separate from the Mosaic covenant,

> The fact that it remains when the Mosaic Covenant was rendered obsolete speaks even louder for its standing as a separate covenant." He then makes an astute observa-tion which unless one adopts the position taken in this book seems to be true, "This passage has been a *crux interpretum* for expositors. It is especially difficult for those who hold an amillennial position in eschatology [since he says this priestly covenant "continues into the Millennium"]. The only resort for them is in allegorization of the text or the use of a dual hermeneutic. Simply stated, the passage assures that just as the Davidic covenant (2 Sam 7) is guaranteed by God's promise, so is the Levitical priesthood. But whereas the amillennial system can find room for the Son of David to reign now and in the future by transferring the earthly throne to the heavenly one at the Father's right hand, it is not so easy to find Levitical priests with their ministra-tions in the same framework" (p. 189).

Busenitz is correct that the *everlasting* priesthood must continue on into the future. If it doesn't, how can it be everlasting? Those who miss this cove-nant have no explanation for this. But Busenitz uses the Levitical covenant as justification for the reestablishment of a national Levitical priesthood in a

---

covenant with the night, so that day and night no longer come at their appointed time, then my covenant with David my servant--and my covenant with the Levites who are priests ministering before me--can be broken and David will no longer have a descendant to reign on his throne. I will make the descendants of David my servant and the Levites who minister before me as countless as the stars of the sky and as measureless as the sand on the seashore.'"

[164] "Remember them, O my God, because they defiled the priestly office and the covenant of the priesthood and of the Levites."

rebuilt temple during the millennium. We take a different view. Instead of going back to the types and shadows of a Jewish Levitical priesthood and a physical temple, we see the continuation of this covenant in the church of Jesus Christ who is our Great High Priest and the new covenant Temple.

It is our opinion that most people get hung up here because they read Hebrews and Jesus' priestly "genealogy" as coming from Melchizedek rather than the Levitical priesthood (Heb 5:6; 7:17). The assumption is that since Jesus is from a different priesthood, he does not have to "fulfill" Levitical sacrificial and ceremonial laws. Yet, no one actually believes that the OT ceremonies continue. Why not?

The whole reason Melchizedek comes up in Hebrews is precisely because Jesus *is* fulfilling Levitical covenantal laws, yet is not himself biologically descended from the tribe of Levi. There has to be an explanation for how Jesus could do this. The Jews repeatedly wrote that Messiah would come from Levi (cf. *Jub* 31:14; *TLevi* 8:11; *TBen* 11:2). But this is not the NT answer.

Hebrews understands the OT properly. It therefore makes a more astounding claim to Jesus' priesthood, because it recognizes that Jesus is in fact not biologically of the seed of Levi. The reason Jesus is able to fulfill ceremonial and sacrificial law is (ironically) because he is *not* from the order of Aaron. Aaron's covenant, like that of Moses', was a covenant of law that makes no man perfect. So Hebrews 7:11 says, "If perfection had been attainable through the Levitical priesthood (for under it the people received the law), what further need would there have been for another priest to arise after the order of Melchizedek, rather than one named after the order of Aaron?" Christ is from the "lineage" of Melchizedek because Scripture says, "The LORD has sworn and will not change his mind, 'You [the Lord of David; vs. 1] are a priest forever after the order of Melchizedek'" (Ps 110:4).

If our temple discussion has taught us anything, it is that the pattern shown to Moses on the mountain is a reflection of heavenly things. So, in entering a tabernacle *not* made with hands and offering the sacrifice of his body rather than that of an animal, Christ fulfills the legal requirements of the Levitical covenant (Heb 9:11-12) "once for all." The Levitical sanctuary and code were the shadow. Jesus is the substance. And if the substance comes, the shadows flee away.

This is the reason why bloody sacrifices, sprinklings, and the rest of it have ceased. They have been fulfilled in Christ. Now, we serve not in the old way of the law, but in the new way of the spirit. This is exactly the point of Colossians 2 (where the circumcision-baptism connection comes up) when it concludes, "When you were dead in your sins and in the uncircumcision of your sinful nature, God made you alive with Christ. He forgave us all our sins, having cancelled the written code, with its regulations, that was against us and that stood opposed to us; he took it away, nailing it to the cross" (Col 2:13-14).

Paul did not write this as a proof-text for baptism replacing circumcision. It is simply there to show that the shadow of the law is fulfilled in Christ. We serve God as new covenant Levitical priests; priests born not of natural lineage, but of the Spirit. This is where Isaiah's discussion of the Levitical covenant is so important.

The third portion of Isaiah's prophecy (chs. 56-66) has the priestly covenant as the beginning and ending of a giant chiasm (Isa 56:3-8; cf. Matt 21:13-14 and Isa 66:19-21; cf. 1 Pet 2:9).[165] This makes the Levitical covenant very important to Isaiah. Though not called "the covenant of Levi," the chiasm makes it clear that this is what he is referring to. Isaiah 56:3-8 says,

> Let not the foreigner who has joined himself to the LORD say, "The LORD will surely separate me from his people"; and let not the eunuch say, "Behold, I am a dry tree." For thus says the LORD: "To the eunuchs who keep my Sabbaths, who choose the things that please me and hold fast my covenant, I will give in my house and within my walls a monument and a name better than sons and daughters; I will give them an everlasting name that shall not be cut off." And the foreigners who join themselves to the LORD, to minister to him, to love the name of the LORD, and to be his servants, everyone who keeps the Sabbath and does not profane it, and holds fast my covenant-these I will bring to my holy mountain, and make them joyful in my house of prayer; their burnt offerings and their sacrifices will be accepted on my altar; for my house shall be called a house of prayer for all peoples." The Lord GOD, who gathers the outcasts of Israel, declares, "I will gather yet others to him besides those already gathered."

It appears that this passage finds its fulfillment in Christ during Passover Week inside *the temple*. Matt 21:13 says, "'It is written,' he said to them, 'My house will be called a house of prayer,' but you are making it a 'den of robbers.'" This is taken in part from Isa 56:7. Beale comments on Jesus' cleansing of the temple in Matthew 21,

> Jesus' violent act in the temple would briefly have stopped the offering of sacrifices by shutting down the procedure by which animals were bought and sacrificed. If the temporary ceasing of sacrifices is to be inferred to any degree from the passage, then in performing this action, Jesus would have been indicating that the temple's purpose in offering sacrifices for forgiveness was passing away and that the temple was awaiting judgment.
>
> (Beale 2004b: 179)

---

[165] For different proposals on the chaism, see Oswalt 1998: 462-465.

Matt 21:14 goes onto say, "The blind and the lame came to him at the temple, and he healed them." This healing of sick people in front of the temple is extremely significant in light of the same section of Isaiah 56, which teaches that foreigners and eunuchs will bind themselves to serve the LORD. But this comes within the context of these same foreigners and eunuchs becoming *priests* as they "minister" before the LORD. So Beale continues,

> Directly after this episode, those who were forbidden to enter the temple because of their deformity were now accepted by Jesus: the 'blind and the lame came to Him in the temple, and He healed them' (21:14). This suggests further that he is beginning to clear the way for the eschatological temple, since the Old Testament prophesied that in the future sanctuary eunuchs and other outcasts could worship even together with Gentiles. That which was formerly unclean will be considered clean for worship in the true temple (Is. 56:3-8).

Some of the very last words of Isaiah most certainly concern the NT fulfillment of *this* covenant (and also chiastically inform the meaning of Isaiah 56),

> I will set a sign among them, and I will send some of those who survive to the nations-- to Tarshish, to the Libyans and Lydians (famous as archers), to Tubal and Greece, and to the distant islands that have not heard of my fame or seen my glory. They will proclaim my glory among the nations. And they will bring all your brothers, from all the nations, to my holy mountain in Jerusalem as an offering to the LORD -- on horses, in chariots and wagons, and on mules and camels,' says the LORD. 'They will bring them, as the Israelites bring their grain offerings, to the temple of the LORD in ceremonially clean vessels. And I will select some of them also to be priests *and Levites*," says the LORD (Isaiah 66:19-21).

Augustine writes about the fulfillment of this passage,

> God promised that from among them He would choose for Himself priests and Levites, which also we see already accomplished. For we see that priests and Levites are now chosen, not from a certain family and blood, as we originally the rule in the priesthood according to the order of Aaron, but as befits the new testament, under which Christ is the High Priest after the order of Melchisedec, in consideration of the merit which is bestowed upon each man by divine grace. And these priests are not to be judged by their mere title, which is often borne by unworthy men, but by that holiness which is not common to good men and bad.
>
> (Augustine, *City of God* 20.29)

In this way the covenant of Levi continues on forever, in the ordaining of Gentile Levitical priests in the new covenant. The way these Gentiles are ordained is by undergoing the baptism-clothing ceremony of the priesthood, which was typified in the laws of the Levitical covenant in Exodus 29:4-9, but which are fulfilled now when we are baptized into Christ. We will have more to say about this in Part V when we look at the inclusion of Gentiles, eunuchs, women and others into the new covenant priesthood.

Jews and the Priestly Covenant

Now that our study of the explicit biblical passages that talk about the Levitical covenant is complete, we want to mention here that this priestly covenant is not only attested as a separate covenant from the Mosaic covenant by Christians. Jews from as long ago as the Tannaitic period (70 – 200 A.D.) talked about this as a covenant. Lawrence Schiffman discusses several commentaries in this regard.

In the Tosefta (the earliest commentary and supplement to the *Mishnah*) we find that "God's covenant with the descendants of Aaron to provide them the twenty-four priestly emoluments [gifts] is the subject of *t. Halla 2:7*. Behind this lies the wider concept that there is a covenant with the sons of Aaron giving them eternal priesthood" (Schiffman 1987: 291).

In the Tannaitic Midrashim *(Mek Pisha' 1)*—besides the Abraham covenant (i.e. "the covenant of circumcision") and the Sinaitic covenant—you come across the "priestly covenant." On this commentary Schiffman says,

> The priestly 'covenant of salt,' a biblical expression denoting a permanent covenant, is to be eternal [and is] based on citation of Numbers 18:19. Indeed, this covenant is singled out along with that of Sinai as being unconditional, as opposed to those pertaining to the Land of Israel, the Temple, and Davidic kingship *(Mek. 'Amaleq 2)*. While the Land of Israel, the Temple, and Davidic kingship can be taken away temporarily as a consequence of the transgressions of Israel, the Torah and the priestly status of the sons of Aaron can never be cancelled, even temporarily.
>
> (Schiffman 1987: 294-295)

Then there is *Sifre Num 117-119*, which repeatedly mentions the covenant God made with Aaron. Here we see that,

> Aaron's covenant is greater than that of David. Whereas David can only devolve his kingship on those of his descendants who are righteous, the Aaronide pedigree of priesthood can be passed on even to those who are not righteous. This difference results from the nature of the priestly office, which is representative of Israel and not dependent on the character of the individual priest. Further, we learn that God also entered into a covenant promising the Levites that they would serve before him eternally.
>
> (Schiffman 1987: 295)

For the Jewish Rabbis, the priestly covenant was viewed as a separate and important covenant alongside of the Noahic, Abrahamic, Mosaic, and Davidic covenants mentioned in the OT. It is high time that the church of to-day recaptures this covenant in their systematic discussions of the Bible.

Covenant of Levi and Baptism

We want to bring Part IV to a conclusion by mentioning an interesting fact about the seemingly irrelevant subject of ancient Jewish marriages. Ancient (and even modern) Jewish weddings had deep baptismal associations. This gives us insight into the meaning of baptism today.

Jewish marriages are broken up into two stages. The first is the betrothal stage where the bride price is paid. The second is when the bridegroom returns for the marriage ceremony. One of the steps taken during the betrothal stage was/is a *mikveh* baptism. Both the bride and the bridegroom would undergo this mikveh. Rabbi Isidore Epstein translated part of the Babylonian Talmud that pertains to this.

> And how do we know that the service of the son of a divorced woman or a *haluzah* is [retrospectively] fit? – Said Rab Judah in Samuel's name, Because Scripture saith, *and it shall be unto him, and to his seed after him, [the covenant of an everlasting priesthood]*: this applies to both fit and unfit seed. Samuel's father said, [It is deduced] from the following: *Bless, Lord, his substance [helo], and accept the work of his hands*: accept even the profaned [*hullin*] in his midst. R. Jannai said, [It is deduced] from this: *And thou shalt come unto the priest that shall be in those days*: now, could you then imagine that a man should go to a - But this [must refer to one who] was [originally assumed to be] fit, and then became profane.
>
> How do we know that the service of a man with a blemish is [retrospectively] invalid? – Said Rab Judah in Samuel's name: Because Scripture saith, *Wherefore say, Behold, I give unto him my covenant of perfection*: when he is perfect, but not when he is wanting. But *shalom* [peace] is written! – Said R. Nahman: The *waw* of *shalom* is broken off [in the middle].
>
> (Mas Kiddushin 66b)

Curiously, the passages cited by Rabbi Judah include Num 25:12-13 and Deut 33:11, both of which we have seen in this chapter pertain to the Levitical covenant. Phil Howell interprets the meaning of the Talmud and these passages. "Here Moses is recounting God's words towards the tribe of Levi, the tribe from which the Priests and temple workers would come. God will bless and accept the hands of the one who is baptized... These verses relate water baptism with the Messiah and priesthood" (Howell 2005: 70).

We are not claiming here that Numbers 25:12-13 and Deut 33:11 themselves talk about baptism. Rather, we are showing how the Talmud justifies the *mikveh* of a bride and groom based upon the *Levitical covenant*. In other words, the relationship of baptism to the Levitical covenant goes back hundreds and thousands of years in some circles.

Perhaps this is yet another significance of Christ's and our baptism. As the bridegroom, Jesus underwent a mikveh. As the bride of Christ, his people also undergo the mikveh baptism. This is done for each other as part of the betrothal before the great consummation day, the marriage and wedding supper of the Lamb.

Though Hywel Jones probably did not have this in mind when he explained the meaning of Malachi 2, it is probable to us that this is part of the fulfillment that takes place here. For it is not Christ alone (i.e., the "seed") who is in mind in Malachi, but also his priestly *servants* who are given to him as a gift by God (John 6:39; 10:29; cf. Num 8:19) to serve at his side. But the bride of Christ is not a mere Levite. For we are allowed now to enter into the Holy Place itself as we boldly approach the throne of grace through the Lord Jesus Christ.

Conclusion

The phrase "covenant of Levi" is important to our study of the covenants. Since Levi came over 400 years before Moses was born, calling it the "covenant of Levi" rather than the "covenant of Aaron" or the "covenant of Phinehas" or even the "covenant of Zadok" proves conclusively that this covenant is *not* an addendum to the Mosaic covenant. There are several covenants tightly woven together in the tapestry of the Pentateuch. Adam, Noah, Abraham, Moses, and Levi (perhaps even the roots of the Davidic covenant; cf. Gen 49:9-11; Deut 17:14-20) are all here. So Williamson says,

> The priestly covenant was closely related to the Mosaic covenant, serving the same general purpose: the priests facilitated the maintenance of the divine–human relationship between Yahweh and Abraham's descendants... the priestly and Mosaic covenants, *while remaining distinct, run in parallel with one another, and are closely related in purpose:* the perpetuity of the relationship between God and Israel [emphasis added].
> (Williamson 2000)

This in turn means that it is probably not appropriate to equate the tabernacle with the *Mosaic* covenant. Moses has his own "tabernacle" upon which the Mosaic covenant was cut. That sanctuary is Mt. Sinai. Since the actual tabernacle belongs to the priests and since the priestly covenant actually existed prior to Moses' birth, it is probable in our estimation that this is the sanctuary of the priestly covenant.

We have seen that there is a history in the church of identifying the Levitical covenant as a separate covenant, worthy of discussion in the great covenants of the OT. Aaron (rather than Moses), Phinehas (rather than Ithamar), and Zadok (rather than Abiathar) are the specific men through whom God chooses to give the inheritance of the Levitical promise. This parallels the way that Isaac (rather than Ishmael) and Jacob (rather than Esau) inherit the covenantal promise first given to Abraham. In both cases we see God confirming the same covenant with men who come later, yet are from the original seed of the covenant head.

This Levitical covenant is absolutely necessary to ensure that the people would understand the work of the Seed and his servants (or bride) to come must be *priestly* work. Christ's priestly work is *covenantal* work. Without this covenant, such an understanding would be blurry at best. But it is also important to note that this Seed would come from a different line than Levi;[166] through Melchizedek - the man that Levi paid tithes to in Abraham (Heb 7:9, 11; Ps 110:4). It is through this lineage that the priestly covenant is actually kept and fulfilled by Christ.

Finally, we can see that baptism becomes codified in law as part of *this* covenant. It is in the establishing of a laver outside of the tabernacle (Ex 30:18) that the idea of baptism—as the first necessary sacrament for entering the sanctuary of God—becomes crystal clear for the first time in redemptive history. Up until this point it was not so easy to see. But in the coming of the priestly code, such a procedure becomes as clear as the glassy sea that surrounds the throne of heaven. As we will see in the next Part, this has direct bearing upon the circumcision/baptism connection. The Abrahamic covenant is not the place to go to decide ultimate questions about baptism.

It is here, in the Levitical covenant, that baptism is first regulated in sacramental form as a permanent and lasting ordinance in the OT (Ex 29:4). This is the rite that Jesus fulfills at his own baptism. The Christian rite therefore flows out of the ordination ceremony of the priest, as we become Levitical priests of the new covenant, servants who are baptized into Christ. Thus, is it here—in *BAPTISM*, and not in circumcision—that NT baptism has its OT covenantal counterpart.

---

[166] There is perhaps evidence that Christ is biologically descended from Levi! If Mary and Elizabeth are cousins (Luke 1:36), and if Matthew is tracing Jesus' kingly heritage through Joseph's maternal grandfather while Luke is tracing it through Joseph's father rather than from Mary as is so often assumed (see Nettlehorst 1988), then it is possible that Christ was from the tribe of Levi on his mother's side. But since it is through the father that the legality of a line matters, this is rather beside the point.

Part V - Implications for Christian Baptism

It is time to synthesize and apply the fruits of this study to more practical matters. We are now able to make an informed decision as to the proper recipients, the mode, and the meaning of baptism. We'll work from the last of these to the first.

Meaning of Baptism

Baptism *means* a great many things. It signifies to us that God will not leave his people drowning in a floody wave. Instead, he will raise us up [up out of the water] with him at the last day. When Noah was baptized, he did not die like the rest of mankind. He made it through safely in the Ark. When Israel was baptized, they did not perish like Pharaoh and his army in the baptismal flood of God's wrath. Rather, they crossed safely to the other side. Thus, baptism signifies to God's people that they have escaped *the ordeal of God's judgment* through faith in Jesus Christ.

Escape from judgment is made possible because we have the forgiveness of sins. Through faith we are baptized into Christ's bloody tide, and thereby cleansed of our sins. Escape and forgiveness are as distinct as the baptisms that represent them. The former is understood from our water baptism. The later is understood from Christ's second baptism.

This second baptism corresponds to the sprinkling baptisms of the OT. There were many sprinkling baptisms in the Levitical Law. Most of them were associated with blood, but a few were also done with water (cf. Num 8:7; 19:18-19).[167] *All* signified purification. In line with these kinds of baptisms, the prophet said that a time was coming when,

---

[167] J. Ligon Duncan has an excellent series on covenant theology available at the present time online (see Bibliography). His seventh lecture is called "The Reformed Doctrine of Baptism and New Testament Practice." In this lecture he goes through almost all of the OT legal baptisms, actually calling them *baptisms!*

    This lecture follows right in line with the arguments we are giving here for baptism as something found in the Law. It is rare to find this acknowledgement in the literature. The only problem we would find is that he entirely misses the correct understanding and significance of the only legal baptism that matters for *Christian* baptism: Ex 29:4. He calls it (along with Ex 40:12 and Num 8:7) a "repeatable baptism." (Ex 40:12 is the same rite as 29:4, but Num 8:7 is not the same, since it is given to an entirely different group of people—namely the Levites rather than the sons of Aaron). Though it may have been repeated *throughout the generations,* it most certainly was *not* repeated *for an individual.* The other washings that take place prior to entering the sanctuary (cf. Ex 30:19-21; Lev 16:4) were not the same ritual as the one in Ex 29:4; 40:12.

    This, of course, colors his theology as we have seen with Jay Adams and others. It keeps him in the "sprinkler system." For some reason, even though many paedobaptists have seen baptism in the OT and applied (incorrectly) the mode of the OT to the NT, they have not done so on the more general level of *who receives* the mode. If they were consistent, they would see that it was not infants, but adults who received OT legal priestly baptisms.

25I will sprinkle clean water on you, and you will be clean; I will cleanse you from all your impurities and from all your idols. 26 I will give you a new heart and put a new spirit in you; I will remove from you your heart of stone and give you a heart of flesh. 27 And I will put my Spirit in you and move you to follow my decrees and be careful to keep my laws.

(Ezek 36:25-27)

Notice that the sprinkling of water is clearly associated with cleansing, with sin, with the new heart, and with the Spirit that comes into us.[168] The problem we have had thinking about baptism is that water baptism is always closely associated in the NT with repentance and faith (Acts 2:38, 8:12, 9:18 etc.). Even the baptism of Christ had repentance close at hand.

But as we have seen, Christ gave another reason for baptism. Yet, this does not mean that cleansing from sin was dismissed by Christ as something that he did not have to bear for the sake of his people. Instead, this was reserved for his *second* baptism. We have noted these verses before. "Are you able to drink the cup that I drink, or to be baptized with the baptism with which I am baptized?" (Mark 10:38). "I have a baptism to be baptized with, and how great is my distress until it is accomplished" (Luke 12:50).

Many commentators try to soften the words here, suggesting that Jesus was just using baptism as a figure of speech. This comment is typical, "This is the first instance of 'baptism' being used metaphorically of suffering in our literature. 'Baptism' expresses Jesus' solidarity with sinners and his willingness to bear their judgment before God" (Edwards 2002: 323). There are several problems with this statement. First, Isa 21:4 (LXX) uses "baptism" metaphorically. It says, "My heart has gone astray and lawlessness has baptized me, my soul has come into terror." Therefore, this is not the first time baptism is being used metaphorically in our literature.[169] More to the point,

---

[168] There appear to be three events followed by three results in the passage quoted (four, if you count the next verse). The first is sprinkling of clean water, which is followed by becoming clean from all uncleannesses. The second is receiving a new heart, which is followed by a receiving a new spirit. The third is removing the heart of stone, which is followed by receiving a heart of flesh. These are separated in the Hebrew by the *vav* consecutive ("and"), which is translated either as a sequential ("and then") or consequential ("and so") relationship (Kelley 1992: 145). Since the language of "removing the heart of stone" and "giving a heart of flesh" is clearly cutting language rather than washing language (sprinkling water will not result in the removal of a heart of stone), it is best to understand this as *sequential* differentiation. That is, God does several related but distinct things here rather than one identical thing said three different ways. The first thing God does is cleanse. The second thing he does is surgery. The third thing he does is give the ability and desire to follow him (vs. 27). This is important because it shows *similarity* but not *identity* between baptism and circumcision in this passage.

[169] Another interesting example of this is Deborah's song (Judges 5). The song gives a very different perspective on the events of the battle of Barak over Sisera's army from the one described in chapter 4. It uses the motif of the Exodus. From Mt. Sinai to the chariots that drown in the "torrent Kishon," there are many exodus images employed to explain the battle in theological terms, even though it is clear that there was no "torrent Kishon" in

it might be true that Jesus was speaking metaphorically, were his death not a *literal* sprinkling in blood and water.

Christ's death baptism was the fulfillment of the *sprinkling* baptisms of the Old Testament. The pouring of the Spirit at Pentecost is the outworking of this in the new covenant. This is why it is written of Christ's death, "One of the soldiers pierced Jesus' side with a spear, bringing a sudden flow of blood and *water*" (John 19:34). Obviously, there was not enough to be immersed. But it is quite easy to see how the mode of sprinkling could be associated with this baptism.

We have been sprinkled with his blood if we have faith in Jesus Christ. This is purely an act of grace and each time we remember our baptism, we must think of the forgiveness of our sins that comes from the Spirit's baptism. In this way, *cleansing* is high on the list of meanings given to baptism.

But when we are baptized *in water*, it teaches us most of all that we are now made fit vessels through the *sanctifying and washing effects of those waters* (Eph 5:26), to serve before God as his priests. Baptism is our *ordination* ceremony into the priesthood, and every believer needs to grasp the practical implications of this important truth. When we are baptized, God expects us to behave as holy, sanctified priests who serve his holy sanctuary (i.e., Christ and the Church; cf. John 2:21; 1 Cor 6:19; Eph 2:21) as new creations in obedience and purity. Our obedience is obligatory.

Mode of Baptism

Earliest Christian Evidence

Christians have debated the *mode* of baptism for centuries. Most of the Church has concluded that sprinkling is the appropriate mode for the rite. This is because they have confused OT baptismal ceremonies. But archaeological studies have demonstrated that the earliest churches had pools, fit best for the immersion of the disciple in a body of water.[170]

There is also evidence from the writings of the earliest Christian sources that something like immersion was the practice of NT Christians. For example, The *Didache* (120 A.D.) teaches,

---

the battle in Ch. 4! The song therefore employs baptism in a symbolic manner. Like the Red Sea baptism that drown Pharaoh and his chariots, this battle was another baptism into death for the enemies of God.

[170] For more, see two similar studies; one done by a Baptist (Buhler 2004), the other by two paedobaptists (Stander-Louw 2004).

And concerning baptism, baptize this way: Having first said all these things, baptize into the name of the Father, and of the Son, and of the Holy Spirit, *in living water*. But if you have no living water, baptize into other water; and if you cannot do so in cold water, do so in warm. But if you have neither, pour out water three times upon the head into the name of Father and Son and Holy Spirit."

(*Didache* 7:1-3)

F. Gavin concludes from this, "It is clear that the *Didache* contemplates as normal, baptism by immersion in living water" (Gavin 1969: 42).

Almost certainly referring to baptism, the *Shepherd of Hermes* (late 1st – 2nd century A.D.) says several things. "I have heard from certain teachers that there is no other repentance beyond that which occurred when we descended into the water and received forgiveness of our previous sins" (*Mandate* 4.3). Referring to the church as a "tower being built upon the waters out of shining square stones," he says that each stone was "dragged from the deep" and "placed in the building just as they were" (*Vision* 3.2). Picking up the same metaphor, he later asks, "Why did the stones come up from the deep, and why were they put into the building?" The answer is, "It was necessary for them to come up through water in order to be made alive, for otherwise they could not enter the kingdom of God. . . So even those who had fallen asleep received the seal of the Son of God. . . The seal, therefore, is the water; so they go down into the water dead and they come up alive. . . they went down into the water, and came up again. . . this is why they came up with them and were fitted together with them [the Apostles] into the structure of the tower" (*Parable* 9.16).

Another of the earliest works we have is the *Canons of Hippolytus* (circa 220 A.D.). It is also clear from this work that the mode of the early church was immersion. "Let them have them to go to the water of a clean and running stream"... "In the following way let them be baptized, when they come to the water which should be both clean and flowing" ... "women shall loose their hair, and they shall be forbidden to wear their ornaments and their gold; and none shall go down having anything alien with them into the water" (*CHipp*, ch. 19-21).

In the Pseudepigrapha (which are usually overlooked in discussions concerning baptism, but which are *invaluable* because of their early date and Christian redaction), book's six and seven of the *Sibylline Oracles* (both 2nd Century A.D.) explain that Jesus was not sprinkled. "I speak from my heart of the great famous son of the Immortal, to whom the Most High, his begetter, gave a throne to possess before he was born, since he was raised up the second time according to the flesh, when he had washed in the streams of the river Jordan, which moves with gleaming foot, sweeping the waves" (*SibOr* 6:1-5). Again, "You did not recognize your God, whom once Jordan washed in its streams, and the spirit flew like a dove" (*SibOr* 7:66-67). The *Odes of Solomon* (late 1st or early 2nd century A.D.) recall when "The dove fluttered over the head of our Lord Messiah" and "the chasms were submerged in the submersion of the Lord" (*OdesSol* 24:1, 7).

Jewish Roots as Witness

Strikingly, immersion was (and is to this day) the practice of the Jews. In *Fragments of a Zadokite Work* (1st century B.C.), it notes how Levitical purifications were to be done. "As to being cleansed in water. No man shall wash in water (that is) filthy or insufficient for a man's bath" (*Zad*, 12).[171]

Jewish Proselyte baptism (from which many people think John the Baptist was borrowing), dating from at least around a couple of centuries before Christ (Katzenelson argued for a date in the Persian period – see Gavin: 37), did not arise out of thin air. They took their practice straight from the Levitical Law (especially Lev 14:9 and the like).[172] There are many surviving commentaries on proselyte baptism from the Tannaitic period (the first and second centuries A.D.).

For example *m. Sotah* 12:b, tells us that Pharaoh's daughter went down to the river "to wash off the defilement of her heathen descent" (cf. *m. Pesahim* VIII.8). *Yeb.* 47 and *Gerim* 1 (a manual *On Proselytes*) each give parallel instructions on what to do with proselytes. First there is the presentation and examination of the candidate. Next comes the instruction of the candidate. This is followed by a circumcision (meaning baptism did not replace circumcision, see below) after which the candidate is "brought to baptism" (*Yeb* 47 a, b). He is completely naked, but is soon "covered with water to his genitals" (*Gerim* 1).[173] Then, "He immerses himself and when he comes up he

---

[171] In the Talmud they said the same thing. Erub 4b, "Since it is written in Scripture: Then he shall bathe all his flesh (Lev 14:9) [its follows] that there must be no interposition between his flesh and the water; In water implies, in water that is gathered together [lit. mikveh]; all his flesh implies, water in which all his body can be immersed [lit. 'goes up in them']" (see also Pes. 109a and Suk 6a).

[172] See Gavin: 55. Gavin's conclusion regarding the practice of the early church is spot on. "How significant this estimate of the proselyte's status is, and how thoroughly it penetrated every aspect of the rules in regard to proselytes, is of profound importance for the interpretation of characteristically Christian views of the place and function of Christian Baptism. In short, for the interpretation of early Christian belief and practice in regard to Baptism we need look no farther than contemporary Rabbinic Judaism" (p. 58).

[173] See also the summary on proselyte baptism in Kim 2004: 98.

is in all respects an Israelite" (*Yeb* 47b), or "he immerses himself, and when he comes up they address him (with) 'comforting words'" (*Gerim* 1).

Mikwaoth VIII.5 relates how a master had to lay his hand upon his slave if the slave was baptized in which case, "his hand would go under the water too, to avoid invalidating the rite by reason of an 'element of separation.'" A *tebilah* (purificatory bath) had to be of "living water" if possible, "and sufficient in quantity to allow complete immersion of the body" (Gavin 1969: 37; cf. 4Q266ᵃ 8 III, 10-11; 4Q270ᵉ 6 IV, 20). There was even a difference of opinion between Bet Hillel and Bet Shammai as to how much "artificial" (or drawn) water would invalidate a *tebilah*. Those differences were not about sprinkling vs. immersion, but unclean vs. clean water during the immersion. The Puritan Andrew Willet, writing in 1633 comments on a view held by a turn of the millennium Rabbi,

> They were washed, not only their hands and feet, as in their daily ministrie, chap. 40:33. but in their whole bodie, as thinkesth Rabbi Salomon [Jarchi - 1040-1105 AD]: Because their first consecreation required a more solemne oblation, and washing, than their daily ministration... And this washing was a figure of Christ's baptisme, who went into the water when he was baptized, Matth. 3.
> (Willet 1633: 547-48)[174]

The *Targum of Jonathan* (written from the second temple period through the early Middle-Ages) says that temple baptisms took place in "four measures of living water."[175] At Qumran we find, "He cannot be cleared by mere ceremonies of atonement, nor sanctified by immersion in lakes or rivers, nor purified by any bath" (1QS III, 4; cf. V, 13).

Josephus refers to assembling together, clothing in white veils, and "bathing their bodies in cold water" (Josephus, *Wars* 2.129). It seems obvious that this was needed because the whole body was being immersed.

The Temple's "sea of cast metal" (1 Kgs 7:23) was vastly larger than the tabernacle laver, probably for the practical reason of performing multiple immersions. All of this evidence led I. Abrahams to conclude almost 100 years ago, "It seems to me that there is no adequate ground for doubting that Jewish baptism in the first century was by total immersion" (Abrahams 1911: 612). Indeed. The same Jewish practice continues today.

A Jewish Sibylline Oracle explains how to forestall judgment. "Wash your whole bodies in perennial rivers" (*SibOr* 4:165). One commentary re-

---

[174] See also John Gill, Exposition of Exodus 29:4.

[175] *Targ. Jon.*, http://www.tulane.edu/~ntcs/pj/pjex28-30.htm

lates this to John the Baptist, though the oracle was written prior to John. "The most obvious parallel to the baptism of *SibOr* 4 is provided by John the Baptist, who also preached a baptism of repentance in the face of imminent eschatological destruction. Baptism and eschatology are also linked in the Ebionite and Elcasaite sects (*PseudClemRec* 1.54-65; Hippolytus, *Ref* 9, Ephiphanius, *AdvHaer* 19, 30)" (Collins 1983: 388).

<u>Passing Through Waters</u>

Then there is the idea common in ancient literature of people having to pass through the waters on their way to the other-world. Interestingly, these are all *immersions*. Adela Collins explains that "The journey passes through a river of fire into heaven, where the seer must be immersed three times in Lake Acherusia[176]" (Collins 1979: 94; see *The Book of the Resurrection of Christ* (Bartholomew). So we read in the *Vision of Paul* (31-32) of a "river of fire, and in it a multitude of men and women immersed up to the knees, and other men up to the navel, and others even up to the lips, others moreover up to the hair." Again in the *Revelation of Paul* there is a "bubbling river" beyond the Acherusian lake where "a great multitude of both men and women who had been cast into it, some up to the knees, others up to the navel, and many even up to the crown of the head." They had been cast there because of their "unrepenting in fornications and adulteries."[177] The *Testament of Isaac* records a "river of fire... throbbing, with its waves rising to about thirty cubits; and its sound was like rolling thunder. I looked upon many souls being immersed in it to a depth of about nine cubits. They were weeping and crying out with a loud voice and great groaning, those who were in the river. And that river had wisdom in its fire: It would not harm the righteous, but only the sinners by burning them" (*TIsaac* 5:21-26). These varied sources demonstrate beyond a shadow of a doubt how the ancients understood baptism. It was by immersion. It is not until later centuries that sprinkling (introduced because of the utter confusion regarding OT baptismal rites) was introduced into the church.

---

[176] Lake Acherusia sits before the city of Christ according to *The Apocalypse of Paul*. Plato (in *Phaedo*) sees it as a lake where the souls of dead go before they are reincarnated as animals. It sits next to a gigantic lake of fire boiling with water and mud.

[177] It continues that in another river (a river of fire), there was a multitude of many people. These "thieves, slanderers, and flatterers" were cast into the river of "immeasurable depth." This same scene is depicted almost verbatim in the *Apocalypse of the Holy Mother*, V.

Baptism by Immersion

It is intriguing to read John Calvin's views on the mode of baptism, "But whether the person being baptized should be wholly immersed, and whether thrice or once, whether he should only be sprinkled with poured water – these details are of no importance, but ought to be optional to churches according to the diversity of countries" (Calvin, *Institutes* 4.15.19).[178] We will start no war over mode, and I have no great objection to being tolerant here—depending upon circumstance—especially in light of harsh weather or persecution.

But... if we want to talk about the ideal *biblical* mode, then the answer has to be something akin to immersion. This is not because the word "baptize" means "immerse," for in actuality the word has a broad semantic range (though its most common meaning is immersion). Rather, it is because in the corresponding OT sacrament (Ex 29:4), the correct baptismal counterpart occurred as a *"rachats"*: a full body washing, as in what Bathsheba was doing on top of her house (2 Sam 11:2). This was also the word used to describe Naaman's baptism in the Jordan River (2 Kgs 5:10).

As already discussed, immersion is surely the plainest reading of the words, "he went up out of the water" in Matthew 3:16 (cf. Mark 1:8; Acts 8:39). It is also the simplest explanation for John's comment, "John [the Baptist] was baptizing at Aenon near Salim, *because water was plentiful there* [italics added]" (John 3:23).

Those with a sprinkling axe to grind will give reasons for why these passages cannot be immersions. But, when the proper OT counterpart is identified *correctly*, all of these arguments melt away like winter ice surrounding the Morning Glory pool at Yellowstone. When Jesus comes "out of the water," he becomes "The Land" upon which God will prepare his new creation. He is the antitype of the Ark that alone was atop the waters of the flood. The very act of appearing out of the water fulfills the land typology appearing in original creation, the flood, and the Sea/River crossings. None of these events were sprinklings (rain?). They were all dramatic epochal flood events where God poured out his wrath like water (cf. Hos 5:10).

Finally, we might add that immersion (and not sprinkling) is a perfect symbol to picture the salvation of the believer from the drowning wrath of God (Ps 18:16, 69:1-3; Jonah 2:3). Sprinkling baptisms don't signify this particularly well. Though we stay under the water for a moment, we do not lin-

---

[178] We have already noted that Meredith Kline (a paedobaptist) seems to think immersion is best to picture the ordeal of baptism. See Kline 1968: 83.

ger there, but are raised up with Christ to newness of life (Rom 6:3-4). Though there *were* sprinkling baptisms in the OT (this is surely where the idea came from in the first place), they differed vastly in meaning from the immersion of the priest. Sprinkling vs. immersion is the difference between cleansing for sin and cleansing for ordination. The former is taken care of in regeneration (sprinkling by the Spirit); the later is dealt with in the waters of Christian baptism. Figuring out the proper OT sign gives important yet clear biblical instruction on the mode of baptism.

Recipients of Baptism

The same thing can be said about the *recipients* of baptism. Of the three items being discussed in this chapter, this one has been far and away the most divisive in church history. It has been so divisive that Christians have murdered each other over it. We no longer live in times like that. Yet, the Christian church still stands divided over these deep waters, disagreeing over just who it is that should receive this sign of the new covenant.

The two main positions are that infants should receive the sign of baptism, or that they should not. It seems to us that at least two errors were made very early on in the development of the infant Baptist argument. The first is that children should be considered covenant members *in the new covenant* (cf. verses like Matt 19:14; 1 Cor 7:14 etc., contra the majority Baptist position that says they should not be considered covenant members from verses like Jer 31:31-34).

Covenant membership is the arena upon which both paedobaptistic *and baptistic* arguments have been staged in recent times. But this first error is the problem with *all* of our arguments. We believe it is a mistake to fight the battle on the field of covenant membership. In fighting on this arena, everyone has forgotten to look at the origin of baptism, and how this might inform our (and the NT) practice of the rite. It has also caused us to miss the covenantal relationship that Christian baptism has in the OT.

Because we cannot agree on who is in the covenant, this has caused the two sides to speak past each other for lo these many centuries. It is sort of like we are showing up to play a football game on two different fields. We all want to play the same game, but our opponents are actually nowhere in sight. But when the origins of baptism are taken into account, the question of who is or is not in the new covenant becomes a moot point. That is, whatever your conclusions are about infants being in the covenant, it really is irrelevant to the argument we are making from the OT. Whether you believe that only believers are in the new covenant, or if you argue from the continuity of the (proper) old covenant administration, the same result obtains. The next point makes this clear.

The second assumptive error of the paedobaptistic argument is the essential component. This assumption is that the old covenant had one—and only one—"membership" sign attached to it. That is, only one sign got an Israelite "in" to the covenant of grace. This has several sub-points. 1. This sign was circumcision. 2. The recipients of this sign were infants. 3. Since we believe in the continuity of the covenants, we must continue to give infants the sign, unless there is clear and convincing proof that the NT has abrogated it. This is the hinge upon which the whole of the infant Baptist argument turns.[179]

There are several counter-arguments that we will make to show the falsity of the assumption. First, it is not true to say that recipients of the sign of circumcision were "infants." Rather, they were "*male* infants." This is critically important, because no infant Baptist wants to say that little girl Israelites were left outside of the covenant. Yet, they never received "the sign of the covenant." So here we have some infants being in covenant without ever receiving the sign of the covenant. The assumption is imprecise.

Second, there is not just one covenant administration in the Old Testament covenant of grace. In another administration of the same covenant of grace (Noah), the children of Noah did not receive the sign until they were at least 100 years old (Gen 11:10). Yet, they were still in the covenant, even prior to receiving the sign (Gen 6:18). The conclusion is threefold. First, circumcision was not the sign of this covenant. Second, circumcision must not always be "the" sign of the covenant of grace in the OT. Third, receiving the sign is not always *immediately* necessary for covenant membership. It all depends upon the particular covenant administration, even in the OT. (Notice also how Noah seems to have waited 120 years from covenant initiation to

---

[179] The common language is therefore that baptism has "replaced" circumcision. The Belgic Confession (BC Art. 34) says, "Having abolished circumcision, which was done with blood, [Jesus Christ] established *in its place* the sacrament of baptism [emphasis added]." Paedobaptists today almost universally follow suit saying, "Those who subscribe to covenantal infant baptism maintain that baptism has now *replaced* circumcision as the mark of covenant membership, and that baptism's meaning and application are essentially the same as circumcision's in the Old Testament period [emphasis added]" (Ross 2003: 97), "Baptism *replaces* circumcision [emphasis added]" (Riddlebarger 2007), "*The rite of circumcision that once signified the benefits of Abraham's covenant has been **replaced** by baptism* [italics original, bold added]" (Chapell 2003: 17), "Baptism is the New Testament *equivalent* of circumcision [emphasis added]" (Wagner 1996: 4), "Baptism is the circumcision of the New Testament" (Murray 1980: 5), "Baptism *fulfills* circumcision [emphasis added]" (Leithart 2003: 89). In light of this evidence, Paul Jewett is certainly correct when he notices, "Paedobaptists... equate the two rites, as those every time the word 'circumcision' occurs in the Old Testament one might substitute 'baptism' and have a perfect theological fit" (Jewett 1978: 93).

the receiving of the covenant sign – Gen 6:3.[180] Also, Abraham and his son Ishmael were at least 13 years removed from the initiation of the covenant with the reception of the covenant sign – cf. Gen 16:16; 17:1; 15:18; 17:23).[181]

Too much is made by paedobaptists of Abraham, to the exclusion of the other covenant federal heads.[182] To make the Abrahamic covenant the first and last word on how we baptize in the NT is arbitrary, and does not arise out of a fully unified view of the Scripture. It is rather akin to a Dispensational reading of the Scripture, in that it ignores thousands of years of covenant history with the OT church prior to Abraham. (Baptists should take the force of this point very seriously, because they get charged by paedobaptists with being Dispensational in their interpretation of baptism. This is not entirely without justification in our opinion, since most baptistic arguments ignore even more history than the paedobaptists do. But the point is, paedobaptists do the same basic thing). The arbitrary nature of the paedobaptists hermeneutic is demonstrated in at least three specific ways.

First, God chose Abram because he was descended from the proper line (Gen 9:26). If Abraham was in the church, it was only because his ancestors were also in the church (Gen 3:21; 4:3 [cf. Heb 12:24]; 4:26; 5:24 [cf. Jude 1:14]; Gen 6:8; 9:26-27). Yet, they did not receive circumcision. But if circumcision is "the sign" of the old covenant and of its church, how can we really say that Adam and Noah were in the church in *any* sense? Were they not part of "the covenant" like Abraham? Were they not *really* in the church of the OT? If they were not in the church, then why was it so important for Abraham to come from their line? But if these people were in the church, and if they did not receive the sign of Abraham but another sign(s), this means that there is not just one sign of the Covenant of Grace in the OT.

The differences between the *Westminster Confession of Faith* and the *London Baptist Confession of 1689* at this point are illuminating. *Westminster*, and her paedobaptist authors, clearly has a bias towards Abraham. Meanwhile, the

---

[180] The idea in this verse is not that man will only live to be 120 years old, because after the flood men were living much longer than that. Rather, Noah preached to the people of the world for 120 years while he was building the Ark (see 2 Pet 2:5).

[181] If Gen 12:1-7 is viewed as the first cutting of the covenant with Abram (here God promises to Abram land, a great name, many descendants, and a seed), then the number of years increases to at least 24 years.

[182] Often the paedobaptists literature will talk about Abraham as if his is the primary and central covenant in Scripture. It is not the place to develop these thoughts here, but our contention is that "world" language which is used often in the NT is actually covenantal language stemming from *Noah* (For example, compare the language of John 3:16-17 with 1 Pet 3:20-21, 2 Pet 2:4-5, and 2 Pet 3:6). "Law" language refers to Moses rather than Abraham, and this language is very common in the NT (see Gal 3:17). Priestly and kingly language refers to yet other OT covenants. "Election" language actually has its origin with Adam and Eve, and prior to that in the covenant of redemption. Thus, it is simply not accurate to depict Abraham as the end-all covenant in the OT.

London Baptist Confession begins with Adam (compare *WCF* 7.5 with *LBC* 7.3). *WCF* is arbitrary, since it does not start at the beginning.[183] We ask, in as much as it pertains to baptism, which system has biased itself from the start against letting the whole of Scripture influence its theology?

Second, the church in its most mature form in Genesis did not even begin with Abraham, but his grandson Jacob and his twelve sons. It was *Jacob* whose name was Israel, not Abraham. Thus, if Adam and Noah were not really in the church, because it did not exist yet, the same must be true of Abraham. It would therefore not be technically correct to say that circumcision was the sign of entrance into the OT church.

Finally, the church of the OT is at *no stage* the mature church of the NT. So if you say that Adam and Noah were only typologically in the OT church (in order to argue that it is really acceptable to start the OT church with Abraham), you have shot yourself in the foot, because Israel also was only typologically in the church as well, because strictly speaking Jesus hadn't founded the church yet (or to put it another way, only in the NT does the church of redemptive history begin to flower).[184] This is why Jesus appoints 12 Apostles to sit along-side of the 12 sons of Jacob, as he begins the ushering in of his Kingdom.

In the NT, the induction sign is baptism. But such a radical change (from circumcision to baptism)—if that is what it is—cannot take into account the simple fact that baptism was *already present* in each of the OT covenants. It is arbitrary to say that baptism now replaces circumcision, when no one claims this happened in the OT, even though baptism was present prior to, during, and after circumcision.

Now we are ready to understand the full importance of the *Levitical* covenant. The Levitical covenant is just as much its own distinct covenant as the Abrahamic covenant. Both are separate administrations of the covenant of grace. It has its own head: Levi. It has its *own* sign. This sign is... baptism, at least as far as the ordination and induction rite of the federal head (i.e., the priest) is concerned. And it is *this* sign that Jesus Christ is receiving, and fulfilling, at his own baptism. And Christian baptism follows after the Lord's baptism. Our baptism does not, strictly speaking, follow the flood or the Red Sea or any other *sign*. It follows the Levitical ordination *sacrament*.

---

[183] One paedobaptist inadvertently makes the point for us. He says we need to get "back to the beginning" by "learning from *Abraham*." So, "let's start with Abraham then" [emphasis added]" (Green 1987: 10).

[184] We recognize here that Jesus takes his "church" language from the LXX of the OT. But the point is, Jesus is establishing something new or at least mature as compared to any OT form that the people of God took.

Our contention has been all along that baptism comes from the Old Testament (read "old *covenant*"), and that baptism comes from *baptism*. Baptism does not come from, is not akin to, and/or does not replace circumcision. It is not the fulfillment of circumcision. It is not the NT equivalent of circumcision. Antitypes come from types, not from things that are only sort of like them.[185] Do dogs come from cats, even though both are animals? The physical element is every bit as important as the spiritual meaning. Having this macro-evolutionist view of the change in sacraments (i.e. baptism is the new equivalent of circumcision) is not biblically justifiable.

Like the paedobaptist, our argument rises out of the *continuity* and *similarity* between the Old Testament covenants and the new covenant. This is very different from the approach usually taken by Baptists. In each OT covenant, baptism is there, because baptism is "the sign" of the new creation. In each of these OT covenants, God is creating something new. In the Levitical covenant, baptism is codified into a ritual or sacrament for a particular group of people within Israel, and this is to be a lasting ordinance throughout the generations.

But even Israel herself was baptized in the waters, in order to set her apart as a priestly nation (Ex 19:6). What need was there for Israel to receive the sign of baptism if she was still under the sign of circumcision? Or to put it another way, why should the sign of circumcision continue after Israel was baptized?

The answer is that even in the OT, the two rites served completely different functions. The fundamentally essential thing about water baptism is that it was there before, during, and after the sacrament of circumcision. Does this not tell us something about the relationship between the two? They never did, and still do not, replace one another, even in terms of covenantal initiatory equivalence.[186]

Though the *sign* of baptism was given to all Israelites, the *ritual* or *sacrament* was given only to the High Priest (in the Law). He now had to serve as a mediator between the nation and God. Does this mean the people could not

---

[185] Here we will simply note that circumcision and baptism have some things in common. Both signify cleansing. Both signify purity. Both signify being set apart. Kline even notes a relationship between the cutting off of all flesh in the covenant with Noah and the cutting nature of circumcision (Gen 9:11; 17:14). But similarity does not translate into equality and identity. Colossians 2:11-12 at best only demonstrates that the signs are similar. Circumcision is like the Sabbath sign of the Mosaic covenant in that both rites relate to "cutting off" (Gen 17:14; Ex 31:14). Both rites are related to the days of the week. Does this mean that the Sabbath replaces circumcision? For more, see Appendix Two.

[186] Nothing changed even by the time of Christ in Jewish practice. It is informative here to note how the Jews were giving *both* circumcision and baptism to proselytes, thus demonstrating how they viewed the two as connected, but positively *not* the same spiritual rite (see *Yeb* 47 a, b; *Gerim* 1, pgs. 143-44 above).

partake in the benefits of the Levitical covenant? Of course not. Rather, they were allowed to participate in sacrifices themselves, *because* of the sacrament of another. The thing about this priest was that he was already circumcised years before his baptism (just like Christ). Yet, it was not until he was baptized that he could enter into the privileges of this priestly covenant.

Circumcision has a NT counterpart, just like bloody sprinkling baptisms and animal sacrifices. All find their terminus in the *death of Christ*. When we receive a new heart, we are circumcised by the Spirit (Rom 2:29). Spiritual heart circumcision is the antitype of Jewish male circumcision. Water baptism is not. This was prophesied by Moses himself in Deut 30:6, "The LORD your God will circumcise your hearts and the hearts of your descendants, so that you may love him with all your heart and with all your soul, and live." Circumcision continues today, but in *spiritual* form. When the destination is arrived at, the need for the sacramental sign is finished.

The very fact that we are commanded to baptize in water means that the same is not true for all types of baptism. Christian baptism into the waters continues in physical form, as a sign and seal of the promise that God will wash us and sanctify us, even when we sin. This hope instills in the NT believer a confidence that his or her every day priestly ministry will be acceptable to God, because of Jesus Christ and faith in him. Once we are glorified, there will be no more need of baptism *as a sacrament* either. Yet, we will always be able to look back upon our baptism, and see that God's promises were faithfully carried out, even to the day of our redemption. There is a river in heaven to keep this always in our minds (Rev 22:1-2).

Thus, our argument for credobaptism actually turns the paedobaptist argument upon itself. This has not been done before in baptistic arguments. Since it was adults who were baptized in the older administration, since Jesus himself was an adult at his own baptism, and since all of the explicit NT references to baptism are adults, we need explicit evidence proving that things have changed from OT to NT. If we cannot demonstrate conclusive evidence of this fact, then we dare not change it.

This is the reason why we do not find infants being baptized in the NT. They never were in the OT sacramental counterpart. Perhaps this is why even Martin Luther[187] and Ulrich Zwingli[188] admitted at some point in their lives that infant baptism is nowhere to be found in the NT.

---

[187] Luther said, "There is not sufficient evidence from scripture that one might justify the practice of infant baptism at the time of the early Christians after the Apostolic period. But so much is evident that none may venture with a good conscience to reject or abandon infant baptism which has for so long a time been practiced"

Change between the OT and NT Baptism

There is evidence that some things have changed. Among these is *not* the inclusion of infants to now receive this sacrament. How can priests serve God as infants today, anymore than they could in the OT? Things stay as they always were for girls and Levitical infant boys. That is, our little children still receive the outward blessings of the covenant,[189] without receiving the induction sign, until they profess faith and are able to serve before God as priests. This follows the typical pattern of the Levitical infant boys. These boys were heirs to the Levitical priesthood, but they were not yet able to serve before God as his priest.

So what *has* changed? Let us go back to our list of qualifications for the Aaronic Ministry. In that list we saw the following seven items:

1. They had to be descended from Aaron (Ex 28:1).
2. They could not begin ministry until age 30 (Num 4:3; 47).
3. They (especially the High Priest) had to be called of God as was Aaron (Ex 28:1).
4. They had to be washed by one already a priest (Ex 29:9; Num 25:13).
5. They had to be without defect in several specific ways (Lev 21:16-23).
6. They had to be male (Num 3:15).
7. They began their ministry immediately after being baptized (Ex 29:1).

With Christ as our High Priest, these qualifications are fully met in him. Yet, he commands baptism, because the church is given as a gift to Christ, just as the Levites were given as a gift to Aaron (Num 8:19). Baptism continues the OT *idea* of ritual ordination, while changing the *circumstances* of the rite. So, what has changed?

(Luther, cited in Bainton 1952: 204). So much for *sola scriptura!* There is no evidence that Luther ever retracted the statement.

[188] Zwingli said, "Nothing grieves me more than at the present I have to baptize children, for I know it ought not to be done. If however I were to terminate the practice, then I fear that I would lose my prebend [a salary given by the state]... If we were to baptize as Christ instituted it then we would not baptize any person until he has reached the years of discretion for I find it nowhere written that infant baptism is to be practiced. However one must practice infant baptism so as not to offend our fellow man" (Zwingli, cited in Verduin 1964: 199). Zwingli did retract, but not because of any conviction of Scripture. Rather, it was because, like Luther, the politics of the day demanded that he not become a Baptist (Anabaptist).

[189] These blessings would include the hearing of the gospel regularly, participating in and receiving the benefits of the prayers of the saints, being surrounded by the fellowship of the believers etc. For differences of opinion on whether or not these children are actually *in* the covenant of grace, or merely stand in the shadow of the covenant of grace, compare Conner 2007: 41-51 (his view is that new covenant "children" only include the elect who have believed upon Christ, but that biological children of believers are in the shadow of the covenant) and Pratt 2003: 156-74 (his view is that the new covenant still has a physical component that includes more than the elect, but less than the whole world. Pratt does not believe that an infant is saved just because it is in the covenant).

First, *they had to be descended from Aaron.*[190] This is no longer true. Isaiah predicted this in the very last thing he ever wrote, "*I will select some of them [Gentiles] also to be priests and Levites,*" says the LORD" (Isa 66:19-21). This prediction came true. Thus, God tells his "elect, strangers in the world, scattered throughout Pontus, Galatia, Cappadocia, Asia and Bithynia" (1 Pet 1:1) that *they* [including Gentiles] are "a holy priesthood, offering spiritual sacrifices acceptable to God through Jesus Christ" (1 Pet 2:5).

Second, *they could not begin ministry until age 30.* We have examples of young and old alike being baptized in the NT. (For a special treatment on Timothy's Baptism, see Appendix 3). It seems to us that the NT testimony of age requirements follows the OT example at this point: all those baptized are conscious of their baptism. Thus, you might find a youth being baptized, but not an infant. You will find elderly people being baptized, but not infants.[191] It is up to the infant Baptist to come up with conclusive, explicit evidence (as we are doing in this section) that the OT law concerning the age of the priests (not to mention prophets and kings, which we have not looked at in any detail in this book) has changed to include infants. What priest has ever served as an infant? Until that time, we have no right to change the rite.

Third, *they had to be called of God.* This particular element remains, though there is an important change. In the OT, priests were called corporately by God, so that any who was qualified to serve, did serve—irregardless of professed faith. In the NT, priests are called individually, effectually, through the word, to believe in Christ. Thus, baptism always follows a profession of faith, because it is only through faith that one enters the kingdom of heaven.

Fourth, *they had to be washed by one already a priest.* This element has changed slightly. We do not believe there is evidence that just anyone can baptize another person. This is a rite that still belongs to the Community of Faith (the Church). It is always performed by Apostles or elders in the NT (elders in the NT correspond to the elders of Israel in the OT – Ex 3:16, 18:21 etc.). As such, it is proper that those doing the baptizing be ministers of the gospel (or elders in the church), and not laity. This follows the pattern set in the

---

[190] As we noted earlier, Christian baptism follows Christ's example, and it is best to correspond these things to the Aaronic priesthood. However, if we were to take the broader Levitical priesthood as the example (seeing a distinction between Aaronic priests and the broader Levitical priesthood), then certain of these six things would change slightly. For example, rather than being descended from Aaron, the qualification was to be descended from Levi. Rather than be baptized into service at age 30, the age became 25 (Num 8:24), etc. None of these things change the application of who may *now* be baptized.

[191] I have always found it curious that paedobaptists who bring household texts (cf. Acts 16:31; 18:8; 1 Cor 1:16 etc.) into the discussion refuse to baptize unbelieving *adults* who live with and are therefore under the authority

OT, with this slight change: ministers of the gospel are not priests *as* the Aaronic Priests were priests. This is not Romanism. That is, the NT teaches the priesthood of all believers. But the priesthood of all believers does not mean that everyone is a pastor, or called to service the assembled church. Therefore, laity do not have the official (here we mean "related to the office," having nothing to do with their own intrinsic worth) qualifications to baptize. God puts his servants in positions of authority in the church, and distinguishes them as teachers and preachers; when they serve the office, they are held doubly accountable, and are worthy of double honor. They are the ones who appropriately baptize disciples, according to both the Old and New Testament standards.

Fifth, *they had to be without defect, spot, or blemish.* This is no longer true. The baptism of the Ethiopian eunuch (Acts 8:27-39) is instructive on both this and the first point.[192] It is astonishing that this eunuch was reading the book of Isaiah, for as we have seen, Isaiah concludes with remarks that are quite pertinent to baptism. As soon as he finishes he asks Phillip, "Why shouldn't I be baptized?" Read in light of this particular qualification for baptism, the question takes on a whole new light. This man was blemished. According to Levitical law, he could not be baptized (besides the fact that he was also a Gentile). Phillip knows the truth of these things, and so he says "there is no reason." The eunuch immediately goes to the water for baptism.

Sixth (following our pattern from an earlier chapter, the fifth point will be last), *they had to be male.* This is no longer true. Acts 8:12 says that both men and women were baptized by the Apostles. Now they too serve before God as priests. This is why Paul says that in Christ there is no longer male or female (Gal 3:28).

How Long to Wait Until Baptism?

The seventh point brings up one final question about application. While paedobaptists insist that we are to baptize at a very young age,[193] many other Christians believe that baptism is sort of a "badge" of true faith. Thus, they

---

of believing children. For some reason "households" only go one way—towards the infants—and not towards older unbelievers in a household. This is arbitrary to say the least.

[192] It seems to us that the whole of Acts 8 is blowing several of the Levitical rules of baptism out of the water. Their fulfillment has come in Christ and as such they no longer pertain to the new covenant.

[193] Compellingly, paedobaptists do not baptize *only* 8 day old infants, as per the law (we'll grant them the change excluding females), even though this is what the law required (Lev 12:3). Though a council led by Cyprian (third century) declared that one need not baptize on the eighth day (see Epistles of Cyprian, 53.2), such a conclusion is completely arbitrary and totally unwarranted, because we do not find explicit examples of infants at *any time*

wait years and years to make the disciple prove that he/she is actually saved, serious about the faith, and right about all the important doctrines. But this fails to understand the meaning of baptism as an ordination into the priesthood. Baptism should not be the baptistic equivalent of confirmation. We do not want to make professing Christians serve God illegally.

Baptism is much more than what *we* do to prove to the world that we are saved. It is what *God* does to his priests, so that they may serve before him legally, biblically, and in sanctified purity (hence, it is a sacrament—or a means of grace—rather than a freewill offering, or bare memorial). It is more than our pledge of honor to him; it is God's pledge of good-will towards us.

Now, we should have some litmus test in place for the sake of the disciple that he or she believe the basics of the faith, and understand the purpose of baptism. Phillip did this with the Ethiopian Eunuch. But it did not take the eunuch years to pass the test. A test is probably more important with smaller children than with adults, but children are every bit as capable as professing real faith in Christ as are adults. So, this waiting around for years and years must be evaluated by the light of Scripture.

The seventh point is that ministry begins immediately upon baptism. Of course, the priests had to be of a certain age in order to perform his duties, and this at least speaks about the fact that priestly duties are *conscious* duties. But, there is not one instance of a long waiting time in either Testament. It is because of the OT practice that the eunuch story is the norm for today: "Repent and be baptized." It is not lawful to minister to God apart from baptism. So, it is actually very important that those who profess faith be baptized soon, because they cannot help but be priests as they serve God in the NT way. If we wish to be biblical, we must be honest about our practices, and seek to conform them to the text.[194]

CONCLUSION

Baptism points us forward, even as it keeps us remembering our past. Baptism teaches us about a mighty creation, and the new creation begun in Christ. Baptism shows us leaving the wilderness, and entering the Promised Land through the waters of the Jordan. Baptism shows us leaving the old world of sin, and entering the cleansed world through Noah's flood. Baptism shows us in our need to be cleaned in the washing basin in the courtyard of

---

being baptized. But if we could, wouldn't this support the need to do it on the *eighth* day? We see nowhere that we are allowed to change one part of the law arbitrarily, but not the other.

God's NT tabernacle, before we may enter the Holy Place. Isaac Watts sets our baptismal hope to poetry. He writes,

> There is a land of pure delight, where saints immortal reign;
> Infinite day excludes the night, and pleasures banish pain.
> There everlasting spring abides, and never with'ring flow'rs;
> Death, like a narrow sea, divides this heav'nly land from ours.
> Sweet fields beyond the swelling flood stand dressed in living green;
> So to the Jews old Canaan stood, while Jordan rolled between.
> But timorous mortals start and shrink to cross this narrow sea;
> And linger, shivering, on the brink, and fear to launch away.
> O could we make our doubts remove, those gloomy doubts that rise,
> And see the Canaan that we love with unbeclouded eyes;
> Could we but climb where Moses stood, and view the landscape o'er,
> Not Jordan's stream, nor death's cold flood, should fright us from the shore.
> (Watts, "There is a Land of Pure Delight")

Most of all, baptism allows us to be consecrated into the priesthood that is ours through Jesus Christ, so that we might serve before him, offering our bodies as living sacrifices in his holy temple. Is it any wonder that Augustine wrote, "Would ye know the Holy Ghost, that He is God? Be baptized, and ye will be His temple" (Augustine, *On the Creed*, 1.13).

Christian baptism is a wonderful gift that God has given to his people to confirm their faith in him. In baptism, the whole gospel is signified, remembered, and re-lived. The "out there" story becomes lived out in the community every time a new Christian is baptized. Baptism is a celebration, remembrance, and ministry of God to the community—a review of the very gospel that saved the person being baptized.

---

[194] An important book on this from a Baptistic perspective advocating the baptism of smaller children (but not infants) is Ted Christman's, *Forbid Them Not* (n.d.).

Appendix One
The Mode of Various Old Testament Baptisms

R ay Stedman recounts a long standing joke about baptismal mode,

> There is an old and rather tired story of a Presbyterian and a Baptist who were arguing this question. The Presbyterian said, "Tell me this. You're a Baptist. If a man goes into the water up to his knees, is he baptized?" The Baptist said "No, he is not." "Well if he goes in up to his waist, is he baptized?" "No, he's not." "If he goes in up to his shoulders?" "No." "Well, suppose he goes in clear up to the top of his head, is he baptized then?" "Yes!" the Baptist said. "Ah," said the Presbyterian, "you see, it's the water on top of the head that counts!"
>
> (Stedman 1970)

He goes on to say that this joke displays the foolishness of our arguments. Water is a symbol, and it is the symbol, not the mode, that matters. After putting this discussion into its proper OT context, we must confess that this study of baptism has convinced us—now more than ever—that immersion is the most faithful expression of Christian baptism. Calvin himself admitted, "Yet the word "baptize" means to immerse, and it is clear that the rite of immersion was observed in the ancient church."[195]

So many studies on the "proper mode of baptism" have been written that you could not fit them all in a small warehouse. Rather than add yet another word study of *baptizō*, we want to do a word study of the various OT modes of baptism. When the correct OT word correlating to NT baptism is identified, it becomes clear that NT practice was almost certainly immersion.

There are seven Hebrew words that deal with the mode of baptism. They are רָחַץ (*rachats*), כָּבַס (*kabas*), זָרַק (*zaraq*), נָזָה (*nazah*), שָׁפַךּ (*shapake*), נָסַךּ (*nasake*), יָצַק (*yasaq*). As we saw in Chapter One (p. 18), *baptismos* is used in Hebrews (6:2 and 9:10) to described various kinds of OT baptisms. We believe that each of these OT words is included in Hebrews' meaning.

Rachats is defined in *BDB* as to "wash, wash off, away, bathe." It is related philologically to an Akkadian word (*ra-asu*), an Egyptian and Ugaritic word (*rḥṣ*). All have the meaning "to overflow" or "flood." It is used over 75 times in the OT. It is used in a common or cultic (i.e. ritualistic) sense. Concerning the cultic sense Elmer Martens tells us,

---

[195] Calvin, *Institutes*, 4.15.19. For an in depth and objective study of the baptism in the early church from two *paedobaptist* scholars who conclude, like Calvin, that immersion was the practice of the early church, see Stander & Louw 2004.

The vb. is frequent in priestly legislation with instructions for the ceremonial washing of priests, and sometimes the washing of parts of the sacrifice (Num 19:7, 8; Lev 1:9, 13; 9:14). At their investiture and also on the Day of Atonement priests were to wash their bodies (Ex 29:4; Lev 8:6; 16:4, 24, 26). Before stepping to the altar or into the tent of meeting, priests were to wash hands and feet on penalty of death (Ex 30:19-21). Lavers for the tabernacle (30:18) and a brass "Sea" in Solomon's temple (2 Chron 4:6) facilitated the ritual.

(Martins, 'rachats,' NIDOTTE 3:1098-99)

Whether for ceremonial or common use, the word is regularly used in the context of bathing the body. For example, this is the same word used of Bathsheba when she "bathed" on the roof in front of David (2 Sam 11:2), of Pharaoh's daughter when she "bathed" in the Nile (Ex 2:5), and of the leprous Naaman who was commanded by Elisha to "bathe" in the Jordan seven times (2 Kings 5:10). This last occurrence is of particular interest to us, and we will come back to it momentarily.

Kabas is the same word used in Lev. 14 in the laws for washing leper's clothes. In fact, it is always used of clothing (as in laundering) and never of washing the body. The root occurs 51 times. It is found in Arabic and Akkadian where it means something like "treading down" or "stamping." Thus, the *TWOT* Lexicon defines it as making things "clean and soft by treading, kneading and beating them in cold water." *Kabas* is used entirely in a cultic sense (e.g. Lev 6:27, 11:25, 15:5, Num 8:7), the lone exception being 2 Sam 19:24. While this word is a bathing in water, it is never used in any way that could be comparable to baptism as we have come to know it; for baptism is first and foremost for the *body* (Heb 10:22), and not the clothing.

Zaraq basically means to "toss or throw or scatter abundantly." We have come to call this the mode of sprinkling. Its mode is therefore quite different from that of *rachats* or *kabas*. Victor Hamilton explains,

Although used most often with the sprinkling or throwing of blood, it is used 3x to refer to the sprinkling of water (Num 19:13, 20; Ezek 36:25). The two references in Num 19 are to purification from impurity resulting from contact with or proximity to something dead. It is such procedures that more than likely inspired Ezekiel to speak of God's forthcoming purification of Israel as a sprinkling of pure water on them. In fact, the Targum makes the connection clear, 'And I will remit your sins like those that are cleaned with the water of sprinkling and with the ashes of the heifer of the guilt offering.' If Ezekiel drew from Numbers, then the Qumran community drew from the language of Ezekiel, as can be seen in the promise, 'And he will sprinkle upon him the spirit of truth like waters of purification' (1QS IV, 21).

(Hamilton, 'zaraq', NIDOTTE 1:1153-1154)

"The sprinkling of blood, conveyed by *zaraq*, is used (a) with the burnt offering (Lev 1:5, 11; 8:19; 9:12; 2 Kgs 16:15; 2 Chron 30:16; Ezek 43:18); (b) with the peace offering (Lev 3:2, 8, 13; 9:18; 17:6; 2 Kgs 16:13); (c) with the sin/purification offering (2 Chron 29:22 [2x]); (d) with the guilt offering (Lev 7:2, 14)."[196] Sprinkling baptisms are thus intimately linked to sacrifices.

Nazah sprinklings differ from *zaraq* sprinklings in that the later were usually performed with the whole hand (Ex 9:8; 29:20-21; Lev 4:6) while the former were performed with a finger (Lev 4:6) or a "sprinkler" (Lev 14:7). This kind of sprinkling is done with oil (Lev 8:11), oil and blood (Ex 29:21), and water (Num 8:7).

The last three words are versions of *pouring*, and they will not be looked at in detail by us here, for these were most often used of anointing with oil and are closely associated (though not identical) with sprinkling. What is true of sprinkling is also usually true of pouring, and we need not be redundant in our explanation.

When blood for the forgiveness of sins is involved, it is *always* the case that the priest was to *zaraq* (sprinkle) the blood. Covenants were ratified by the sprinkling of blood or water. "The ceremony of covenant ratification at Sinai concludes with Moses "sprinkling" half of the blood on the altar (Ex 24:6) and then "sprinkling" the remaining half on the assembled people (Ex 24:8).[197] In Ezekiel we read of the new covenant, "For I will take you out of the nations; I will gather you from all the countries and bring you back into your own land. I will sprinkle (*zaraq*) clean water on you, and you will be clean" (Ezek 36:24-25, see also for example Ezek 39:29 and *pouring*).

When was the new covenant ratified? Jesus said about the Communion ceremony, "The cup is the new covenant in my blood which is shed[198] for you" (Luke 22:20, 1 Cor 11:25). The cup refers to his death on the cross that was to take place the next day. In this way, the new covenant is ratified by Christ on the cross, through the shedding of his blood (see also Hebrews 9).

But as Jesus himself says, his death (as both priest and sacrifice) is also a *baptism*. This should be taken literally. At his death, blood and water (the combination of Exodus 24 and Ezekiel 36) poured forth from his body, as the spear pierced his side (John 19:34). At least two times the New Testament refers to this same "pouring" as if it were a sprinkling. "To God's elect... for

---

[196] Ibid.

[197] Ibid.

[198] The Greek "shed" is *ekxeo*, which can mean "to pour out" or "shed."

obedience to Jesus Christ and *sprinkling* by his blood" (1 Pet 1:1-2). "To Jesus the mediator of a new covenant, and to the *sprinkled* blood that speaks a better word than the blood of Abel" (Heb 12:24).

Forgiven people owe their cleansing to the sprinkled blood right there at the cross. This is why the author of Hebrews tells us, "Let us draw near to God with a sincere heart in full assurance of faith, having our hearts sprinkled to cleanse us from a guilty conscience" (Heb 10:22). The bloody baptism of Christ sprinkles his people clean of their sins once for all. His death baptism is a fulfillment of all the types and shadows effected by the sprinkling baptisms in the Levitical law (Heb 9:13, 19, 21). Since the sprinkling baptisms find their fulfillment in the death of Christ (as does circumcision), they no longer serve as signs and seals, and therefore pass away with the dawning of the new age of Christ and his Holy Spirit.

But Hebrews 10:22 continues, "...and our bodies washed with pure water." It distinguishes between two baptisms. Many Christians argue that Christian baptism should be a sprinkling. We believe this is a serious confusion of the two baptisms of Christ (sprinklings have passed away), and also a failure to identify the correct OT counterpart to Christian baptism.

The problem of mode is solved by understanding that Christ fulfilled a very specific law at his own baptism—the ordination of the priest in Exodus 29:4. In this text, the priest was to be washed (*rachats*).[199] But what exactly did this priest do in Exodus 29:4? Was it merely a rinsing? Or, could it have been an immersion? It is probable that it was the latter. There are several reasons for thinking this. The most important has to do with the baptism of Naaman, the same event in which we find the only use of *baptizō* in the LXX.

Baptists love 2 Kings 5:14, because the LXX actually uses the word *baptizō*. The Hebrew it translates is the word *tabal*. *TWOT* says, "The verb [*tabal*] conveys the immersion of one item into another: bread in vinegar (Ruth 2:14), feet in water (Josh 3:15), a coat in blood (Gen 37:31). *Baptō* is the common LXX rendering of this root." English Bibles universally translate the word as "dipped." Naaman dipped himself in the water. Since this is the only instance of the LXX actually using the verb *baptizō*, it is possible that many Baptists assume that "baptism" isn't in the Law.[200] It is as if no other

---

[199] *Zaraq* (sprinkle) is used three times in the chapter, but each time it refers to the sprinkling of sacrificial blood of animals, and this is *after* the ordination part of the ceremony has been completed (see Exodus 29:9). Thus, we have in Exodus 29 two types of baptisms being performed in two very different stages with separate purposes. This is parallel to the two different baptisms that take place in two different stages in the life of our Lord Jesus.

[200] Paedobaptists do seem to admit that baptism is in the Law. This is why they sprinkle. As Jay Adams and others have (incorrectly) asserted, Jesus is fulfilling the sprinkling baptism of Numbers 8:7.

Hebrew word could be considered a baptism in the OT. But we have seen already that Paul and Peter both see baptism in the OT, though the OT itself never calls the flood or the Red Sea crossing a baptism.

What is not often noticed is the surrounding context of the Naaman story, and how it relates to *rachats*. Though Naaman *dips* in the Jordan, Elisha had told him to *rachats* (LXX: *louō*) in it (2 Kgs 5:10). Naaman understands perfectly well, and uses the same word himself in vs. 12. His servants repeat the command to *rachats* in vs. 13. Only then do we read that Naaman dipped himself in the Jordan. But it adds that Naaman did this, "according to the word of the man of God." That is, Naaman did not do something different from the commandment. He did exactly what Elisha told him to do. This is why he was healed. Therefore, in the context of 2 Kings 5, *rachats*, *tabal* and *baptizō* are synonyms. *Rachats* in this instance does not mean a rinsing, but a bath that can only occur when the person is dipped into the water.

There is a probable legal precedent for Elisha's actions. Leviticus 14:8 says, "He who is to be cleansed shall wash (*kabas*) his clothes and shave off all his hair and bathe (*rachats*) himself in water, and he shall be clean. And after that he may come into the camp, but live outside his tent seven days."[201] When a person *rachats* his whole body, he does it like Naaman, by dipping himself in the water. This also corresponds with the idea that rachats is related to a "flood" in other languages. This also matches the purpose for the Tabernacle-Laver and Temple-Sea. Both were big enough to take a bath in. In fact, the Scripture explicitly tells us that Moses and Solomon made their basins to *rachats* in them (Ex 30:18; 2 Chron 4:6).

This short study demonstrates that we do not have to rely solely upon the meaning of the term baptize to prove immersion.[202] The OT counterpart of NT baptism was an immersion too. No church has the right to modify or dispense with the persistent and regular teaching of this baptismal rite as it was practiced *for thousands of years* of Old Testament history, as commanded by God to the Aaronic priests of Israel in their ordination ceremony, as fulfilled by Jesus in his Jordan baptism, and as he commanded his disciples to follow in his wake.

---

[201] "Seven days" and "seven times in the Jordan" are interesting parallels in the two passages.

[202] As any lexical analysis will quickly demonstrate, the term "baptism" has a broader semantic range than immersion, as paedobaptists are always pointing out, though immersion is still its first definition.

Appendix Two

Typology and Allegory, Substance and Identity

We have offered several arguments for why baptism cannot be the NT equivalent of circumcision. Here we want to explore one more reason. The *physical* signs are not equivalent. It appears from paedobaptists' own writings that for signs to be equivalent, not only must there by spiritual equivalency, but also physical.

Paedobaptists compare other signs and sacraments in the following manner. John Murray states, "It is far from irrelevant *to observe the difference* between baptism and the Lord's supper *in respect to the elements used* and the actions involved [emphasis added]" (Murray 1980: 75). In talking about why Peter sees the flood as a baptism (1 Pet 3:20-22), Meredith Kline says,

> The most natural assumption is certainly that Peter was led to bring the deluge and the rite of baptism together *because of* the *common element* of the waters. And surely, then, that exegesis will most commend itself which succeeds in maintaining a genuine parallel between the role played by the waters in the two cases [emphasis added].
> (Kline 1968: 65)

It is common sense to think this way. In explaining how Ephesians can tell us there is only one baptism when clearly there is both a physical and spiritual baptism (two baptisms), Jay Adams says,

> Ephesians 4:4-5 emphatically asserts that there is but one. The only possible conclusion that one may reach is that the two must be but different aspects of the same thing. *Identity of mode* shows that this is precisely the case... *The ritual must symbolize the real*, or it is no symbol at all, and has no point [emphasis added].
> (Adams 1975: 22)

Let us not miss the point of what these paedobaptist men are suggesting to us. John Murray made his statement in the context of explaining why infants may participate in baptism but not the Lord's Supper. We know (according to his position) that infants may be baptized because,

> Baptism is washing with water, something necessary and appropriate to the infant in the earliest stages of life. There is nothing in the element or the action incongruous with earliest infancy. The Lord's supper is the partaking of bread and wine. We can readily detect that there is in the elements used and the actions involved something that is not congruous with early infancy.
> (Murray 1980: 75-76)

In other words, the elements in and of themselves, because they are different physically and because of their application to infants demonstrate that the sacraments of baptism and of the Lord's Supper are not identical, but are rather different. Because of the different *elements* involved, one is unjustified to make an argument that baptism and the Lord's Supper should be applied in the same way because they are not identical sacraments.

Kline is saying that Peter had a very good reason for connecting the flood with baptism. It is because the physical element of water is common to both. The identical language of baptism is directly tied to the parallel/identical physical elements.

Finally, Adams is saying that if the ritual does not symbolize the real, then there is no symbol at all. If the water of baptism did not really wash anything physically, then to call the washing of the Spirit a baptism would make no sense. Identity of mode in both real and spiritual baptism tells us that they are really "different aspects of the same thing."

So here we have three paedobaptists telling us in three different ways that the identity/non-identity between any two symbols is determined by likeness of the elements used, actions involved, and mode administered. We cannot make this point strongly enough, for this is the criteria used by paedobaptists themselves with everything *except circumcision/baptism*.

This is more than just a philosophical point. It is also hermeneutical. Especially as hermeneutics seeks to understand typological relationships correctly, paedobaptists insist that we must be careful to make sure that the fuller sense (usually in the NT) is organically related to the original meaning (usually in the OT). Dan McCartney writes,

> If the divine plan gives early indication of later events through typology, when we look at the older revelation from the standpoint of the completed revelation in Christ, we may expect to find there a "fuller sense" than would have been evident to the first hearers. "*Sensus plenior*"[i.e., fuller sense] is thus simply another way of looking at how later revelation relates to earlier... True *sensus plenior* is organically related to the historical meaning. That is, it should be a "fuller" sense, not an entirely "other" sense. It is like the oak tree within the acorn. Just looking at an acorn, one could not see the full end result, though one could tell that the acorn is intended to grow into something bigger, and from a later standpoint one can look back and see how the oak tree gradually grew out of the acorn.
>
> (McCartney 2002: 164-165)

We agree with this insistence. One of the scores of biblical examples of this is how Paul understands Isaiah 60:1 which reads, "Arise, shine, for your light has come, and the glory of the LORD rises upon you." Paul "quotes" this verse in the following way, "This is why it is said: 'Wake up, O sleeper, rise from the dead, and Christ will shine on you" (Eph 5:14). Christ is the *sensus plenior* of the sun. What is the organic relationship? Christ said elsewhere, "I am the light of the world" (John 8:12). There is a play on "light" going on later in Isaiah where the fulfillment of the sun in the sky takes place in the light of Christ (see Isa 60:19-20; cf. Rev 21:23, 22:5). There is an organic relationship between the physical lights of the sky and the spiritual light of Christ. In this way, the *sensus plenior*—the fuller meaning—is organically related to the former meaning.

Some church fathers got carried away with allegory, not because they shouldn't have been looking for types, but because they didn't fully appreciate the organic relationship that must exist for an allegory to be legitimate.[203] A classic example of the blurring between typology and allegory that has sometimes occurred is Justin Martyr and many other early fathers' understanding that the scarlet thread hung by Rahab from her window typified the blood of Christ. According to McCartney, this is not a proper type-antitype relationship for the reason that there is no organic relationship between a piece of thread and the blood of Christ. The redness of the thread (if not also the blood) is accidental to the substance.[204] Thread and blood are substances and there is no organic continuity between them.

In light of this, Kevin Vanhoozer's explanation of the difference between the typology and allegory is well noted. "The crucial difference between figural or typological interpretation and its allegorical counterpart is that the former relates two items that stand in a historical relation of anticipation and fulfillment, whereas no such relation regulates the connection between the literal and spiritual senses in allegory" (Vanhoozer 1998: 119). How does a piece of thread anticipate the blood of Christ on the cross? This is difficult to understand. But how does a water baptism of a priest anticipate the baptism of Christ in water? This is simple to understand and self-evident.

---

[203] Bryan Estelle suggests that in allegorical interpretation, "the literal sense (not to be confused with the literalistic interpretation) is dismissed and history takes a back seat, so to speak" (Estelle 2005: 69). No doubt that for many it often does, though we doubt that Paul sees history taking a backseat in one of the rare biblical allegories of the OT (Gal 4:24-31). History taking a backseat should never be the case in proper typological interpretation. Indeed, without an actual historical event, the antitype fulfillment makes no sense! Typology presupposes that God authored real history to point to future historical things.

[204] "Accident" is being used philosophically here. By it we mean that *redness* is not inherent to *threadness*. One can have a blue thread or a yellow thread yet still have a thread. Redness is also not inherent to blood (though to human blood it probably is). Some creatures have different color blood (the Vulcan Spock and his green blood not going into our consideration). Therefore, red cannot be a proper type, because it is only *accidental* to the stories.

Today it is popular to allegorize all sorts of things. One of the most common is to take the literal historical story where David slays Goliath and spiritualize it, so that the deeper (and more important) meaning is for you to take whatever "Goliaths" are in your life and slay them. Notice how there is no need for the event to actually be historical. If it were a myth, this same meaning could be derived without missing a beat. Allegory works not on the level of history, but on the level of metaphor.

On the organic (typological) level, there is a problem too. For example, Goliath the man is not related in any way to Joe Smith's financial blunders in the stock market, which have become his personal "Goliath" in life. This is not at all what we have attempted in this book.

From a basic hermeneutical point of view, we have been using typology. We have never done so with unrelated organically disconnected substances, or given diminishing importance to the historical events. Our argument is simply that NT baptism comes from the OT type of... baptism. To think that circumcision is the OT counterpart of baptism because they are both "signs of the covenant" completely disregards the substances and the organic relationships that always go into biblical type-antitype relationships.[205] It fundamentally messes up typology as it is found throughout Scripture.

Therefore, it seems fair to us to conclude that if three giants in the paedo-baptist community can appeal to the nature of the elements used and actions involved in understanding relationships between two signs (whether they be the discontinuity between baptism/communion, or the actual continuity between baptism/flood, or real/spiritual baptism), and if good biblical hermeneutics from paedobaptist's own writings say that we need organic relationship to see true *sensus plenior*, then surely we are on safe ground when we inspect circumcision and baptism to see if they are actually related to each other *as signs*—the two signs and seals that are supposedly "identical," "interchangeable," and "prototypical" of each other.

We conclude that they are not. It is as illegitimate to think that Christ would "replace" baptism with circumcision as it is to think that Rahab hung

---

[205] Thus, in the Bible NT meals are related to OT meals. The NT sacrifice is related to OT sacrifices. Days are related to days. Light fulfills light. The NT Door fulfills OT sanctuary doors. Water-rites fulfill water-rites. Crossings fulfill crossings. Circumcision fulfills circumcision. Wilderness ordeals fulfill wilderness ordeals. The NT Law intensifies the same OT law. The Resurrection event (and subsequent believer's resurrection[s] first to spiritual life and then to bodily life) intensifies OT resurrection events. It is never the case that the physical substances are melded into one another in such a way that Sabbath's fulfill circumcision or Communion fulfills Light or whatever.

a type of the blood of Christ upon her window. Baptism comes from baptism, and no place else.

Appendix Three

Timothy's Baptism

Jesus was baptized in water by a Levitical priest (John the Baptist) at age thirty because he was entering the time of his priestly ministry on earth. This was done in compliance with the law of ordination given in Ex 29:4 – "to fulfill all righteousness." Since baptism arises out of baptism, we expect that NT baptisms will also be done according to the pattern established in the Old Testament unless we have explicit examples showing differences taking place from the established Law.

Of course, we do find such examples. The baptism of the Ethiopian eunuch shows how new covenant priests can be both foreigners and physically deformed. The baptism of women in Acts shows how the regulations for males only have also been transformed. All new covenant believers may offer their priestly sacrifices before God, as they honor him with the sacrifice of their lives (Rom 12:1-2).

Yet, we never find infants being baptized in the New Testament. Since infants were not baptized in the Old Testament either, we have no justification for baptizing them in the new. This is the great distinctive of Reformed credo-baptism over and against our Reformed paedobaptist bretheren. We need more than simple "household" passages to justify the practice of infant baptism, because baptism does not arise out of circumcision, is not equivalent to it, but is instead a completely different sacrament entirely.

Curiously, rather than finding explicit examples of infants being baptized, we find exactly the opposite in the story of one very special young man in the New Testament who was reared in a Christian home from his infancy. We learn of Timothy the following. Paul says, "I have been reminded of your sincere faith, which first lived in your grandmother Lois and in your mother Eunice and, I am persuaded, now lives in you also" (2 Tim 1:5). It is not speculation to say that Timothy's mother and grandmother were converted prior to his birth. For Paul elsewhere says, "But as for you, *continue* in what you have learned and have become convinced of, because you know those from whom you learned it, and how *from infancy* you have known the holy Scriptures, which are able to make you wise for salvation through faith in Christ Jesus" (2 Tim 3:14-15).

If the Scripture records Timothy's baptism, then if paedobaptism is the correct New Testament position, we would expect to find reference to it being performed when he was an infant, since he was raised from infancy with the Holy Scriptures in a Christian home.[206]   Curiously for the paedobaptist, yet expectedly for the credobaptist, we find something very different taking place.   There is very good reason to believe that Paul does mention Timothy's baptism, his baptism as one old enough to profess his own faith.

1 Timothy 6:12 says, "Fight the good fight of faith. Take hold of the eternal life to which you were called when you made your good confession in the presence of many witnesses." At first glance, this verse appears quite irrelevant to our discussion. Yet, first impressions can be very deceiving. Commenting on this verse Philip Towner says,

> The Greek sentence continues without a break, and attention shifts to Timothy's past commitment to God. It may be (as the NIV interprets it) that the phrase *good confession in the presence of many witnesses* relates directly to God's calling (to eternal life), indicating the time when realization of this occurred. In this case, the event in mind would probably be Timothy's baptism.
>
> (Towner 1994: 143)

Follow the line of thought carefully here. At some point in time, when he was old enough, Timothy made a public confession of faith. It was done "in the presence of many witnesses." This good confession related specifically to his calling to eternal life. A calling to eternal life can be nothing less than a calling to salvation. In other words, Timothy was converted near the time of his public confession, even though he was raised in a Christian home.

In the New Testament there was no waiting time between recognition of conversion and the gift/act of faith and one's baptism. Rather, we see profession of faith and baptism taking place nearly simultaneously. Public confessions were those places where the person stated before the congregation that they had believed upon Christ. At this same time, they were baptized. Thus, Paul is referencing Timothy's baptism in this verse. Strikingly, paedobaptists like John Stott[207] and William Hendriksen[208] believe that this verse is talking about Timothy's baptism.

---

[206] We know his home was a Christian home because he was exhorted to "continue" in what he had learned from infancy, rather than turning from it to Christ. If Timothy were only learning Judaism (because his mother and grandmother were simply Jews and not Christians), would Paul really want him to continue in this doctrine? Would he not rather desire for Timothy to become a Christian instead? Thus, it is self-evident that Timothy was raised *as a Christian* from *infancy*.

[207] Stott says, "The reference to 'many witnesses' has suggested to some that the occasion recalled is not Timothy's baptism but his ordination (cf. 4:14; 2 Tim. 2:2). But the combination of the calling (inward and private) and the confession (outward and public) more naturally refers to Timothy's conversion and baptism. Every convert was expected to make a solemn public affirmation of faith" (Stott 1996: 157).

The close connection between baptism and public confession in the midst of the church assembly is also found in Hebrews 10:22-23. "Let us draw near with a sincere heart in full assurance of faith, having our hearts sprinkled clean from an evil conscience and our *bodies washed* with pure water. Let us *hold fast the confession* of our hope without wavering." Here we understand "bodies washed with pure water" to be referring to baptism.[209] The "confession of our hope" is the confession of the faith (not our subjective conversion testimony when Jesus "came into our hearts," but an objective public assent to the core doctrines of the Christian faith) that we do at the time of our baptism and that we continue to uphold whenever we meet together with the brethren. The same idea is also found in Acts 15:22-23.

John 3:33-34 is another place where the idea of confessing and baptism may go hand in hand. While in the process of baptizing others, John the Baptist says, "He who has received His witness has set his *seal* to this, that God is true. For He whom God has sent speaks the words of God; for He gives the Spirit without measure."

Some understand "seal" in this passage as a man's confession that he believes the truthfulness of Christ's witness (cf. Morris 1995: 217). This is interesting in light of the broader context. Seven times in the passage the word "witness" or "testimony" have been used. This verse says that a man who receives the witness or testimony "sets his seal" to this. What is that seal? It could just be a verbal assent. But something else is taking place here. People are being *baptized* (John 3:23).

The church has recognized since at least Tertullian that baptism is a seal. But if the word "seal" refers to a believer's confession, why use the word "seal" when the common word of the passage (i.e., testimony) would make more sense? It would be easier to say, "The one receiving the testimony has set *his own testimony* (i.e., given his own confession) to this, that God is true." But if "seal" refers to baptism, then we understand the phrase "The one receiving his testimony" to be referring to the testimony of Christ (vs. 31-32); and the seal, rather than being a believer's word, would refer to the sealing of Christ.[210] But either way, it is clear from these passages that confessing the faith and being baptized are just not separated by great deals of time as they often are today.

---

[208] "When, on Paul's first missionary journey, Timothy was 'called' (both externally and internally), he had in connection with his baptism professed his faith publicly" (Hendriksen 1957: 204).

[209] Dahl (1951: 407).

[210] So the one doing the sealing is not the person receiving, but Christ who is the one witnessing.

As credobaptists (i.e., "professing," from *credo* where we get our English word "creed"), we should *expect* to find that Timothy was baptized only upon his ability to profess the faith publicly with his mouth. This is exactly what we *do* find. Timothy's baptism is thus a very important portion of Scripture that all Baptists should become familiar with as they seek to mount a defense of their position.

Chart 1—Biblical Sanctuaries Compared

Archetypal Temple:
Isa 6, Dan 7; Zech 3-4; Rev 4-5

SANCTUARY w/
COVENANT HEAD
HEAVENLY
TEMPLE

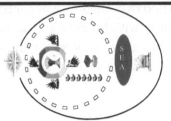

Good Space = Myriads & Myriads
(Sea of Glass, Sacrificial Altar, Creatures)

Holy Place = 24 Elders
(7 Blazing Lamps, Golden Altar of Incense and Smoke, Angels, Wall of Thrones)

Holy of Holies = Throne
(Ark, 4 Living Creatures, Lamb, Lightning/Thunder, Emerald Rainbow)

Prototypical Temples:
Two perspectives

HEAVEN &
EARTH

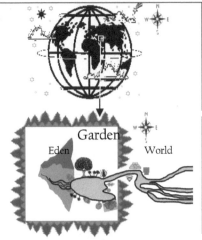

Good Space = Earth/World
(East Sunrise, Waters, Land, Animals)

Holy Place = Sky/Heaven
(Atmosphere, Birds, Clouds, Shiny Sun, Moon, and Stars, Trees)

Holy of Holies = Heaven
(Righteousness, Sacrificial Lamb, Throne, Living Creatures, Rainbow)

GARDEN OF
EDEN:
ADAM

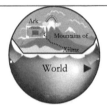

Good Space = World
(East Gate, River, Sacrifice, Animals)

Holy Place = Garden
(Sword and Wall, Rain-cloud, Cherubim, Gold, Tree of Life, Food)

Holy of Holies = Eden
(Tree of Knowledge, Sacrificial Skins, God's Presence, Mountain, Priest etc.)

Ectypal Temples:
Made by God

ARARAT:
NOAH

Good Space = World
(In East, Waters, Land, Animals)

Holy Place = Mountains
(Birds, Clouds, Branch of Tree)

Holy of Holies = Ark
(Law, Sacrifice, God's Presence, Mountain Top, Priest, Rainbow)

SINAI:
MOSES

Good Space = Bottom-Mt.
(East Wind, Water from Rock, Sacrifices, People and Animals)

Holy Place = Mid-Mt.
(Boundaries, Eagle-Spirit, Angel of Lord, Burning Bush, Table by Shiny Pavement)

Holy of Holies = Top-Mt.
(Law, God's Presence, Lightning/Thunder on Mt., Prophet-Priest)

PROMISED
LAND:
ABRAHAM

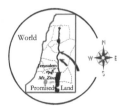

Good Space = World
(East Entrance, Great River, Sacrifices, People)

Holy Place = Promised Land
(Boundaries, Smoking Pot, Angel of Lord, Trees, Bread & Wine)

Holy of Holies = Jerusalem
(Law, Sacrifices, God's Presence, Mt. Moriah, King-Priest)

Chart 1—Biblical Sanctuaries Compared (Cont.)

Ectypal Temples:
Made by man at God's Command

SANCTUARY w/ COVENANT HEAD

TABERNACLE:
LEVI

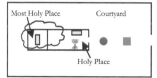

Good Space = Courtyard
(East Entrance, Laver, Bronze-Earthen Sacrificial Altar, All People)

Holy Place = Holy Place
(Wall, Angels on Curtains, Incense, Golden Items: Lampstand, Showbread Table for Bread and Wine)

Holy of Holies = Most Holy Place
(Law, Sacrifice, Ark, Glory of God, Heavenly Embroidery, Priest)

TEMPLE:
DAVID

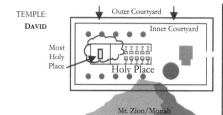

Good Space = Courtyard
(East Entrance, Sea, Bronze-Earthen Sacrificial Altar with Inlaid Animals, All People)

Holy Place = Holy Place
(Wall, Angels on Curtains, Incense, Golden Items: Lampstands, 10 Showbread Tables with Bread and Wine)

Holy of Holies = Most Holy Place
(Law, Sacrifice, Ark, Glory of God, Heavenly Architecture, Priest)

Antitypical Temples:
Two Eschatological Perspectives

EZEKIEL'S TEMPLE:
JESUS CHRIST

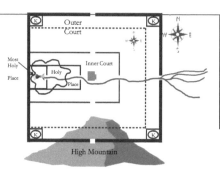

Good Space = Courtyard
(Entrance on N-S-E, River, Altar, Kitchens)

Holy Place = Holy Place
(Wall, Cherubim and Tree Carvings)

Holy of Holies = Most Holy Place
(Throne, Priest)

JOHN'S TEMPLE:
JESUS CHRIST

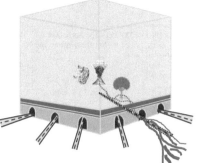

Good Space = World
(Entrance on all Sides, River of Life, All Believers)

Holy Place = City
(Wall, Precious Stones, Golden Streets, Tree of Life)

Holy of Holies = Throne
(Throne, Lamb, Ark, Presence of God)

Chart 2—Creation Stories Compared

ORIGINAL CREATION	NOAH'S FLOOD	RED SEA/EXODUS	JESUS' BAPTISM
GEN 1:1 In the beginning, God created the heavens and the earth.	GEN 7:11 The windows of the heavens were opened.		MATT 3:16c The heavens were opened to him.
GEN 1:2b The earth was without form and void.		DEUT 32:10 He found him in a desert land, and in the howling waste of the wilderness.	MATT 3:1 In those days John the Baptist came preaching in the wilderness.
LUKE 3:38 Adam, the son of God (cf. **Gen 1:26-27, 28-30**).	LUKE 3:36 ...Noah, the son of... God.	EXO 4:22 "Thus says the LORD, Israel is my firstborn son."	MATT 3:17 A voice from heaven said, "This is my beloved Son."
GEN 1:2b And darkness was over the face of the deep.	GEN 7:19 The waters prevailed so mightily on the earth that all the high mountains under the whole heaven were covered.	EXO 15:10 The sea covered them.	MATT 3:16a, Jesus was baptized (i.e. was covered by the water).
GEN 1:2 And the Spirit of God was hovering over the face of the waters.	GEN 1:17, 8:8 The ark floated on the face of the waters... He sent forth a dove from him, to see if the waters had subsided from the face of the ground.	DEUT 32:11-12 Like an eagle that stirs up its nest, that hovers over its young... The LORD alone guided him, no foreign god was with him.	MATT 3:16d He saw the Spirit of God descending like a dove.
GEN 1:2 A wind from God swept over the face of the waters (NRS).	GEN 8:1 God made a wind blow over the earth, and the waters subsided.	EXO 14:21 The LORD drove the sea back by a strong east wind all night.	
GEN 1:9 "Let the dry land appear."	GEN 8:13 The face of the ground was dry.	EXO 14:21 And made the sea dry land.	MATT 3:16b He went up from the water.
GEN 1:11 'Let the earth sprout vegetation."	GEN 8:11 The dove came back to him in the evening, and behold, in her mouth was a freshly plucked olive leaf.		
GEN 1:24 'Let the earth bring forth living creatures according to their kinds- livestock and creeping things and beasts of the earth according to their kinds.'	GEN 8:17 "Bring out with you every living thing that is with you of all flesh- birds and animals and every creeping thing that creeps on the earth- that they may swarm on the earth."	EXO 12:38 A mixed multitude also went up with them, and very much livestock, both flocks and herds.	MATT 3:5 Jerusalem and all Judea and all the region about the Jordan were going out to him.
GEN 1:22 'Be fruitful and multiply."	GEN 8:17 ...and be fruitful and multiply on the earth.'	EXO 1:7 The people of Israel were fruitful and increased greatly; they multiplied and grew exceedingly strong.	
GEN 2:2 God finished his work that he had done, and he rested on the seventh day from all his work that he had done.	GEN 8:4 On the seventh month... the ark came to rest on the mountains of Ararat.	EXO 16:30 So the people rested on the seventh day.	MATT 3:16e Coming to rest on him.
	GEN 7:21 And all flesh died that moved on the earth, birds, livestock, beasts, all swarming creatures that swarm on the earth, and all mankind [from the flood] .	EXO 15:1 The horse and his rider he has thrown into the sea.	MATT 3:11-12 He will baptize you with the Holy Spirit and with fire. His winnowing fork is in his hand, and he will clear his threshing floor and gather his wheat into the barn, but the chaff he will burn with unquenchable fire.

What can we conclude from this chart? Original creation was a pattern for new creation(s). The new creation takes place in stages. In the OT it is in the anticipatory stage, like a Presidential caucus. In the NT it is in the inaugural stage, like the day after the election. At the Second Coming, it is in the consummate stage, like the day the President takes his oath of office. Original creation always stood as a pattern for the new creation to come. Today, it has come in Christ so that Scripture may say, "In Christ, you are new creation."

Bibliography

Abba, R. (1978), 'Priests and Levites in Ezekiel', *VT* 28, 1-9.

Abrahams, I. (1911), 'How Did the Jews Baptize?', *JTS* XII, 609-612.

Adams, J. (1975), *The Meaning and Mode of Baptism*, Phillipsburg, NJ: Presbyterian and Reformed.

Adamson, James T. H. (1970), 'Malachi', in D. Guthrie and J. A. Motyer (eds.), *The New Bible Commentary: Revised*, Grand Rapids, MI: Eerdmans, 806-809.

Adler, C. and J. Greenstone, *'mikweh'*, *JE* at:
http://www.jewishencyclopedia.com/view.jsp?artid=608&letter=M

Alexander, Hartley B. (1920), *The Mythology of All Races in Thirteen Volumes*, Louis Herbert Gray (ed.), Boston: Marshall Jones.

Alexander, P. (1983), '3 Enoch', in James H. Charlesworth (ed.), *The Old Testament Pseudepigrapha: Apocalyptic Literature and Testaments*, Vol. 1, New York: Doubleday.

Alexander, T. D. and Brian S. Rosner (eds.) (2000), *New Dictionary of Biblical Theology*, Downers Grove, IL: InterVarsity Press.

_____, and Simon J. Gathercole (eds.) (2004), *Heaven on Earth*, Carlisle, England: Paternoster Press.

Archer, G., R. L. Harris and B. Waltke (eds.) (2003), *Theological Wordbook of the Old Testament*, Chicago: Moody.

Badia, L. (1980), *The Qumran Baptism and John the Baptist's Baptism*, Lanham, MD: University Press of America.

Bainton, Roland H. (1952), *The Reformation of the Sixteenth Century*, Boston: Beacon Press.

Barcellos, Richard C. (2005), 'An Exegetical Appraisal of Colossians 2:11-12', *RBTR* 2:1, 3-23.

Barclay, W. (1975a), *The Gospel of Matthew*, Vol. 1, Philadelphia: Westminster Press.

_____. (1975b), *The Letter to the Romans*, Philadelphia: Westminster Press.

Barrick, William D. (1999), 'The Mosaic Covenant', *MSJ* 10:2, 213-232.

Baugh, Stephen M. (2000), 'Covenant Theology Illustrated: Romans 5 on the Federal Headship of Adam and Christ', *MR* 9:4, 17-23.

Beale, G. K. (1999), *The Book of Revelation*, NIGTC, Grand Rapids, MI: Eerdmans Publishing Company.

_____. (2004a), 'The Final Vision of the Apocalypse and Its Implications for a Biblical Theology of the Temple', in T. D. Alexander and S. J. Gathercole (eds.), *Heaven on Earth*, Carlisle, England: Paternoster Press.

_____. (2004b), *The Temple and the Church's Mission: A Biblical Theology of the Dwelling Place of God*, Downers Grove, IL: InterVarsity Press.

_____. (2005), 'Eden, The Temple, and the Church's Mission in the New Creation', *JETS* 48:1, 5-32.

_____. and Sean M. McDonough (2007), 'Revelation', in G. K. Beale and D. A. Carson (eds.), *CONTUOT*, Grand Rapids, MI: Baker, 1081-1161.

Beasley-Murray, George R. (1963), *Baptism in the New Testament*, Milton Keynes, UK: Paternoster.

Beeke, Joel R. and Ray B. Lanning (2003), 'Unto You, and To Your Children', in Gregg Strawbridge (ed.), *The Case for Covenantal Infant Baptism*, Phillipsburg, NJ: P & R.

Berkhof, L. (1979), *Systematic Theology*, Grand Rapids, MI: Eerdmans.

Black, David A. (1998), *It's Still Greek to Me: An Easy-to-Understand Guide to Intermediate Greek*, Grand Rapids, MI: Baker.

Block, Daniel I. (1995), 'Reviving God's Covenant with Levi: Reflections on Malachi 2:1-9', *RAR* 4:3, 121-136.

Blomberg, Craig L. (2007), 'Matthew', in G. K. Beale and D. A. Carson (eds.), *CONTUOT*, Grand Rapids, MI: Baker Academic, 1-109.

Bock, Darrell L. (1994), *Luke 1:1-9:50*, Vol. 1, BECNT, Grand Rapids: MI: Baker Books.

Boston, T. (1848), *The Whole Works of the Late Reverend and Learned Mr. Thomas Boston*, 12 vols., Aberdeen: George and Robert King.

Brown, C. (ed.) (1978), *New International Dictionary of New Testament Theology*, 3 vols., Grand Rapids: Zondervan.

Brown, J. P. (1969), 'The Mediterranean Vocabulary of the Vine', *VT* 19, 146-70.

Brown, William P. (1996), *Obadiah through Malachi*, WBCS, Louisville, KY: Westminster John Knox Press.

Buhler, F. M. (2004), *Baptism, Three Aspects: Archaeological, Historical, Biblical*, Dundas, Ontario: Joshua Press.

Burkitt, F. C. (2003), 'The Debt of Christianity to Judaism', in Edwyn R. Bevan (ed.), *The Legacy of Israel*, Whitefish, MT: Kessinger Pub. First Printing 1927.

Busenitz, Irvin A. (1999), 'Introduction to the Biblical Covenants: The Noahic Covenant and the Priestly Covenant', *MSJ* 10:2, 173-198.

Calvin, J. (1960), *Institutes of the Christian Religion*, John T. McNeill (ed.), Philadelphia: Westminster Press.

Carnagey, G. (1998), 'Balaam: A Light to the Gentiles?', *CTSJ* 4:4, 18-27.

Chapel, B. (2003), 'A Pastoral Overview of Infant Baptism', in Gregg Strawbridge (ed.), *The Case for Covenantal Infant Baptism*, Phillipsburg, NJ: P & R.

Charlesworth, James H. (ed.) (1983), *The Old Testament Pseudepigrapha* in 2 Vols, New York: Doubleday.

Christman, T. (n.d.), *Forbid Them Not: Rethinking the Baptism and Church Membership of Children and Young People*, Greenwell-Chisholm Printing Company, 1-800-844-1876.

Clines, D. J. A., (1974), 'The Tree of Knowledge and the Law of Yahweh', *VT* 24, 8-14.

Clouse, Robert G. (1977), *The Meaning of the Millennium: Four Views*, Downers Grove: IL: InterVarsity Press.

Clowney, Edmund P. (1973), 'The Final Temple', *WTJ* 35:2, 156-189.

Collins, Adela Y. (1979), 'The Early Christian Apocalypses', *Semeia* 14, 61-120.

Collins, J. J. (1983), 'Sibylline Oracles', in James H. Charlesworth (ed.), *The Old Testament Pseudepigrapha: Apocalyptic Literature and Testaments*, Vol. 1, New York: Doubleday.

Conner, A. (2007), *Covenant Children Today: Physical or Spiritual?*, Owensboro, KY: Reformed Baptist Academic Press.

Cross, Anthony R. (2002), 'The Meaning of "Baptisms" in Hebrews 6.2', in Stanley E. Porter and Anthony R. Cross (eds.), *Dimensions of Baptism: Biblical and Theological Studies*, London: Sheffield Academic Press.

Dahl, Nils A. (1955), 'The Origin of Baptism', in *IaVTPSM*, Oslo: Forlaget land og kirke.

Dale, James W. (1874), *Christic Baptism and Patristic Baptism*, Vol. 4, Philadelphia, PA: Perkenpine & Higgins.

_____. (1869), *Judaic Baptism*, Vol. 2, Philadelphia, PA: Perkenpine & Higgins.

Davies, W.D. and D.C. Allison (1988), *The Gospel According to Saint Matthew*, Vol. 1, ICC, Edinburgh: T. & T. Clark.

Day, J. (2003), 'Why Does God "Establish" rather than "Cut" Covenants in the Priestly Source?', in A. D. H. Mayes and R. B. Salters (eds.), *Covenant as Context: Essays in Honour of E. W. Nicholson*, New York: Oxford University Press, 91-106.

Dhorme, É. (1907), 'L'arbre de verite et l'arbre de vie', *RB* 4, 271-274.

Dillard, Raymond B. (1999), *Faith in the Face of Apostasy: The Gospel According to Elijah and Elisha*, Phillipsburg, NJ: Presbyterian and Reformed.

Duncan, J. L. 'The Reformed Doctrine of Baptism and New Testament Practice', http://www.fpcjackson.org/resources/apologetics/Covenant%20Theology%20&%20Justification/Ligons_covtheology/07.htm)

Durand, G. (1995), *God's Covenant and the Community of Believers: A Defense of Infant Baptism*, Aurora, CO: Crown Rights Book Company.

Edwards, J. (2002), *The Gospel According to Mark*, PNTC, Grand Rapids, MI: Eerdmans.

Epstein, I. (1936), *The Babylonian Talmud*, London: The Sonineo Press.

Estelle, Bryan D. (2005), *Salvation Through Judgment and Mercy: The Gospel According to Jonah*, Phillipsburg: NJ: Presbyterian and Reformed Publishing.

Farrer, A. (1964), *The Revelation of St. John the Divine*, Oxford: Clarendon Press.

Feinberg, Charles L. (1982), *Jeremiah: A Commentary*, Grand Rapids, MI: Zondervan.

Fretheim, Terence E. (1991), *Exodus*, Louisville, KY: John Knox.

Futato, Mark D. (1998), 'Because It Had Rained: A Study of Gen 2:5-7 with Implications for Gen 2:4-25 and Gen 1:1-2:3', *WTJ* 60:1, 1-21.

Gavin, F. (1969), *The Jewish Antecedents of the Christian Sacraments*, New York, KTAV Publishing House.

Gill, J. (n.d.), *Exposition of the Entire Bible*, online at:
http://eword.gospelcom.net/comments/1samuel/gill/1samuel2.htm

Ginzberg, L. (1954), *Legends of the Jews: Moses in the Wilderness*, Vol. 3, trans. Paul Radin, Philadelphia: Jewish Publication Society of America.

Glazier-McDonald, B. (1987), *Malachi: The Divine Messenger*, Atlanta: Scholars Press.

Goodblatt, D. (2006), *Elements of Ancient Jewish Nationalism*, New York: Cambridge University Press.

Goppelt, L. (2002), *Typos: The Typological Interpretation of the Old Testament in the New*, Eugene, OR: Wipf & Stock.

Goulder, M. (1974), *Midrash and Lection in Matthew: The Speaker's Lectures in Biblical Studies, 1969-71*. London: SPCK.

Green, M. (1987), *Baptism: Its Purpose, Practice and Power*. Milton Keynes, UK: Paternoster.

Hahn, Scott W. (1995), *Kinship by Covenant: A Biblical Theological Study of Covenant Types and Texts In the Old and New Testaments*, Ann Arbor, MI: UMI Research Press. Available online: http://mufederalist.com/scott_hahn_dissertation.pdf

Hamilton, Victor P. (1990), *The Book of Genesis Ch. 1-17*, NICOT, Grand Rapids: Eerdmans.

_____. (1997), 'Zaraq', *NIDOTTE*, 1:1153-1154.

Hancock, G. (1995), *Fingerprints of the Gods*, New York: Three Rivers Press.

_____. (1998), *Heaven's Mirror: Quest for the Lost Civilization*, New York: Crown Publishers.

Hannan-Stavroulakis, N. (2002), 'The Waters of Life Mikveh', at: http://www.etz-hayyim-hania.org/_resources/articles_pdf/article0010.pdf

Hastings, J., John A. Selbie and John C. Lambert (eds.) (1918), *Dictionary of the Apostolic Church*, 2 vols., Edinburgh: T. & T. Clark.

Hellerman, J. (2003), 'Purity and Nationalism in Second Temple Literature: 1-2 Maccabees And Jubilees', *JETS* 46:3, 410-421.

Hemer, C. (1986), *The Letters to the Seven Churches of Asia in their Local Setting*, Sheffield: JSOT.

Hendriksen, W. (1957), *Exposition of the Pastoral Epistles*, NTC, Grand Rapids, MI: Baker.

Henry, M. (1960), *Matthew Henry's Complete Commentary in One Volume*, Grand Rapids, MI: Zondervan.

_____. (n.d.), *Treatise on Baptism*, in RBCD, Vol. 28, Edmonton: Still Waters Revival Books.

Himmelfarb, M. (2006), *A Kingdom of Priests: Ancestry and Merit in Ancient Judaism*, Philadelphia, PA: University of Pennsylvania Press.

Hodge, A. A. (1999), *Outlines of Theology*, Carlisle, PA: Banner of Truth Trust.

Holloway, Steven W. (1991), 'What Ship Goes There: The Flood of Ancient Near Eastern Temple Ideology', *ZAW* 103, 328-254.

Hooke, S. H. (1918), 'Sea of Glass,' *DAC* 2:464-465.

Hooper, F. J. B. (1861), *The Revelation of Jesus Christ by John in Two Volumes*, London: J. & F. H. Rivington.

Horton, M. (1994), *Putting Amazing Back into Grace: Who Does What in Salvation*, Grand Rapids, MI: Baker Books.

_____. (2002), *A Better Way: Rediscovering the Drama of God-Centered Worship*, Grand Rapids: Baker Books.

Howell, P. (2005), *John the Great: John the Baptist, His Relationship with Jesus and You*, Summerville, SC: Holy Fire Publishing.

Hultgren, Arland J. (1994), 'Baptism in the New Testament: Origins, Formulas, and Metaphors', *W&W* 14:1, 6-11. Online at: http://www.luthersem.edu/word&world/archives/14-1_baptism/14-1_Hultgren.pdf

Hummel, Horace D. (1964), 'The Old Testament Basis of Typological Interpretation', *BR* 9, 38-50.

Iannelli-Smith, D. (2004), 'The Progress of Redemption through the Covenants', at: http://bellsouthpwp2.net/e/p/eph61820/documents/ArticleRedemptionthroughCovenants.pdf

Jewett, Paul K. (1978), *Infant Baptism & the Covenant of Grace*, Grand Rapids: Eerdmans.

Jones, Hywel R. (1999), 'Remembering A Forgotten Covenant', *BT* 429:1. Also available at: http://www.wscal.edu/faculty/wscwritings/06.04b.php

Jordan, James B. (1984), *The Law of the Covenant: An Exposition of Exodus 21-23*, Tyler, TX: Institute for Christian Economics. Also available at http://www.biblicalhorizons.com/pdf/jjlc.pdf

Kaiser, Walter C. Jr. (1988), *Malachi: God's Unchanging Love*, Grand Rapids, MI: Baker Books.

Katzenelson. (1885), 'Die Rituellen Reinheitsgesetze in der Bible und im Talmud', *MFWJ*, 113.

Kelley, P. (1992), *Biblical Hebrew: An Introductory Grammar*, Grand Rapids: Eerdmans Publishing Company.

Keown, Gerald L., Pamela J. Scalise and Thomas G. Smothers (1995), 'Jeremiah 26-52', *WBC*, Dallas, TX: Word Books.

Kim, Jung H. (2004), *The Significance of Clothing Imagery in the Pauline Corpus*, New York: Continuum International.

Kingdon, D. (1973), *Children of Abraham--a Reformed Baptist View of Baptism, the Covenant, and Children*, Haywards Heath, Carey Press.

_____. (2002), 'John the Baptist – The Silence that Breaks the Silence', *FJ* 50, 5-16.

Kittle, G. and G. Friedrich (eds.) (1964-76), *Theological Dictionary of the New Testament*, 10 vols., Grand Rapids: Eerdmans.

Kline, Meredith G. (1958), 'Because It Had Not Rained', *WTJ* 20, 146-157.

_____. (1968), *By Oath Consigned*, Grand Rapids: Eerdmans Publishing Company.

_____. (1996), 'Har Magedon: The End of the Millennium', *JETS* 39:2, 207-222.

_____. (1999), *Images of the Spirit*, OR: Wipf & Stock.

_____. (2006a), *God, Heaven, and Har Magedon: A Covenantal Tale of Cosmos and Telos*, Eugene, OR: Wipf & Stock.

_____. (2006b), *Kingdom Prologue*, Eugene, OR: Wipf & Stock.

Knibb, Michael A. (1987), *The Qumran Community*, New York: Cambridge University Press.

Lawler, Michael G. (1987), *Symbol and Sacrament: A Contemporary Sacrament Theology*, Mahwah, NJ: Paulist.

Leithart, P. (2003), *The Priesthood of the Plebs: A Theology of Baptism*, Eugene, OR: Wipf and Stock.

Lightfoot, J. (1643), *A Handful of Gleanings out of the Book of Exodus*, in PBCD, Vol. 20, Edmonton: Still Waters Revival Books.

Longman, T. (2001), *Immanuel in Our Place: Seeing Christ in Israel's Worship*, Phillipsburg: Presbyterian and Reformed.

Lundquist, John M. (1984), 'The Common Temple Ideology of the Ancient Near East', in T. G. Madsen (ed.), *The Temple in Antiquity*, Religious Studies Monograph Series 9, Salt Lake City: Brigham Young University.

Luther, M. (1996), 'To the Christian Nobility of the German Nation Concerning the Reform of the Christian Estate', Jaroslav J. Pelikan, in Hilton C. Oswald, Helmut T. Lahmann (eds.), *Luther's Works*, Vol. 44, Philadelphia: Fortress Press.

Luz, U. (2005), *Studies in Matthew*, Grand Rapids, MI: Eerdmans.

Marshall, I. H. (1978). *The Gospel of Luke*, NIGTC, Grand Rapids, MI: Eerdmans Publishing Company.

Martens, E. '*Rachats*', NIDOTTE, 3:1098-1099.

Martin, E. L. (2004), 'The Temple Symbolism in Genesis', http://askelm.com/doctrine/d040301.htm# ftnref2

Martinez, Florentino G. and Tigchelaar, Eibert J. C. (eds.) (1997), *The Dead Sea Scrolls: Study Edition (Transcriptions and Translations)*, Boston, MA: Brill.

Massaus, E. (1990), *The Influence of the Gospel of Saint Matthew on Christian Literature before Saint Irenaeus. Book 1: The First Ecclesiastical Writers*, Arthur J. Bellinzoni (ed.), trans. Norman J. Belval and Suzanne Hecht, Macon, GA: Mercer University Press.

Mayhue, Richard L. (1996), 'Heb 13:20: Covenant of Grace or New Covenant? An Exegetical Note', *MSJ* 7, 251-258.

McCarter, P. K. (1973), 'The River Ordeal in Israelite Literature,' *HTR* 66:4, 403-412.

McCartney, D., Clayton, C. (2002), *Let the Reader Understand: A Guide to Interpreting and Applying the Bible*, Phillipsburg, NJ: P & R.

McCormack, A. (1969), 'Christian Initiation', in Henri Daniel-Rops (ed.), *TCEC* 50:20, New York: Hawthorn Books.

McCurdy, J. Frederic, K. Kohler and R. Gottheil, 'Adam', *JE* at: http://www.jewishencyclopedia.com/view.jsp?artid=758&letter=A&search=adam#1 859

McGrath, Alister E. (2007), *Christian Theology: An Introduction*, Malden, MA: Blackwell Publishing.

McKim, Donald K. (1996), *Westminster Dictionary of Theological Terms*, Louisville, KY: Westminster John Knox Press.

Mclean, John A. (1994), 'The Prophets as Covenant Enforcers: Illustrated In Zephaniah', *MTJ* 5, 5-24.

Meier, S. '*sîm*', NIDOTTE, 3:383-385.

Merrill, Eugene H. (1994), *An Exegetical Summary: Haggai, Zechariah, Malachi*, Chicago: Moody Press.

Micks, M. (1996), *Deep Waters: An Introduction to Baptism*, Boston: Cowley Publications.

Morris, L. (1992), *The Gospel According to Matthew*, PNTC, Grand Rapids, MI: Eerdmans.

_____. (1995), *The Gospel According to John* (Revised), NICNT, Grand Rapids, MI: Eerdmans.

Moseley, Ron. (n.d.), 'The Jewish Background of Christian Baptism', Sherwood, AR: Sherwood Institute of Holy Land Studies. http://www.scribd.com/doc/52903/Baptism-Resources

Motyer, J. A. (2005), *The Message of Exodus*, BST, Downers Grove, Ill: InterVarsity Press.

Mueller, H. (1967), 'Baptism (in the Bible)', in William J. McDonald (ed.), *TNCE* 2:55, New York: McGraw-Hill.

Müller, H. *'type, pattern'*, *NIDNTT*, 3:903-907.

Munday Jr., John C. (1996), 'Eden's Geography Erodes Flood Geology', *WTJ* 58.1, 123-154.

Murray, J. (1980), *Christian Baptism*, Phillipsburg, NJ: Presbyterian and Reformed.

Myers, Paul E., (1985), *A Study of Baptism in the First Three Centuries*, Ann Arbor, MI: UMI Dissertation Information Service.

Neale, John M., Littledale, Richard F. (1871), *A Commentary on the Psalms: From Primitive & Mediaeval Writers*, London: Joseph Masters.

Nettlehorst, R. P. (1988), 'The Genealogy of Jesus', *JETS* 31:2, 169-172.

Opeke, A. *'baptō, baptizō'*, *TDNT*, 1:529-546.

Oswalt, J. (1998), *The Book of Isaiah: Chapters 40-66*, NICOT, Grand Rapids, MI: Eerdmans.

Owen, J. (ed.) (1848), *Calvin's Commentaries*, Vol. 15, translated by John Owen, Grand Rapids: Baker.

Owen, J. (2004), 'The Doctrine of the Perseverance of the Saints' Explained and Confirmed', in *Works of John Owen*, Rio, WI: Ages Software.

Packer, J.I. (1990), 'Introduction on Covenant Theology', in *The Economy of the Covenants Between God and Man: Comprehending A Complete Body of Divinity* by Herman Witsius, Phillipsburg, NJ: Presbyterian and Reformed. Also available at: http://www.pcabakersfield.org/articles/Introduction_On_Covenant_Theology.pdf

Pipa, J. (2003), 'The Mode of Baptism', in Gregg Strawbridge (ed.), *The Case for Covenantal Infant Baptism*, Phillipsburg, NJ: P & R.

Pococke, E. (1692), *A Commentary on the Prophecy of Malachi*, in PBCD, Vol. 26, Edmonton: Still Waters Revival Books.

Pohlig, James N. (1998), *An Exegetical Summary of Malachi*, Dallas, TX: Summer Institute of Linguistics.

Poythress, V. (1991), *The Shadow of Christ in the Law of Moses*, New Jersey: Presbyterian and Reformed.

Pratt, R. (2003), 'Jeremiah 31: Infant Baptism in the New Covenant', in Gregg Strawbridge (ed.), *The Case for Covenantal Infant Baptism*, Phillipsburg, NJ: P & R. Also at *IIIM Magazine Online*, Vol. 4:1, Jan 7-13, 2002, http://thirdmill.org/newfiles/ric_pratt/TH.Pratt.New.Covenant.Baptism.pdf

Rehm, Merlin D. (1992), 'Levites and Priests', *ABD*, New York: Doubleday, 297-310.

Reymond, Robert L. (1998), *A New Systematic Theology of the Christian Faith*, Nashville: Thomas Nelson Publishers.

Riddlebarger, K. (2007), 'The Sacraments: Lecture 3A – The Biblical Case for Infant Baptism', http://christreformedinfo.squarespace.com/lecture-3a/

Riesen, Richard A. (1988), 'Book Review: Typos,' *Kerux* 3:1, 40-42.

Rivkin, E. (2003), *The Unity Principle: The Shaping of Jewish History*, Springfield, NJ: Behrman House.

Robertson, O. P. (1980), *Christ of the Covenants*, Phillipsburg, NJ: P& R.

Rose, Ben L. (1949), 'Baptism by Sprinkling', reprint *SPJ*.

Ross, M. (2003), 'Baptism and Circumcision as Signs and Seals', in Gregg Strawbridge (ed.), *The Case for Covenantal Infant Baptism*, Phillipsburg, NJ: P & R.

Ryle, J. C. (1997), *Luke*, CCC, Wheaton, IL: Crossway Books.

Scalise, Pamela J. (1987), 'To Fear or Not to Fear: Questions of Reward and Punishment in Malachi 2:17-4:3', *RevExp* 84:3, 409-418.

Schiffman, Lawrence H. (1987), 'The Rabbinic Understanding of Covenant', *RevExp* 84:2, 289-298.

Schreiner, T. (1993), *The Law and Its Fulfillment: A Pauline Theology of Law*, Grand Rapids, MI: Baker.

Sclater, W. (1650), *A Brief and Plain Commentary with Notes: not more useful, than seasonable, upon the Whole Prophecy of Malachi*, in PBCD, Vol. 26, Edmonton: Still Waters Revival Books.

Shafer, B. E. (1997), 'Temples, Priests, and Rituals: An Overview,' in B. E. Shafter (ed.), *Temples of Ancient Egypt*, Ithaca, NY: Cornell University Press.

Singer, I. (1901), 'Baptism', *JE*, 12 vols., New York: KTAV Publishing House Inc.

Skehan, Patrick W., Di Lella, Alexander A. (1980), *The Wisdom of Ben Sira*, New York: Doubleday.

Slonim, R. (1996), *Total Immersion: A Mikvah Anthology*, Northvale, NJ: Jason Aronson. Available online at:

http://www.chabad.org/theJewishWoman/article_cdo/aid/1541/jewish/The-Mikvah.htm

Small, Dwight H. (1959), *The Biblical Basis for Infant Baptism: Children in God's Covenant Promises*, Westwood, NJ: Fleming H. Revell.

Smith, Ralph L. (1984), 'Micah-Malachi', *WBC*, Waco, TX: Word Books.

Speiser, E. A. (1955), "ed in the Story of Creation', *BASOR* 140, 9-11.

Spurgeon, Charles H. (1868), 'Consecration to God Illustrated by Abraham's Circumcision', in *The Metropolitan Tabernacle Pulpit*, Vol. 14, London: Passmore and Alabaster.

Stander, Hendrick F. and Johannes P. Louw (2004), *Baptism in the Early Church*, Leeds, England: Carey Press.

Stedman, Ray C. (1970), 'The Meaning of Baptism', Discovery Publishing, http://www.pbc.org/dp/stedman/misc/0278.html.

Stock, R. (1641), *A Learned and Very Useful Commentary upon the Whole Prophesy of Malachi*, in PBCD, Vol. 26, Edmonton: Still Waters Revival Books.

Stordalen, T. (2000), *Echoes of Eden*, Leuven: Peeters.

Stott, J. (1996), *Guard the Truth: The Message of 1 Timothy & Titus*, Downers Grove, Ill: InterVarsity Press.

Strawbridge, G. (ed.) (2003), *The Case for Covenantal Infant Baptism*, Phillipsburg, NJ: P & R.

Stuart, D. (1998), 'Malachi', in Thomas McComiskey (ed.), *The Minor Prophets, Vol. 3*, Grand Rapids, MI: Baker Books.

Tate, Marvin E. (1987), 'Questions for Priests and People in Malachi 1:2-2:16', *RevExp* 84:3, 391-408.

Taylor, Richard A. and E. R. Clendenen (2004), 'Haggai, Malachi', *NAC*, Nashville, TN: Broadman & Holman.

Towner, P. (1994), *1, 2 Timothy and Titus*, IVPNTC, Downers Grove, Ill: InterVarsity Press.

Tsumura, David T. (1996), 'Genesis and Ancient Near Eastern Stories of Creation and Flood: an Introduction Part 2', *BSP* 9.2, 33-40.

Turretin, F. (1997), *Institutes of Elenctic Theology, Vol. 3*, James T. Dennison Jr. (ed.), trans. George Musgrave Giger, Phillipsburg, NJ: P & R.

van der Waal, C. (2003), *The Covenantal Gospel*, Pella, Iowa: Inheritance Publications.

VanderKam, James C. (2002), *From Revelation to Canon: Studies in the Hebrew Bible and Second Temple Literature*, Boston: Brill Academic Pub.

Vander Zee, Leonard J. (2004), *Christ, Baptism and the Lord's Supper: Recovering the Sacraments for Evangelical Worship*, Downers Grove, IL: InterVarsity Press.

VanGemeren, Willem A. (ed.) (1997), *New International Dictionary of Old Testament Theology and Exegesis*, 5 Vols., Grand Rapids: Zondervan.

Vanhoozer, K. (1998), *Is There a Meaning in This Text?*, Grand Rapids, MI: Zondervan.

Venema, Cornelis P. (2003), 'Covenant Theology and Baptism', in Gregg Strawbridge (ed.), *The Case for Covenantal Infant Baptism*, Phillipsburg, NJ: P & R.

Verduin, L. (1964), *The Reformers and Their Stepchildren*, Grand Rapids, MI: Eerdmans.

Vos, G. (1994), The Pauline Eschatology, Phillipsburg, NJ: Presbyterian and Reformed.

Wagner, M. (1996), *Baptists and Infant Baptism*, In RBCD, Vol. 28, Edmonton, CA: Still Waters Revival Books.

Walton, John H. (2001), *Genesis*, NIVAC, Grand Rapids: Zondervan.

_____, V. H. Matthews and M. W. Chavala (eds.) (2000), *IVP Bible Background Commentary: Old Testament*, Downers Grove, IL: InterVarsity Press.

Wenham, G. J. (1994), 'Sanctuary Symbolism in the Garden of Eden Story', in R. S. Hess and D. T. Tsumara (eds.), *'I studied Inscriptions from before the Flood'*, Winona Lake, IN: Eisenbrauns.

Westerink, H. (1997), *A Sign of Faithfulness: Covenant and Baptism*, translated by J. Mark Beach, Neerlandia Alberta, Canada: Inheritance Publications.

Weyde, Karl W. (2000), *Prophecy and Teaching: Prophetic Authority, Form Problems, and the Use of Traditions in the Book of Malachi*, New York: Walter de Gruyter.

Willet, A. (1633), *Hexapla in Exodum, That is, A Sixfold Commentary upon the Second Booke of Moses called Exodus*, London, Afsignes of Thomas Man, in PBCD, Vol. 20, Edmonton, CA: Still Waters Revival Books.

Williams, Michael D. (2005), *Far as the Curse is Found: The Covenant Story of Redemption*, Phillipsburg, NJ: P & R.

Williamson, Paul D. (2000), 'Covenant', *NDBT*, electronic edition.

Wright, Christopher J. H. (2001), *The Message of Ezekiel*, BST, Downers Grove, Ill: InterVarsity Press.

Young, Edward J. (1961), 'The Interpretation of Genesis 1:2', *WTJ* 23:2, 151-178.

Author Index

Verse Index

Exodus

Leviticus

Numbers

Potentially Forthcoming Endorsements (Just for Fun):

What we are pretty sure they might say about the book:

"Perhaps he should try writing children's books." C. S. Lewis

'I've burned people for less. Servitus would be proud of this work.' John Calvin

'He may have a Dutch surname, but he's clearly Swedish. Anabaptists everywhere are dancing in the streets.' Cornelius Van Til

'Try to nail THAT to the door!' Martin Luther

'Reminds me of something I wrote in 1643.' Shirley McLaine

'The field of theology is really evolving.' Chuck Darwin

'I couldn't put it down fast enough.' B.B. Warfield

'Bring him to me, and we shall draw and quarter him. He may not be a heretic, but he ticks us off.' -- The Grand Inquisitor

'Over the top.' Silvester Stallone

'A cut above.' -- O. J. Simpson

'Blew my mind.' John F. Kennedy

"Van Dorn spins a real web of mischief in this comic book." Spiderman

"It was a bit of a stretch." Mr. Fantastic

"It's clobberin' time." The Thing

"Flame on." The Human Torch

"   ,   ?   !" Sue Richards and the Invisible Man

'I'll recommend it to 130 million of my best friends.' Oprah Winfrey

'I especially liked the part after the last potential endorsement.' Augustine

'Quo est reliquum?' (tr: 'Where's the rest of it?')' -- Thomas Aquinas

'A real page burner.' Hitler

'I'm glad I don't know how to read.' Baby Infant Baptist

"A comedy and a tragedy at the same time. Something I never managed to write." William Shakespeare

"Huh?" Socrates

"This really makes a lot of sense, which is the biggest problem with the whole thing!" Søren Kierkegaard

"Among the great fantasy books ever written. Tops in the genre." JRR Tolkien

'RUINED!!! OUR RELIGION IS BUNK!!!' Pope John Paul

'RUINED!!! OUR RELIGION IS BUNK!!!' Jerry Falwell

'Another blurb for the back of yet another book that I just skim at best. Cause. I mean, come on. Who on earth has time to read as many books as I endorse? I'm sure it's great.' JI Packer

"Reading it was like the sound of one hand clapping." The Dalai Lama

"I had no idea that this theory was out there until my husband woke me up and told me one night. I cried for a week." Hillary Clinton

'Two books on the shelf, and I took the one less read.' -- Robert Frost

'We decided that full immersion was bad news, so we used it to line the dove's cage.' -- Noah

'My biggest ally in the fight against fundamentalists.' Bishop John Shelby Spong

"A Tour de Force this is. Read it you should." Yoda

"I've read it 7 times. A real Tour de France." Lance Armstrong

'The greatest Satan since Satan hisself.' The Very Rev. John Hagee

'If this is all there were to print, I'd have been out of a job.' – Gutenburg

"It's a killer." Stephen King

"Explosive." Sheik Muhammad

"I love that he's a Baptist, but I cried for eighteen days when I found out the he's a reformer and hates little children." Jan Crouch, TBN

"I think I should cut my eyes out next." Van Gogh

"I screamed." Edvard Münch

'Try Again Later.' -- Magic 8-ball

'ZZZZZZZZ.' Dr. Paul D. Simmons, author's friend

'I really probably should have read it.' Stephen Charles Van Dorn, author's brother

"Giving birth was more fun than reading this." Janelle Van Dorn, author's wife

"I really have no idea why I wrote this thing." Doug Van Dorn, author